After the Arab Uprisings

The Arab uprisings that began in 2010 removed four presidents and made more mobilized mass publics an increased factor in the politics of regional states. The main initial problematic of the Arab uprising was how to translate mass protest into democratization and ultimately democratic consolidation; yet four years later, there was little democratization. This book explores various aspects of this question while comparing outcomes in three states, Egypt, Syria and Tunisia. The introduction by Raymond Hinnebusch explores how far different starting points—the features of the regime and of the uprising—explain these pathways. Morten Valbjørn then considers the consequences of the Arab uprisings for the credibility of rival democratization and post-democratization paradigms. Vincent Durac examines the efficacy of anti-system social movements in challenging regimes and their inability to steer a democratic transition. Joshua Stacher examines the increased violence deployed by more coercive authoritarian regimes to prevent such a transition. Frédéric Volpi and Ewan Stein examine the consequences of the relative balance between different kinds of Islamists for outcomes. Jamie Allinson then examines the impact of workers' movements on democratic potentials. Adham Saouli assesses the mobilization of communal identities by ruling elites and counter-elites. Raymond Hinnebusch focuses on the negative impact on democratization of competitive external interference inside the uprising states. In Hinnebusch's conclusion, the combined effects of the agency of these forces and the political, cultural and economic contexts in which they operate are summarized. This book was previously published as a special issue of *Democratization*.

Raymond Hinnebusch is a Professor of International Relations and Middle East Politics at the University of St Andrews, UK. His works include *Egyptian Politics under Sadat* (1985), *Syria: Revolution from above* (2001) and *Syria from Reform to Revolt: Politics and International Relations* (2014), edited with Tina Zintl.

Democratization Special Issues

Edited by
Jeffrey Haynes, *London Metropolitan University, UK*
Aurel Croissant, *University of Heidelberg, Germany*

The journal, *Democratization*, emerged in 1994, during "the third wave of democracy", a period which saw democratic transformation of dozens of regimes around the world. Over the last decade or so, the journal has published a number of special issues as books, each of which has focused upon cutting edge issues linked to democratization. Collectively, they underline the capacity of democratization to induce debate, uncertainty, and perhaps progress towards better forms of politics, focused on the achievement of the democratic aspirations of men and women everywhere.

After the Arab Uprisings
Raymond Hinnebusch

Voting Rights in the Age of Globalization
Daniele Caramani and Florian Grotz

The State Democracy Nexus
Edited by Jørgen Møller and Svend-Erik Skaaning

Democracy Promotion and the Challenges of Illiberal Regional Powers
Edited by Nelli Babayan and Thomas Risse

Religiously Oriented Parties and Democratization
Edited by Luca Ozzano and Francesco Cavatorta

Religion and Political Change in the Modern World
Edited by Jeffrey Haynes

Comparing Autocracies in the Early Twenty-first Century
Two-volume set:
  1 Unpacking Autocracies – Explaining Similarity and Difference
  2 The Performance and Persistence of Autocracies
Edited by Aurel Croissant, Steffen Kailitz, Patrick Koellner and Stefan Wurster

Twenty Years of Studying Democratization
Three-volume set:
1 Democratic Transition and Consolidation
2 Democratization, Democracy and Authoritarian Continuity
3 Building Blocks of Democracy
Edited by Aurel Croissant and Jeffrey Haynes

Political Opposition in Sub-Saharan Africa
Edited by Elliott Green, Johanna Söderström and Emil Uddhammar

Conflicting Objectives in Democracy Promotion
Do All Good Things Go Together?
Edited by Julia Leininger, Sonja Grimm and Tina Freyburg

PREVIOUSLY PUBLISHED BOOKS FROM DEMOCRATIZATION

Coloured Revolutions and Authoritarian Reactions
Edited by Evgeny Finkel and Yitzhak M. Brudny

Ethnic Party Bans in Africa
Edited by Matthijs Bogaards, Matthias Basedau and Christof Hartmann

Democracy Promotion in the EU's Neighbourhood
From Leverage to Governance?
Edited by Sandra Lavenex and Frank Schimmelfennig

Democratization in Africa: Challenges and Prospects
Edited by Gordon Crawford and Gabrielle Lynch

Democracy Promotion and the 'Colour Revolutions'
Edited by Susan Stewart

Promoting Party Politics in Emerging Democracies
Edited by Peter Burnell and Andre W. M. Gerrits

Democracy and Violence
Global Debates and Local Challenges
Edited by John Schwarzmantel and Hendrik Jan Kraetzschmar

Religion and Democratizations
Edited by Jeffrey Haynes

The European Union's Democratization Agenda in the Mediterranean
Edited by Michelle Pace and Peter Seeberg

War and Democratization
Legality, Legitimacy and Effectiveness
Edited by Wolfgang Merkel and Sonja Grimm

Democratization in the Muslim World
Changing Patterns of Authority and Power
Edited by Frederic Volpi and Francesco Cavatorta

Religion, Democracy and Democratization
Edited by John Anderson

On the State of Democracy
Edited by Julio Faundez

After the Arab Uprisings
Between democratization, counter-revolution and state failure

Edited by
Raymond Hinnebusch

LONDON AND NEW YORK

First published 2016
by Routledge
2 Park Square, Milton Park, Abingdon, Oxon, OX14 4RN, UK

and by Routledge
711 Third Avenue, New York, NY 10017, USA

Routledge is an imprint of the Taylor & Francis Group, an informa business

© 2016 Taylor & Francis

All rights reserved. No part of this book may be reprinted or reproduced or utilised in any form or by any electronic, mechanical, or other means, now known or hereafter invented, including photocopying and recording, or in any information storage or retrieval system, without permission in writing from the publishers.

Trademark notice: Product or corporate names may be trademarks or registered trademarks, and are used only for identification and explanation without intent to infringe.

British Library Cataloguing in Publication Data
A catalogue record for this book is available from the British Library

ISBN 13: 978-1-138-65615-4

Typeset in TimesNewRomanPS
by diacriTech, Chennai

Publisher's Note
The publisher accepts responsibility for any inconsistencies that may have arisen during the conversion of this book from journal articles to book chapters, namely the possible inclusion of journal terminology.

Disclaimer
Every effort has been made to contact copyright holders for their permission to reprint material in this book. The publishers would be grateful to hear from any copyright holder who is not here acknowledged and will undertake to rectify any errors or omissions in future editions of this book.

Contents

Citation Information ix
Notes on Contributors xi

1. Introduction: understanding the consequences of the Arab uprisings – starting points and divergent trajectories
   Raymond Hinnebusch   1

2. Reflections on self-reflections – On framing the analytical implications of the Arab uprisings for the study of Arab politics
   Morten Valbjørn   14

3. Social movements, protest movements and cross-ideological coalitions – the Arab uprisings re-appraised
   Vincent Durac   35

4. Fragmenting states, new regimes: militarized state violence and transition in the Middle East
   Joshua Stacher   55

5. Islamism and the state after the Arab uprisings: Between people power and state power
   Frédéric Volpi and Ewan Stein   72

6. Class forces, transition and the Arab uprisings: a comparison of Tunisia, Egypt and Syria
   Jamie Allinson   90

7. Back to the future: the Arab uprisings and state (re)formation in the Arab world
   Adham Saouli   111

CONTENTS

8. Globalization, democratization, and the Arab uprising: the international factor in MENA's failed democratization 131
Raymond Hinnebusch

9. Conclusion: agency, context and emergent post-uprising regimes 154
Raymond Hinnebusch

   Index 171

Citation Information

The chapters in this book were originally published in *Democratization*, volume 22, issue 2 (March 2015). When citing this material, please use the original page numbering for each article, as follows:

Chapter 1
Introduction: understanding the consequences of the Arab uprisings – starting points and divergent trajectories
Raymond Hinnebusch
Democratization, volume 22, issue 2 (March 2015) pp. 205–217

Chapter 2
Reflections on self-reflections – On framing the analytical implications of the Arab uprisings for the study of Arab politics
Morten Valbjørn
Democratization, volume 22, issue 2 (March 2015) pp. 218–238

Chapter 3
Social movements, protest movements and cross-ideological coalitions – the Arab uprisings re-appraised
Vincent Durac
Democratization, volume 22, issue 2 (March 2015) pp. 239–258

Chapter 4
Fragmenting states, new regimes: militarized state violence and transition in the Middle East
Joshua Stacher
Democratization, volume 22, issue 2 (March 2015) pp. 259–275

Chapter 5
Islamism and the state after the Arab uprisings: Between people power and state power
Frédéric Volpi and Ewan Stein
Democratization, volume 22, issue 2 (March 2015) pp. 276–293

CITATION INFORMATION

Chapter 6
Class forces, transition and the Arab uprisings: a comparison of Tunisia, Egypt and Syria
Jamie Allinson
Democratization, volume 22, issue 2 (March 2015) pp. 294–314

Chapter 7
Back to the future: the Arab uprisings and state (re)formation in the Arab world
Adham Saouli
Democratization, volume 22, issue 2 (March 2015) pp. 315–334

Chapter 8
Globalization, democratization, and the Arab uprising: the international factor in MENA's failed democratization
Raymond Hinnebusch
Democratization, volume 22, issue 2 (March 2015) pp. 335–357

Chapter 9
Conclusion: agency, context and emergent post-uprising regimes
Raymond Hinnebusch
Democratization, volume 22, issue 2 (March 2015) pp. 358–374

For any permission-related enquiries please visit:
http://www.tandfonline.com/page/help/permissions

Notes on Contributors

Jamie Allinson is a Lecturer in International Relations at the University of Westminster, UK, with a focus on historical sociology and international relations, political economy and the Arab world. He is the author of the forthcoming book *The Struggle for the State in Jordan*.

Vincent Durac lectures in Middle East Politics in the School of Politics and International Relations at University College Dublin, Ireland. His research is focused on political reform and civil society in the Middle East and Yemeni political dynamics. He is co-author of *Politics and Governance in the Middle East* (Palgrave 2015) and *Civil Society and Democratization in the Arab World: The Dynamics of Activism* (Routledge 2014). His recent work has appeared in Journal of Contemporary African Studies and Mediterranean Politics.

Raymond Hinnebusch is a Professor of International Relations at the University of St Andrews, UK. His books include *International Politics of the Middle East* (Manchester 2015), *Syria: Revolution from above* (Routledge 2001) and *Egyptian Politics under Sadat* (Cambridge 1985). His recent works on the Arab Spring and democratization include "Change and Continuity after the Arab Uprising: The Consequences of State Formation in Arab North African States", *British Journal of Middle Eastern Studies* (2015) and "Toward a Historical Sociology of the Arab Uprising: Beyond Democratization and Post-Democratization", *Handbook of the Arab Uprising*, ed. Larbi Sadiki (Routledge 2015).

Adham Saouli is a Lecturer in International Relations and Middle East Politics at the University of St Andrews, UK. His most recent publications include "Performing the Egyptian Revolution: Origins of Collective Restrain Action in the Midan", *Political Studies* (2014), "Intellectuals and Political Power in Social Movements: The Parallel Paths of Fadlallah and Hizbullah", *British Journal of Middle Eastern Studies* (2014) and *The Arab State: Dilemmas of Late Formation* (Routledge 2012).

Joshua Stacher is an Associate Professor in the Department of Political Science at Kent State University, Kent, OH, USA. He is the author of *Adaptable Autocrats: Regime Power in Egypt and Syria* (2012) and is on the editorial board of MERIP's *Middle East Report*.

NOTES ON CONTRIBUTORS

Ewan Stein is a Lecturer in International Relations at the University of Edinburgh, UK. His interests include political Islam, Egyptian politics and Arab political thought. His works include *Twenty-First Century Jihad: Law, Society and Military Action*, London: IB Tauris (2015) *Representing Israel in Modern Egypt: Ideas, Intellectuals and Foreign Policy from Nasser to Mubarak* (2012).

Morten Valbjørn is an Associate Professor at the Department of Political Science, Aarhus University, Denmark. His work focuses on meta-theoretical issues concerning the role of cultural diversity in international relations, the area studies controversy and the study of Middle East politics. His work has appeared in, among others, *Review of International Studies, International Review of Sociology, Cooperation & Conflict, Mediterranean Politics* and *Middle East Critique*.

Frédéric Volpi is a Senior Lecturer in the School of International Relations of the University of St Andrews, UK. He is the author of *Political Islam Observed* (2010). His work broadly engages questions of democratization, political Islam and contentious politics in the Middle East and North Africa.

Introduction: understanding the consequences of the Arab uprisings – starting points and divergent trajectories

Raymond Hinnebusch

School of International Relations, University of St Andrews, St Andrews, UK

This introduction sets the context for the following articles by first conceptualizing the divergent post-uprising trajectories taken by varying states: these are distinguished first by whether state capacity collapses or persists, and if it persists, whether the outcome is a hybrid regime or polyarchy. It then assesses how far starting points – the features of the regime and of the uprising – explain these pathways. Specifically, the varying levels of anti-regime mobilization, explained by factors such as levels of grievances, patterns of cleavages, and opportunity structure, determine whether rulers are quickly removed or stalemate sets in. Additionally, the ability of regime and opposition softliners to reach a transition pact greatly shapes democratic prospects. But, also important is the capacity – coercive and co-optative – of the authoritarian rulers to resist, itself a function of factors such as the balance between the patrimonial and bureaucratic features of neo-patrimonial regimes.

What are the consequences of the Arab uprisings for democratization in the Middle East North Africa (MENA) area? The Arab uprisings that began in 2010 had, as of the end of 2014, removed four presidents and seemingly made more mobilized mass publics an increased factor in the politics of regional states. It is, however, one thing to remove a leader and quite another to create stable and inclusive "democratic" institutions. The main initial problem of the Arab uprisings was how to translate mass protest into democratization and ultimately democratic consolidation. Yet, despite the fact that democracy was the main shared demand of the protestors who spearheaded the uprisings, there was, four years later, little evidence of democratization; what explains this "modest harvest", as Brownlee, Masoud, and Reynolds[1] put it?

Neither of the rival paradigms – democratization theory (DT) and post-democratization approaches (PDT) – that have been used to understand the Middle East have come out of the uprisings looking vindicated. The PDT theme of authoritarian resilience, in its focus on elite strategies for managing participatory demands, has clearly overestimated their efficacy, neglected their negative side effects and underestimated the agency of populations. Yet, the democratization paradigm has also since suffered from the failure of revolt to lead to democracy.[2] Rather than either a uniform authoritarian restoration or democratization, the uprisings have set different states on a great variety of different trajectories. As Morten Valbjorn argues in his contribution, grasping this complexity requires moving beyond both DT and PDT.

This introductory article first *conceptualizes* the variations in post-uprising trajectories. It then seeks to explain how far the *starting point* – the features of both regimes and oppositions in the uprisings – explain these post-uprising variations, specifically looking at: (1) *anti-regime mobilization*, both its varying scale and capacity to leverage a peaceful transition from incumbent rulers and (2) variations in *authoritarian resistance* to the uprisings, a function of their vulnerabilities, resources and "fightback" strategies. This will provide the context for the following contributions which focus on post-uprising *agency*, that is, the struggle of rival social forces – the military, civil society, Islamists, and workers – to shape outcomes. These contributions give special attention to three states that are iconic of the main outcomes, namely state failure and civil war (Syria); "restoration" of a hybrid regime (Egypt); and democratic transition (Tunisia). In the conclusion of the special issue, the evidence is summarized regarding how the power balance among post-uprising social forces and the political, cultural, and political economy contexts in which they operated explain variations in *emergent regime outcomes*.

Alternative post-uprising trajectories

The various outcomes or trajectories of the Arab uprisings appear best conceptualized in terms of movement along two *separate* continuums: *level of state consolidation* and *regime type*. Moreover variations in the states' starting points on these dimensions at the time of the uprisings will arguably affect trajectories.

As regards *state consolidation*, if uprisings lead to democratization this ought to strengthen states in that it would accord them greater popular consent, hence capacity to carry out their functions. However, the initial impact of the uprisings was state weakening, with the extreme being state collapse or near collapse (Libya, Syria), where democratization prospects appear to be foreclosed for the immediate future. Yet, even amidst such state failure, new efforts at state remaking can be discerned. Such competitive state making in MENA was first conceptualized by the North African "father" of historical sociology, Ibn Khaldun, and adopted by Max Weber, who identified the "successful" pathways to authority building dominant in MENA, notably the charismatic movement which tended to be institutionalized in patrimonial rule, perhaps mixed with bureaucratic authority. Ibn Khaldun's "cycles" of rise and decline in state building appear better suited to MENA than the idea of a progressive increase in state consolidation; indeed the history of state making in MENA has described a bell-shaped curve of rise and decline,[3] with the current state failure merely a nadir in this decline.

As for *regime type*, if one measures variations in regimes along Dahl's two separate dimensions by which power is distributed – level of elite contestation and level of mass inclusion[4] – a greater variety of regime types is possible than the simple authoritarian-democratic dichotomy and this variation may explain both vulnerabilities to the uprising and likely outcomes. Patrimonial regimes low in both proved quite viable in the face of the uprisings, as in the persistence of absolute monarchy in the tribal oil-rich Arab Gulf. Polyarchy, high on elite contestation and mass inclusion, has been rare in MENA. The region has, however, experienced various "hybrids" in which some social forces were *included* in regimes *in order to exclude others*: thus, the populist authoritarian regimes of the 1960s expanding popular inclusion within single-party/corporatist systems, in order to exclude the oligarchies against which they had revolted; when populism was exhausted in the 1980s, they turned "post-populist", marginally increasing elite contestation (for example, by co-opting new elements into the regime and allowing some party pluralism and electoral competition) in order to co-opt the support needed to exclude the masses. Given that the uprisings initially precipitated *both* increased elite contestation and mass inclusion, movement toward polyarchy, that is, democratization, appeared possible. However, rather than linear "progress" toward increased contestation and inclusion, hybrid regimes with different combinations of opening and closing at elite and mass levels are more likely.

Figure 1 adumbrates the alternative trajectories the uprisings have so far taken. Where the state fails, the outcome is an authority vacuum, with extreme levels of elite contestation propelling mass mobilization along identity lines, with rivals competing violently to reconstruct state authority, often pitting the most coercive remnants of state establishments against charismatic Islamist insurgencies (Syria, Libya, Yemen). The rival regimes are likely to be hybrids constructed around

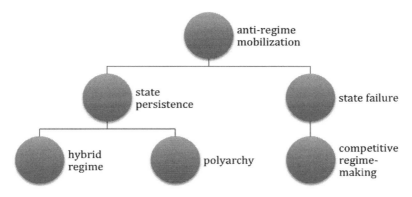

Figure 1. Pathways of post-uprising states.

patrimonial or charismatic leadership and remnants of bureaucratic state institutions, with very limited elite contestation within such regimes-in-formation and with identity groups mobilized around included victors, with the losers coercively excluded.

Where the state does not collapse, two outcomes are possible: the establishment persists and restores its authority or it is taken over by new democratic leadership. In the first case, the new post-uprising regimes are likely to be hybrids, mixing elements of co-optation, coercion, and pluralism – electoral authoritarianism – with middle levels of inclusion. Equally, the state establishments may take advantage of widening identity cleavages within society, such as that between secularists and Islamists, to divide and rule, including one segment in order to exclude the other, as in Egypt. Only Tunisia approximates the second case of democratic transition.

Path dependency: uprising starting points and subsequent trajectories

To understand the starting point from which the uprising trajectories departed, we need to assess their drivers – the vulnerabilities of authoritarian regimes and the dimensions of anti-regime mobilization.

Roots of crisis, authoritarian vulnerability

Two theoretical approaches give us insight into the roots of the crisis that exploded in the Arab uprisings. In modernization theory (MT), the challenge authoritarian regimes face is that once societies reach a certain level of social mobilization (education, literacy, urbanization, size of the middle class) regimes that do not accommodate demands for political participation risk they will take revolutionary forms unless otherwise contained by exceptional means such as "totalitarianism". MENA states were in a middle range of modernization where democratization pressures were significant but could still seemingly be contained and indeed had been in the republics for decades, first by a generation of populist, more inclusive, forms of authoritarianism (diluted imitations of Soviet "totalitarianism"), later by post-populist "upgrading". MT would locate the roots of the uprisings in a growing imbalance between social mobilization and political incorporation.[5] There were some levels of imbalance in all of the republics but the depth of the imbalance arguably affected regime trajectories. Thus, levels of social mobilization as measured by indicators such as literacy and urbanization were lowest in Yemen and highest in Tunisia; yet political incorporation was sharply limited in Tunisia, while co-optation via controlled political liberalization was much more developed in Yemen. The very strong imbalance in Tunisia may help explain the rapid, thorough mobilization and quick departure of the president, as well as the more thorough transition from the old regime; conversely, the stalemated outcome in Yemen may be related to the lower levels of social mobilization combined with still viable traditional practices of co-optation.

Second, Marxist theory locates the crisis in a contradiction between the productive forces and the political superstructure. Gilbert Ashcar[6] argues that the uprisings were stimulated by the contradiction between the imported capitalist mode of production and the blockage of growth by crony capitalist rent seeking patrimonial regimes that failed to invest in productive enterprise, resulting in massive numbers of the educated unemployed. Indeed, the Arab uprisings were a product of the republics' evolution from a formerly inclusionary populist form of authoritarianism to post-populist exclusionary versions under the impact of global neoliberalism; this move was particularly damaging in the republics, compared to monarchies, because they had founded their legitimacy on nationalism and a populist social contract, both of which they abandoned in the transition to post-populism. The cocktail of *grievances* that exploded in the uprisings was produced by the growing economic inequality produced by the region's distinct combination of International Monetary Fund-driven "structural adjustment" and crony capitalism. Inequality was driven by region-wide policies of privatization, hollowing out of public services, reduction of labour protections, tax cuts, and incentives for investors. Yet economic growth remained anaemic, principally because, while public investment plummeted, private investment did not fill the gap and indeed MENA was the region with the highest rate of capital export, in good part because capital was concentrated in a handful of small-population rentier monarchies that recycled their petrodollar earnings to the West. This was reinforced by the loss of nationalist legitimacy as regimes aligned with the West. Protests against this evolution had been endemic, beginning with the spread of food riots across the region in the 1980s – but, at the same time the regimes' strategies of "authoritarian upgrading" meant to make up for the exclusion of their popular constituencies, such as divide and rule through limited political liberalization, co-optation of the crony capitalist beneficiaries of neoliberalism, and offloading of welfare responsibilities to Islamic charities – had appeared sufficient to keep protests episodic or localized enough to be contained by the security forces, preventing a sustained mass movement.[7]

Bringing the modernization and Marxist approaches together, we can hypothesize that in the short term authoritarian upgrading had reached its limits and had begun to produce negative side effects. Thus, the wealth concentration and conspicuous consumption of crony capitalists was paralleled by growth of unemployment among middle-class university graduates – the force that spearheaded the uprisings. The attempts of aging incumbent presidents to engineer dynastic succession and an over-concentration of wealth and opportunities in presidential families alienated elites as well. On the other hand, political liberalization had stalled or been reversed in the years just preceding the uprisings, with, for example, manipulated elections becoming more a source of grievance than of co-optation.[8] In addition, the republics suffered leadership de-legitimation from the very long tenures of many presidents.

Ultimately, the particular depth of the crisis in each country was a function of the relative degree of economic blockage and the imbalance between social mobilization and political incorporation. However, states were set on varying trajectories by the specific initial features of the uprising in each, shaped by the interaction between varying levels of *anti-regime mobilization* and varying levels of *regime resilience* in the face of this mobilization.

Variations in mobilization across cases

While the literature on the uprisings has noted the apparently greater immunity of the monarchies to anti-regime mobilization, as compared to the republics, much less appreciated are the *variations* in levels of mobilization among the uprising states. In Egypt and Tunisia widespread bandwagoning against the regimes led to the relatively rapid departure of presidents. Large cross-class coalitions, involving revolutionary youth, union activists, Islamists, and the urban poor joined to overwhelm by sheer numbers the very substantial security forces and to converge on the centre of power while no social forces – even the constituents of the large ruling parties – seemed prepared to defend the regimes.[9] By contrast, in Syria, Libya, Yemen, and Bahrain there was enough mobilization to destabilize the state, but the regimes had core constituencies prepared to defend them and wider groups unwilling to bandwagon with the opposition, obstructing the irresistible mobilization needed to sweep away incumbent rulers. What explains these variations?

Social movement theory (SMT) identifies two factors – the framing of grievances via a vision of change and the political opportunity structure. Arguably, levels of grievance had reached a tipping point and opportunity structures had become more favourable for challenges to regimes, albeit *not uniformly across different states*. Although grievances were ubiquitous, variations in their intensity affected the ability of movements to mobilize discontent. Given that the uprisings were a reaction to post-populism, a working hypothesis would be that, other things being equal, the earlier post-populism began, hence the more advanced it likely was, the deeper the class inequalities, the more intense the accumulation of grievances, and the more widespread mobilization was likely to be. In MENA the move to post-populism, a main root of grievances, was most advanced in Tunisia and Egypt, which had pioneered it in the 1970s, while in Syria, where it came three decades later, its impact would likely have been lesser. Similarly, the extent of regime nationalist de-legitimation – from alignment with the United States, separate peace with Israel – varied, with notably Syria enjoying a certain nationalist legitimacy as the one regime that had eschewed this foreign policy submission to the West.

However, complicating matters is that populations are divided not just by class inequalities but also by communal (sectarian, ethnic) cleavages. Where class cleavages are not cross-cut by communal cleavages or where there is a substantial overlap between them, especially where identity separates the ruling group from deprived societal majorities, as in Bahrain, mobilization would be expected to be more intense; indeed, perhaps 40% of the population was estimated to have participated in demonstrations at the core of power – Pearl Square – and it evidently took external intervention (by Saudi Arabia) to put an end to it, although the mobilization by the regime of its sectarian minority constituency precluded the sort of total anti-regime mobilization approximated in Egypt and Tunisia. Where communal cleavages *cross-cut* class, with, for example, a cross-communal upper class benefiting from post-populism while retaining clients in the lower classes, as in Lebanon, mobilization against the regime would be limited or divided into pro and anti-regime movements. A middle case would be Syria, where a substantial portion of the Sunni urban upper and middle strata, particularly beneficiaries of post-populism, aligned with the minority dominated regime or at least did not join the opposition, while a substantial anti-regime coalition joining middle-class activists and the rural poor, who had been victimized by post-populism, mobilized large enough numbers to de-stabilize the regime but not to overthrow it, resulting in stalemate.

As SMT argues, mobilization requires not just grievances, but also a permissive *opportunity structure* in which societal opposition can overcome atomization and combine for collective action. Where society is fragmented along identity lines, mass mobilization is obstructed; in a homogeneous society shared identity facilitates it. Also important is the extent of civil society organization – whether it has enough density and autonomy to give people associative experience beyond primordial solidarities, without which people remain atomized. In this regard, why the revolt began in 2010 and not before may be down to the improving opportunity structure owing to the pre-uprising region-wide growth of civil society. But civil society was much more advanced in Egypt and Tunisia because the early onset of neoliberalism had both necessitated greater tolerance for it and had also led to years of protest experience by activists that generated organizational skills and networks that would be crucial in the uprisings. Finally, autonomous communications technology is crucial to overcoming atomization: the new electronic communications had made the public more politically conscious, interconnected, and mobilizable than hitherto, although more so where it was well established than where it was relatively new or information technology (IT) penetration was limited (Syria, Yemen). Social media were sources of networking and mobilization for activists. The pre-existing single Arab public space created by exposure to Arab satellite TV created a powerful demonstration effect: the early success of the uprising in Tunisia led to a re-calculation by alienated individuals elsewhere that they could actually bring down a dictator; similarly, the widespread media depiction of outside intervention against the Libyan regime changed the calculations of actors elsewhere, notably in Syria, where many believed they would be protected by the "international community". Yet, similarly, as further into the uprising the consequences – chaos, civil war – became widely disseminated, calculations changed, with some reverting to political passivity, and others committing to armed struggle – each antithetic to democratic transition.[10]

In summary, higher levels of mobilization against regimes were more likely in homogeneous societies with social mobilization levels far exceeding institutional incorporation, with developed civil society and protest experience, considerable IT penetration, and accumulating grievances generating dominant class cleavages, such as in Egypt and Tunisia. Where mobilization is more rapid, massive, unified, and peaceful, chances increase that presidents go quickly and a democratic transition is possible. Where class and communal (identity) cleavages cross cut each other and mobilization is diluted or rival mobilizations checkmate each other, leaders can hang on, resulting in a failed state or authoritarian restoration. However, the level of mobilization is only one variable shaping outcomes; another is the dynamics of bargaining between regime and opposition.

Explaining the mobilization – democratization disconnect

The Arab uprisings produced substantial pro-democracy mobilization across many states but the outcomes were very different. According to the mass protest paradigm, as delineated notably by Stephan and Chenoweth, peaceful mass protest can readily destabilize authoritarian regimes; *even if* the regime refuses protestors' demands and uses violence against them, this is likely to *backfire*, stimulating wider anti-regime mobilization, precipitating international sanctions and support for the opposition, and, most importantly, causing defections in the security forces, which will be reluctant to use violence against fellow citizens who are not themselves using violence.[11]

All of these phenomena were observable in the Arab uprisings. How regimes responded to protests mattered; indeed one commonality was that the brutal overreaction of security forces against protesters spread rebellion to much wider sections of the population. Videos of beatings and shootings escalated demands for reform into demands for the "fall of the regime". Why then did mass protest not translate into democratization in MENA? The mass resistance literature cannot explain variations in outcome because it ignores differences in the *scale* of mass mobilization (hence pressure on regimes) and the capacity of opposition leaders to split the regime, a requisite of translating mobilization into *peaceful* transition. The *transition paradigm* identifies the pre-condition that allows protest to initiate a democratic transition, namely a *pact* between moderates in the ruling elite and among the opposition,[12] wherein the latter refrain from threatening the vital interests of incumbents who, in return, concede a pluralization of the political system, enabling a transition coalition composed of both insiders and outsiders to preside over democratization. Where protests remain peaceful the chances of such a democratic transition increase since it encourages moderates within the regime to push for reform and/or withdraw their support from hardline authoritarians; democratic transition is less likely when rebels make maximalist demands or resort to violence, thereby empowering regime hardliners against moderates. In Egypt and Tunisia insider-outsider coalitions (for example, the army and the Muslim Brotherhood in Egypt) came together to engineer a peaceful exit of the president, ushering in a possible transition from authoritarianism. However, it is very difficult for the sort of unorganized mass protests, lacking leadership or organization, that characterized the Arab uprisings to bargain with regimes and exploit hardliner-softliner cleavages; as such, they tended to fall back on maximalist all-or-nothing demands which empowered regime hardliners, leading to either regime collapse, or civil wars in Syria and Libya where no mediators could engineer a transition coalition.[13] When revolts turn violent the chances of democratization sharply decline.

Authoritarian resilience

The other side of the coin of opportunity structure – regime capacity to resist – is also important for understanding the great variation in outcomes. Authoritarian regimes had two options for dealing with the uprisings: co-optation or repression, and their resilience was a function of their ability to effectively mix the two.[14] But what explains these capacities?

Variation in regime type is said to explain the reliability of the coercive apparatus. For Stepan and Linz,[15] Weber's "Sultanism", a regime type in which the leader enjoys the absolute loyalty of a personally dependent "staff" explains the inability of protests to separate regimes from their leaders in Libya and Syria; however, unlike the household slaves of Sultans in modern states, elites are not personal dependents of rulers and, indeed, preside over institutional domains. Brownlee et al.[16] argue that *dynasticism* – the transfer of power from father to son – denotes the exceptional intra-elite loyalty to the leader needed to ensure reliable coercive capacity; yet many monarchies suffered coups by their militaries in the 1950s–1960s. Nor does hereditary succession in a republic enjoy even the putative legitimacy it has in actual monarchies. Several of the republican leaders were preparing such a transition but only in Syria had it come about and Syria's Asad never enjoyed undisputed authority, having to share power with other elites who presided over institutional "centres of power".[17]

More useful for understanding MENA is the neo-Weberian concept of *neo-patrimonialism,* a hybrid of personal and bureaucratic authority in which there can be considerable variation in the relative balance between the two sources of authority. Such variations may go some way to explaining how the regimes reacted to the uprisings and the resulting differences in trajectories. Stepan and Linz[18] argued that the more patrimonial the regime, the less likely a peaceful transition in the face of protests since there would less likely be softliners in the regime with enough independence of the leader to ally with softliners in the opposition in order to remove the president; thus, in Syria the security forces were colonized by the presidential clan's clientele network and elites remained cohesive behind the president. Conversely, where the state bureaucratic apparatus enjoyed relative autonomy of the leader and was not colonized by a particular identity group, as in Egypt and Tunisia, it was able to sacrifice the presidential family to save the state via agreement between regime softliners and peaceful protestors. Stacher[19] agrees on the outcome but explains it in almost opposite terms: the relative centralization of power in Egypt allowed the decision to be taken on a swift presidential removal without imperilling the whole regime and also allowing its restoration of control over society; in Syria's more decentralized regime, nobody had the power to decide on a swift transition.

The capability of neo-patrimonial regimes to resist an uprising over the *longer term* probably depends on some *balance* between personal authority and bureaucratic capability. While the personal authority of the president helps contain elite factionalism and his clientalization of the state apparatus helps minimize defections when it is called upon to use force against protestors, a regime's ability to resist longer term insurgencies and to stabilize post-uprising regimes requires that the state enjoy institutional and co-optative capability such as infrastructural penetration of society via the bureaucracy and ruling political party. Thus, the Egyptian state had the bureaucratic capacity to reconstitute its authority over the whole of the country's territory, except for some contestation by Islamist insurgents in Sinai.

Thus, we can hypothesize that the *patrimonial-bureaucratic balance* determines regime resistance capacities. Where the bureaucratic capacity is high relative to the patrimonial authority, loyalty to the leader is low but its capacity to sustain the state establishment is high (Tunisia and Egypt); where the patrimonial side is high and the bureaucratic low, the state apparatus stays loyal but the state collapses, as in Libya, where the leader's clientele networks were far stronger than state institutions. Stalemate is more likely where there is an even patrimonial-bureaucratic balance. In Yemen, splits in the ruling elite core plus weak bureaucratic institutions led to increasing fragmentation of power over state territory. In Syria, state institutions, in spite of colonization by regime in-group *assabiyya*, were too strong to be overthrown by the opposition but too weak to retain control of the whole territory of the state.

Conclusion

Put together, these variables shape two polar opposite starting points: (1) quick relatively peaceful leadership change that does not jeopardize the state or (2) protracted violent conflict that puts the state at risk.

(1) Where grievances and social mobilization were high, political incorporation low, and the opportunity structure had shifted in favour of society, mass mobilization produced a bandwagoning effect; where state institutions had sufficient capacity and autonomy, presidents were rapidly and peacefully removed but state institutions remained intact. This pathway required some minimum form of insider-outsider transition coalition, issuing from negotiations between softliners in the army and bureaucracy and a moderate Islamist-democratic opposition coalition. It requires a broadly mobilized (cross-class, cross-sectarian) opposition coalition to force the regime into negotiations and a sufficient level of bureaucratic over patrimonial authority within the regime to empower regime softliners.

(2) Where social mobilization exceeded political incorporation, and there were enough grievances for anti-regime rebellion to be sustained but insufficient grievances to rapidly remove the patrimonial leader (without external help) owing to the dilution of mobilization by cross-cutting cleavages and insufficient opportunity structure (civil society experience), but where, also, institutions lacked autonomy to turn against the leader and pursue a transition coalition without endangering the whole regime, and had sufficient bureaucratic capacity to stand against rebellion yet not enough to sustain control over the whole territory against rebels, the outcome was *protracted conflict*, with extended *stalemates* between regime and opposition, leading to varying degrees of state failure, as in Syria, Libya, and Yemen. In the Libyan case, external intervention overcame the stalemate but without sufficient conditions for state reconstruction.

These variant starting points generate a path dependency that narrows the chances for some trajectories and enables others. The probabilities are stacked against democratization where the uprising turns into violent revolt and state failure, which fragments authority among rival leaderships. Peaceful removal of the leader allows *either* moves toward democratic transition *or* restoration of a hybrid regime when, despite removal of the leader, a new exclusionary insider-outsider coalition reverses transitions: thus, in Egypt a hardliner coalition of regime and secular opposition re-formed to exclude the Muslim Brotherhood. Nevertheless, such variant outcomes are not predetermined by the starting point and are continually reshaped by the balance of agency among contending social forces, including external powers, and the political economy and political cultural context in which their competition takes place. These variables are examined in the following articles and summarized in the conclusion.

In the next article, Morten Valjborn, surveys the theoretical debates over democratization in the Middle East, considers the consequences of the Arab uprisings for the credibility of rival democratization and post-democratization paradigms and asks how re-conceptualizations can throw light on the actually existing politics in the post-uprising Arab world. Vincent Durac then examines anti-regime movements in the light of social movement theory, assessing how it enables us to understand their relative efficacy in challenging regimes but their inability to steer a democratic transition. Joshua Stacher examines the increased violence deployed by regimes to prevent such a transition, arguing that the outcome, the remaking of more coercive authoritarian regimes, denotes neither transition nor restoration to the pre-uprising period. Next, Frédéric Volpi and Ewan Stein examine the third major category of players, variegated Islamists, assessing consequences of the relative balance between them for post-uprising politics. James Allison then examines the positive effect of a class balance, notably the relative efficacy and autonomy of workers' movements, on democratic potentials. Adham Saouli assesses the opposite, negative scenario, the mobilization of communal identities by ruling elites and counter-elites. Raymond Hinnebusch focuses on the also negative impact on democratization of competitive external interference inside the uprising states. In the conclusion, the combined effects of the agency of these forces and the political, cultural, and economic contexts in which they operate are summarized to understand three main divergent trajectories taken by the post-uprising states.

Disclosure statement

No potential conflict of interest was reported by the author.

Notes

1. Brownlee, Masoud, and Reynolds, "Why the Modest Harvest?"
2. Pace and Cavatorta, "The Arab Uprisings in Theoretical Perspective."
3. Hinnebusch, "Historical Sociology and the Arab Uprising."
4. Sorenson, *Democracy and Democratization.*
5. Hinnebusch, "Authoritarian Persistence," 374–375.
6. Ashcar, *The People Want*; see also Heyderian, *How Capitalism Failed.*
7. Brynen et al., *Beyond the Arab Spring*, 213–232.
8. Ibid., 147–172.
9. Tripp, *The Power and the People*, 95; Ghobashy, "The Praxis."
10. Lynch, *The Arab Uprising*, 43–65, 165; Brynen et al., *Beyond the Arab Spring*, 233–256; Heyderian, *How Capitalism Failed*, 1–33; Weyland, "The Arab Spring."
11. Stephan and Chenoweth, "Why Civil Resistance Works."
12. O'Donnell and Schmitter, *Transitions from Authoritarian Rule.*
13. Weyland, "The Arab Spring," 924.
14. Brownlee, Masoud, and Reynolds, "Why the Modest Harvest?"
15. Stepan and Linz, "Democratization Theory and the 'Arab Spring.'"
16. Brownlee, Masoud, and Reynolds, "Why the Modest Harvest?"
17. Stacher, *Adaptable Autocrats.*
18. Stepan and Linz, "Democratization Theory and the 'Arab Spring.'"
19. Stacher, *Adaptable Autocrats.*

References

Ashcar, Gilbert. *The People Want: A Radical Exploration of the Arab Uprising*. London: Saqi Books, 2013.

Brownlee, Jason, Tarek Masoud, and Andrew Reynolds. "Why the Modest Harvest?" *Journal of Democracy* 24, no. 1 (2013): 29–44.

Brynen, Rex, Pete Moore, Bassel Salloukh, Marie-Joelle Zahar. *Beyond the Arab Spring: Authoritarianism and Democratization in the Arab World*. Boulder, CO: Lynne Rienner Publishers, 2012.

Ghobashy, Mona. "The Praxis of the Egyptian Revolution." *Middle East Report* 258 (2011). www.merip.org/mer/mer258/praxis-egyptian-revolution

Heyderian, Richard Javad. *How Capitalism Failed the Arab World: The Economic Roots and Precarious Future of the Middle East Uprisings*. London: Zed Books, 2014.

Hinnebusch, Raymond. "Authoritarian Persistence, Democratization Theory and the Middle East: An Overview and Critique." *Democratization* 13, no. 3 (2006): 373–395.

Hinnebusch, Raymond. "Historical Sociology and the Arab Uprising." *Mediterranean Politics* 19, no. 1 (2014): 137–140.

Lynch, Marc. *The Arab Uprising: The Unfinished Revolutions of the New Middle East*. New York: Public Affairs, 2012.

O'Donnell, Guillermo, and Philippe Schmitter. *Transitions from Authoritarian Rule: Tentative Conclusions about Uncertain Democracies, Part 4*. Baltimore, MD. Johns Hopkins University Press, 1986.

Pace, Michelle, and Francesco Cavatorta. "The Arab Uprisings in Theoretical Perspective – An Introduction." *Mediterranean Politics* 17, no. 2 (2012): 125–138.

Sorenson, Georg. *Democracy & Democratization*. Boulder, CO: Westview Press, 1998.

Stacher, Joshua. *Adaptable Autocrats: Regime Power in Egypt and Syria*. Standford, CA: Stanford University Press, 2012.

Stepan, A., and J. J. Linz. "Democratization Theory and the 'Arab Spring.'" *Journal of Democracy* 24, no. 2 (2013): 15–30.

Stephan, Maria J., and Erica Chenoweth. "Why Civil Resistance Works: The Strategic Logic of Nonviolent Conflict." *International Security* 33, no. 1 (2008): 7–44.

Tripp, Charles. *The Power and the People: Paths of Resistance in the Middle East*. Cambridge: Cambridge University Press, 2014.

Weyland, Kurt. "The Arab Spring: Why the Surprising Similarities with the Revolutionary Wave of 1848?" *Perspectives on Politics* 10, no. 4 (2012): 917–934.

Reflections on self-reflections – On framing the analytical implications of the Arab uprisings for the study of Arab politics

Morten Valbjørn

Department of Political Science, Aarhus University, Aarhus, Denmark

> The Arab uprisings have not only impacted large parts of the Arab world. They have also left their mark on scholarship about Arab politics. Following the unexpected events, scholars have been engaged in a self-reflective debate on whether their assumptions and theoretical approaches to Arab politics have proven inadequate and their reasoning flawed, and if some kind of rethink is necessary for how this is supposed to take place. The present article, which belongs in the realms of meta-studies, reflects on these self-reflections. By presenting and evaluating some of the specific positions within this more inward-looking part of the Arab uprisings debate, the article brings attention to how this line of more self-reflective questions can – and has been – addressed within very different kinds of "frames" and how these are associated with very different ways of discussing the analytical applications of the Arab uprisings for Arab politics. More specifically, the article identifies three kinds of framing: (i) a *who-has-been-vindicated-and-made-obsolete framing*, where the core interest is in picking winners and losers among the last decades' (post)democratization currents in Middle East studies; (ii) a *how-do-we-synthesize-and-upgrade framing*, where the ambition is to revise and combine insights from the analytical toolboxes of both authoritarian resilience and democratization; and finally (iii) a *how-do-we-get-beyond-the-democratization/authoritarianism-paradogma framing*, which perceives the Arab uprisings as an opportunity to engage in a more basic reflection about how (Arab) politics has been and should be debated and whether it is time to make the study of Arab politics into a "genuine science of *politics*" instead of being reduced mainly to topics of democratization and authoritarian resilience.

Introduction

The Arab uprisings have not only impacted large parts of the Arab world. Since 2011, they have also left their mark on scholarship about Arab politics, which has been preoccupied with discussing the uprisings and their implications. Much of this debate has revolved around the immediate and underlying causes of the Arab uprisings, their nature and different trajectories in various Arab countries, or the broader question about the consequences these dramatic events are going to have for future Arab politics.

This debate has, however, also had a more inward-looking and self-reflective dimension. It concerns the *analytical* implications of the Arab uprisings for the study of Arab politics *as such*.[1] Given that the vast majority of observers and academic experts were, alongside Arab leaders themselves, also taken by surprise in 2011, it has been asked whether scholarship about Arab politics has similarly been undermined by the Arab uprisings: to what extent have the Arab uprisings proved our assumptions and theoretical approaches to Arab politics inadequate and our reasoning flawed, requiring a fundamental rethink of our way of studying Arab politics? This article, which belongs in the realms of meta-studies,[2] reflects on this more self-reflective dimension of the Arab uprisings debate. The aim is not only to present and evaluate some of the specific positions within this more inward-looking debate, which during the last four years have been reflected in soul-searching, scathing critiques as well as rejoinders and rebuttals. The purpose is also to bring attention to how this line of more self-reflective questions can – and have been – addressed within very different kinds of "frames" and how these are associated with very different ways of discussing the analytical applications of the Arab uprisings for Arab politics.

More specifically, the article identifies three different kinds of framing: (i) a *who-has-been-vindicated-and-made-obsolete framing*, where the core interest is in picking winners and losers among the last decades' (post)democratization currents in Middle East studies; (ii) a *how-do-we-synthesize-and-upgrade framing*, where the ambition is to revise and combine insights from the analytical toolboxes of both authoritarian resilience and democratization; and finally (iii) a *how-do-we-get-beyond-the-democratization/authoritarianism-paradogma framing*, which perceives the Arab uprisings as an opportunity to engage in a broader and more basic reflection about how (Arab) politics has been and should be debated and whether it is time to make the study of Arab politics into a "genuine science of *politics*" instead of being reduced mainly to topics of democratization and authoritarian resilience.

From democracy-spotting to post-democratization

Before turning to these framings of the debate about the analytical implications of the Arab uprisings, it is necessary to sketch out how Arab politics previously was discussed and approached. One of the much-debated issues since the late 1980s concerns the prospects for democracy and the resilience of authoritarianism in the Arab world. In simplified terms this debate can be divided into two eras, defined by "democracy-spotting" and "post-democratization".[3]

The era of democracy-spotting

As a reflection of the so-called "Third Wave of Democratization",[4] which began in the early 1970s and gained global momentum after the democratic revolutions in eastern Europe, democratization received tremendous attention in 1990s political science debates. In line with Francis Fukuyama's triumphant statement about the "End of History",[5] political development was increasingly perceived in terms of a dichotomous autocracy/democracy transition scheme. Within the so-called "transition paradigm", the question of how to ensure a successful transition to the "post-historical" world was portrayed almost as a matter of programme design and implementation.

The Middle East at that time did not receive much attention in the *general* academic and more policy-oriented debates on democratization. The region was either simply ignored or perceived as being "out of step with history". The optimistic expectations about a universal democratic transition and the transition paradigm from the general democratization debate did, however, influence parts of Middle East studies. During the 1990s, this was reflected in the emergence of "democracy-spotters". Often by drawing on insights from democratic transitions elsewhere and by applying theoretical models and concepts derived from them, these scholars were busy spotting signs, particularly those emerging from what was perceived as an increasingly "autonomous society",[6] confirming their expectation that the Middle East was also in a transition to democracy. Attention was drawn to how a crisis of legitimacy was eroding autocratic regimes; to the many elections, the (re)instatement of parliaments and the (re)introduction of multi-party systems; to various political liberalizations; and to the emergence of a vibrant civil society and public debates in which *ta'addudiya* (pluralism) and *dimuqratiyya* (democracy) were figuring as the predominant concepts. The process of democratization was seen as being not different in the Middle East than elsewhere – just a bit slower.[7] Others proclaimed that "the defining concept of the 1990s is democracy"[8] and that "the long-term trend will be toward greater liberalization and more representative government in the Arab world".[9]

The era of post-democratization

At the turn of the new millennium, this very optimistic mood had changed. A survey of political reform in the Arab world, concluded that "it is impossible to talk about a democratic paradigm shift in any of the countries discussed"[10] and Holger Albrecht and Oliver Schlumberger argued that waiting for democracy was like "waiting for Godot".[11] Thus, the Middle East not only still figured as the least free region in the world; the democracy gap had, during the 1990s, even widened. The many nominal reforms did not result in the expected democratic transition but only brought the region into what Daniel Brumberg described as a "transition to nowhere".[12]

The hopeful but also rather teleological democracy-spotting of what was now perceived as the "demo-*crazy*" 1990s was therefore met with growing criticism within parts of Middle East studies. Besides the misfit between the optimistic expectations and the depressing reality of resilient authoritarianism, the democracy-spotters were charged with being blind to how the countless but selective and regime-led reforms were not an expression of a democratic transition but part of a regime-preserving strategy following Lampedusa's famous "if-we-want-things-to-stay-as-they-are-things-will-have-to-change" doctrine.[13] Due to a tendency to equate change with democratization, the democracy-spotters were at the same time criticized for being blind to how the absence of change *of* regime is not necessarily synonymous with standstill; one can imagine changes *in* regimes as authoritarianism transforms into new and "upgraded" forms[14] or various changes at the society level without a direct impact on regimes. In this context, calls were made for scholars of Arab politics to enter the "*era of post-democratization*",[15] focusing less on "what ought to be" and more on "what in fact is", which from this perspective was resilient authoritarianism. Thus, instead of engaging in wishful democracy-spotting or debates about the "failure of democratization", one should seek a better understanding of "the success of authoritarianism".

In the decade before the Arab uprisings, this change of perspective first and foremost manifested itself in a major and fertile debate about the durable but also dynamic nature of Arab authoritarianism.[16] This "renaissance in the study of authoritarianism"[17] provided important insights into a variety of forms of authoritarianism, for example, upgraded, monarchical, (post) populist, and liberalized autocracies, and the specific techniques employed by these regimes in the management of elections, parliaments, civil society, external democracy support, and so on.[18]

The major part of the post-democratization trend applied a very regime-centred focus on Arab politics. It paid only limited attention to the society level, which was perceived as marked by political apathy among an increasingly de-politicized population without any ability to challenge regimes in power. A parallel but less influential sub-current did, however, call on Middle East scholarship to move beyond the "democratization and authoritarianism *paradogma*"[19] and look for changes in forms of politics not directly related to the regime level. This more society-centred focus was not, however, associated with any expectation of imminent region-wide upheaval. If anything, they rather expected a growing state/society de-linkage. Instead of trying to bring change of/in their governments, citizens, the argument went, would ignore the formal political institutions in favour of setting up alternative social structures parallel to the official state order.

Despite these differences between the two sub-currents within the post-democratization trend, when it came to the question about prospects for any genuine democratization there was a general consensus that "if the end of history comes with the triumph of democracy, the Middle East has plenty of history ahead of itself yet".[20]

A region of surprises: the Arab uprisings, 2011

When the first decade of the twenty-first century drew to a close, the post-democratization current appeared as a useful lens through which to observe Arab politics. Those interested in the durability and dynamics of Arab authoritarianism were for instance able to explain why two decades of nominal reforms had not produced any genuine democratization. At the turn of 2010, however, the Arab world once again lived up to its reputation for surprising Middle East scholars at least once a decade. Given the stress on resilient authoritarianism and de-politicized populations, few expected that the self-immolation of a Tunisian street vender could ignite a regional "Tunis-ami" that would set in motion peaceful protest movements that could undermine authoritarian rulers such as Egypt's Mubarak or Tunisia's Ben Ali – *the* prototypes of successful upgraded authoritarianism.[21] It is therefore hardly surprising that the unexpected Arab uprisings produced a soul-searching "what-went-wrong" debate, similar to those that followed previous "Middle East surprises".[22] Besides the question about whether it is possible to predict revolutionary events like the Arab uprisings as such,[23] this debate has revolved around the issue of whether our approaches and theoretical assumptions about Arab politics are inadequate and our reasoning flawed. This line of questioning can be approached in quite different ways, and the answers reached depend very much upon how the question is framed.

The who-has-been-vindicated-and-made-obsolete framing

One possible way of framing the question about the analytical implications of the Arab uprisings is by asking who has been vindicated and who now appears obsolete and whether "the democratic Godot" has at last arrived in the region or the "authoritarian Lampedusa" still rules.[24]

The early months of 2011 were characterized by jubilant statements about how this was "the Arab 1989", where the Arab people reclaimed power from their authoritarian rulers and started the "fourth wave of democratization".[25] "Durable authoritarianism" had turned out to be a mirage. Thus, the Arab uprisings had according to this perspective not only brought down a number of Arab rulers, but also those *Gedankenhäuser* who had prophesied their resilience.[26] Michael Hudson rhetorically asked if he and his "democracy-spotting" colleagues of the 1990s really were so "demo-*crazy*" after all, or if they had been vindicated by the Arab uprisings.[27] Gregory Gause listed a range of areas in which the literature on the stability of Arab authoritarianism in his view misread or missed important factors.[28] According to Marc Lynch, the Arab uprisings had destabilized the conclusions developed over the previous decade to explain the resilience of Arab authoritarianism.[29] This literature, too obsessed with understanding the dynamics and durability of authoritarianism, had been too narrowly regime-centred at the expense of attention to the power of the people and those dynamics and changes at the society level that enabled the uprisings. Attention, it was argued, should now be directed to how far various parts of the Arab world had gone in democratic transition and on understanding the actors and dynamics in this democratization process. In doing so, scholars of Arab politics should reopen the analytical toolbox of the general democratization literature, discredited in the previous decade, and draw on experiences from previous democratization processes elsewhere. This renewed interest in the prospects of democracy in the Arab world has already given rise to a considerable literature. Some have reintroduced transitology and, for instance, discussed the role of elites and political parties in democratization processes.[30] Others have returned to the classic debate about civil society and democratization and how social movements can play a significant role in subverting authoritarian regimes.[31] Many of these studies, moreover, adopt a cross-regional perspective by comparing the Arab uprisings with democratization processes in Latin America, southern/eastern Europe or Asia.[32] While these comparisons have sometimes led to an acknowledgement that there might be momentary setbacks, the long-term trend is still assumed to be toward democracy.[33]

In this debate, however, it is also possible to identify another and far less optimistic position, doubting that the Arab uprisings are going to mark the end of Arab authoritarianism and the beginning of a democratic transition. In addition to the existing repertoire of regime-preserving strategies, many regimes have, according to Steven Heydemann and Reinoud Leenders, shown an increasing ability to adapt to these new challenges and to learn from the failures and successes of others.[34] Besides repression and violence in both new and more well-known forms, these strategies also include new versions of the well-known Lampedusan "if-we-want-things-to-stay-as-they-are-things-will-have-to-change" strategy. From this perspective, the nominal concessions some regimes have made to protesters are not necessarily signs of the arrival of the "democratic Godot". They may just as well be an indication of how the "liberalizing autocracies" in the region are continuing the kind of pseudo-liberalizations that were the defining feature of the previous two decades' "transition to nowhere". Carothers warned that comparisons to the democratic revolutions in eastern Europe could be misleading[35] owing to differences in the natures of the *anciens régimes*, the opposition movements and existing societies, and the geopolitical context. Moreover, Arab regimes have previously managed large protests by means very similar to those employed today.[36] In an early discussion of post-Mubarak Egypt, Jason Brownlee and Joshua Stacher called attention to how a *de facto* continuity is also possible in situations where the ruler is forced to resign, ending up with "change of leader, continuity of system"[37] – or "Mubarakism without Mubarak".[38] In situations where the ruling regime, and not just the leader, is unseated, Eva Bellin points out that the fall of an authoritarian regime does not necessary translate into the rise of democracy.[39] Historically, the usual scenario has, in fact, been for one authoritarian regime to be replaced by another. In Lucan Way's view, when the dust settles, some form of authoritarianism is likely to dominate the Arab world for a long time,[40] and according to Heydemann, the future of Arab authoritarianism will even be "darker, more repressive, more sectarian and even more deeply resistant to democratization than in the past".[41] Instead of returning to wishful democracy-spotting, scholars are from this perspective better served by sticking to the well-equipped analytical toolbox of the previous decade on the durability and dynamics of Arab authoritarianism, which according to Brownlee may end up being vindicated.[42]

The popularity of these two perspectives has fluctuated since 2011. In the early days of the Arab uprisings, the former found much support. Its optimism seemed to be supported by region-wide demands for democracy and credible elections in Egypt, Tunisia, and Libya. Subsequently, as many Arab autocracies have proved more resilient than initially expected, the uprisings in Syria, Yemen, and Libya have turned into chaotic civil wars, and Egypt's first democratically elected president was toppled in a military coup, the more pessimistic perspective began to gain ground. Some initial optimists did moreover recognize that "it is probably too early for 'democracy spotters' in the Middle East to claim vindication for their predictions".[43] While the latter and more pessimistic perspective has much to offer in explaining the current situation, the literature on authoritarian resilience can hardly be depicted as completely untouched by the Arab uprisings. That huge popular protests could lead to the overthrow of the leaders of some of the allegedly most stable autocratic regimes certainly poses a challenge to assumptions about autocratic stability. It moreover highlights the problems of a very narrow focus on the regime level at the expense of attention to dynamics at a far less de-politicized society level. Additionally, it is hard to write off all political reforms as nothing but a continuation of the last decades' "transition to nowhere". In Tunisia, hopes for some democratic transition seem warranted, and although many of the recent reform initiatives in for example Jordan and Morocco may be based on Lampedusan logic, old tricks may be less efficient today.[44]

While the two perspectives differ in their views on the nature of Arab politics following the Arab uprisings, both in fact offer valuable insights for understanding Arab politics. At the same time, neither gets the whole picture and both strands of literature have shortcomings. This is easily neglected if the question about the analytical implications of the Arab uprisings is posed in either/or terms, as is the case in this first framing. For another kind of framing this observation constitutes however the basic point of departure.

The how-do-we-synthesize-and-upgrade framing

Instead of perceiving the Arab world as being either in a transition to democracy or "transition to nowhere", the post-uprising process can alternatively be conceptualized as a "transition to somewhere",[45] marked by both important changes and continuity. It is perceived as rather open-ended without any teleology and every part of the Arab world is moreover not expected to follow the same trajectory. In order to grasp this complex transition process, it might be necessary not only to combine and integrate insights from the analytical toolboxes of both democratization and authoritarian resilience, but also to revise and recalibrate some of the assumptions and approaches of these traditions. This idea constitutes the overall point of departure for the second kind of framing. Thus, instead of declaring one or the other analytical approach obsolete or vindicated, subscribers to this framing are "far more interested in the challenge of synthesis"[46] and very intent on not "throwing out the baby with the bath water".[47] As the complexities of the implications of the Arab uprisings become more obvious, this kind of framing has become increasingly prominent but it is possible to identify different strategies as to how upgrading and synthesis should be accomplished.

On revisiting and revising existing approaches

The first strategy basically stays within one or the other of the existing approaches, aiming mainly to remedy some of the analytical shortcomings revealed by the Arab uprisings. While the authoritarian upgrading and liberalizing autocracies' approaches in some respects seemed discredited by the Arab uprisings,[48] instead of throwing the whole approach overboard, the uprisings should from this perspective be taken as an occasion to deepen our understanding of the at times *contradictory* dynamics of authoritarianism. More specifically, more attention should be paid to the *un*intended consequences of Lampedusan strategies: authoritarian upgrading may generate its own problems and weaken the regime as a consequence of underdeveloped political institutions and a lack of political legitimacy.

Another example is the critical rethink of debates about civil society, social movements, and political activism.[49] On the one hand, the important role of mass mobilization and protest movements during the Arab uprisings has brought attention to the fact that Arab societies were less passive and depoliticized, political activism was less inefficient, and civil society more independent from authoritarian regimes than was often claimed in critiques of civil society enthusiasm among the 1990s "democracy-spotters". On the other hand, it is acknowledged that it is important not to throw out the insights of the past decade about "government-organized non-governmental organizations" (GONGOs) and how regimes through various techniques try to control civil society. In order to acknowledge the "rise of civil society" it is, according to Lina Khatib and Ellen Lust, moreover necessary to move beyond the classic civil society literature's narrow focus on formal civil society institutions and pay more attention to new and more informal forms of political activism.[50] Similarly, Paul Aarts et al. have suggested that traditional social movement theory should be complemented by Asef Bayat's theory about non-movements and non-collective collective action.[51]

A final example of this strategy is represented by Alfred Stepan and Juan Linz, who revisited the democratization debate during the "third wave" in order to examine whether the classic concepts and assumptions are applicable to the Arab uprisings.[52] They end up with three suggestions for revisions. The first follows from the observation that because conflict concerning religion, or between religions, did not figure prominently in Latin American or eastern European democratizations, the relationship between religion and democratization is under-theorized. With the Arab uprisings, in which Islam has played a central role, it is however necessary to consider how democracy and religion can flourish through what they call "twin tolerations". The second suggestion concerns their own regime typology, which is supplemented by a new sixth "historically constructed" category: the "authoritarian-democratic hybrid". This regime type is present in contexts where major political actors believe that they will lose legitimacy and their followers' support should they fail to embrace certain core features of democracy, yet are prepared to resort to authoritarian approaches when necessary. Finally, Stepan and Linz suggest that the concept of sultanism should be viewed as a continuum and argue that the more sultanistic the pre-revolutionary regime, the greater the obstacles to democratization.

On combining traditions and integrating insights

Instead of revisiting and revising a single specific approach or issue, the second strategy is more about *combining* different approaches and traditions and *integrating* their insights in order to provide a more nuanced picture of the complexities of this "transition to somewhere". An example of this is Aarts et al.'s discussion of the likelihood of democratic transitions in Tunisia, Egypt, Libya, and Yemen.[53] They emphasize that authoritarian breakdown is an insufficient condition for a democratic transition but by selectively combining insights from a range of classic literature, including Rustow, Lipset, Linz and Stepan, they identify five "indicators of likelihood": the level of economic development, the degree of concentration of national wealth, the institutional power of the state, national unity, and historical experience with political pluralism. Against this background, they conclude that Tunisia is most likely to succeed to some kind of democracy, Egypt has potential but is less certain, and Libya and Yemen are unlikely to experience any democratic transition in the near future.

Another variant of this strategy can be found in Hudson's argument that both schools of thought in the (post)democratization debate before the uprisings have their merits, but that the Arab uprisings and chaotic aftermath cast doubt on the adequacy of both. As such, it is necessary, he argues, "to turn away from these polarities and look to new ways of understanding the complicated new realities".[54] In this endeavour, Hudson identifies three areas for new scholarly (re)thinking: he sees a need for research on the relation of the global level's penetration of the Middle East regional system to the Arab uprisings. Another area concerns social movements and civil society, which could draw on some of the work from the 1990s if the concept of "civil" is further unpacked and the role of tribes, youth, and new information technology is given more attention. Finally, authoritarian resilience literature has according to Hudson much to offer on control capabilities and bureaucratic structures but should in his view be supplemented with investigations into elite-relations, the way regimes (fail to) learn, leadership, and the "idea of a state" as a "state of mind" with moral weight. This requires, Hudson concludes, that we return to the classic question of political legitimacy, which might be difficult to operationalize but nevertheless crucial for our understanding of Arab politics before and after the uprisings.

A final example of this synthesizing effort is present in the discussion about how a nuanced understanding of the degree of change and continuity in the Arab world's "transition to somewhere" requires an – paraphrasing Heydemann – "upgrading of post-democratization studies".[55] To understand what is actually happening it is not only necessary to understand the dynamics of authoritarianism, including the aforementioned *un*intended consequences, but also "what in fact is" going on at the society level. This requires that the post-democratization tradition begins a "dialogue" with more society-centric traditions and integrates their insights about social (non)movement and political culture. By doing so we should be better equipped to recognize dimensions of change in what at first sight appears to be continuity as well as elements of continuity in apparent changes. The efficiency of a continued Lampedusan strategy may for instance be different from before if the Arab uprisings have changed the "audience" – the population and their political culture – so much that they no longer accept the old "reform-theatre". Conversely, a regime change without the emergence of a new political culture may lead to a situation with "new actors, but same script".[56]

On specifying when and where what works

While the previous strategies in this second framing have been about making revisions and synthesizing, the overall aim of the last strategy is more about specifying the circumstances under which different approaches are still useful, in need of an upgrade, or have become obsolete.

An example is provided in Volpi's exploration into the trajectories of democratization and authoritarianism in the Maghreb, in which he asks to what extent it is sensible still to rely on the literature about authoritarian resilience.[57] In answering this question Volpi argues that as this literature is primarily about *institutionalized* mechanisms of authoritarian governance its utility depends upon whether institutionalized political processes obtain. He therefore concludes that while this literature is still useful in explaining the (limited) implications of the Arab uprisings in Morocco and Algeria, we have to look elsewhere for analytical tools to account for the mechanisms of de-and re-institutionalization in Libya and Tunisia.

Upgrades and revisions within an existing debate

Although it is possible to identify different specific strategies as to exactly how an upgrading and synthesizing is going to take place, the overall position of this second framing is that in order to understand the complexities of the Arab world's "transition to somewhere" it is necessary to get out of the oscillation between the (post)democratization poles that has been so dominant not only in past decades but also the early Arab uprisings debate. As reflected in the frequent reference to "democratization" and "authoritarianism" in the titles of many of these revising and synthesizing efforts,[58] this framing does however stay within a "democratization and authoritarianism *paradogma*" and this is exactly what the third and final framing wants to get beyond.

The how-do-we-get-beyond-the-democratization-and-authoritarianism-*paradogma* framing

While disagreements might be the most visible feature of debates in academia and elsewhere, debates usually also rest on a more basic – but sometimes implicit – agreement among the participants on what to disagree about. This defines the limits of the debate and to some extent is necessary in order to have a meaningful debate. But now and then it can be useful to reflect upon the implications of this unspoken agreement and whether the terms of debate should be different.

This general observation constitutes the point of departure for a third possible way of framing the question about the analytical implications of the Arab uprisings. It considers these events as an opportunity to engage in a broader and more fundamental (self)reflection about how (Arab) politics has been and should be debated. More specifically, it asks whether it is time to get beyond the prevalent "democratization and authoritarianism *paradogma*" and make the study of Arab politics into a "genuine science of *politics*" instead of being reduced mainly to topics of democratization and authoritarian resilience.

Searching where the light shines – revisited in a re-politicized Arab world

This ambition can be traced back to Lisa Anderson's critical review of the (post)-democratization debate,[59] which was part of the aforementioned more radical but less influential sub-current of the post-democratization strand. Anderson not only criticized the 1990s "democracy-spotters" for "searching where the light shines", for which reason they came up empty handed. Her critique also extended to the authoritarian resilience literature. In her view it represented "little more than the obverse of the 'inevitability of democracy' inflected with pessimism", as attention was directed to the same research subjects as the democracy-spotters.[60] Both traditions thus represented different aspects of the same "democratization and authoritarianism *paradogma*".[61] According to Anderson, this tendency was closely related to the provincialism of American political science that had confined its field of research to *liberal* politics, with a narrow focus on electoral systems, parliaments, parties, and other liberal institutions, that Anderson argued, would leave us with a very incomplete if not distorted understanding of where to look for the keys to political dynamics in a place like the Arab world.[62] Questions relating to *nation-building and identity formation, insurrection, sectarian and tribal politics, the resilience of monarchies, the dynamics of rentier-states, the role of the military in politics, the politics of informal economies, and transnational networks* were dimensions of political life that might not be directly related to authoritarianism/democratization but were of crucial importance to Arab politics. A focus on them would contribute to (re)making political science into a "genuine science of *politics*".[63]

While Anderson's critique was written well before the Arab uprisings, her call for a broadening of our conception of the political seems directly relevant to the current realities of military rule in Egypt, clashing militias in Libya, sectarian rivalries in Syria, resilient royals in the Gulf, an increasingly fragile Yemeni state, the declaration by the transnational Islamic State of a caliphate in parts of Syria and Iraq, proclamations of "the end of the Sykes/Picot state order" and yet another Israeli-Palestinian war in Gaza.

From this perspective, the most distinctive feature of the Arab uprisings appears so far to be less about democratization or authoritarian resilience than about what can be described as a *multi-dimensional re-politicization of Arab politics*.[64] This has not only been reflected in a (brief?) revitalization of the formal political scene in some Arab countries, where parliaments, elections, and parties have become more meaningful. It is equally expressed in the explosion of various new forms of contentious politics in formal and informal spheres, new forms of intertwinements between religion and politics, the (re)emergence of identity politics based on tribe/sect/kinship, the return of the military (and judiciary) to politics, and an intensification of the interplay between domestic and regional politics. Overall and additionally, there is now a widespread feeling that everything is potentially political.

Rediscovering basic but classic debates and reopening old toolboxes

If the most distinctive outcome of the Arab uprisings so far has been a multi-dimensional re-politicization of Arab politics, what would this mean for the question about the analytical implications of the Arab uprisings? From the perspective of this third framing the broadening of our analytical universe is going to take place through the opening of old analytical toolboxes and the rediscovery of more basic but classic debates from before the study of (Arab) politics was reduced mainly to topics of democratization and authoritarian resilience.

If the Arab uprisings mark the "rebirth of Arab politics" and make it necessary to explore how the "texture in politics" has changed, understand "politics by other means", and examine the struggle for (avoiding) the return to "normal politics",[65] an important classic debate to revisit concerns the very fundamental – but these days somewhat neglected – question of "What is politics?" Depending on which definition one favours, one may end up with very different views on for instance whether the Arab world before the uprisings actually was so de-politicized as often claimed, whether it makes sense perceiving the salafists as apolitical before they entered electoral politics in 2011, and whether the parliament, the street, or the judiciary today should be considered as important sites of Arab politics.

Another classic debate to revisit concerns the basic organizing principle of politics and revolves around the question about the merits of state vs society-centred understandings of politics; in other words, should the state be perceived as an autonomous actor with its own interests and capacity to shape society or is the state little more than an arena of socially engendered conflict and/or an instrument of family, sect, or class domination?[66] This classic and very fundamental question has gained new actuality following the Arab uprisings. Thus, both the state and society have since 2011 already been "brought back in" and "kicked out again" several times. This is for instance the case in the debate about the implications for state/society relations in the Arab world of the initial massive mobilization of the Arab public and the subsequent reassertion in places like Egypt of the (deep) state. It is even more obvious in the controversy about the weakening of Arab statehood following the Arab uprisings. Here one finds a heated discussion about whether it is "fact or fiction" that Arab states are nothing but "tribes with flags", that "the driving organizing principle in Arab politics is not based on national affiliation but sectarian and ethnic identity" and that we are currently witnessing the rise of a "crescent of state weakness" that might be the "end of the Sykes-Picot state system".[67] These are far from brand new topics in the study of Arab politics, but appear rather as the most recent version of a debate with a long history. From the perspective of this third framing we would therefore be well-served revisiting earlier contributions to this debate about state/society relations in order to draw lessons about the implications of "over/under-stating" the Arab state.[68]

In order to address some of the other "new" issues that have (re)gained prominence on the agenda about Arab politics following the Arab uprisings, it may in a similar way be useful to examine promises and pitfalls in how these topics have been addressed in the past by revisiting old analytical toolboxes and rereading some of the associated "classics". In line with this suggestion, Huntington's classic discussion of political order in changing societies has for instance gained new attention. Thus, it provides an analytical lens for understanding how a massive re-politicization in states with underdeveloped political institutions may instead of democracy lead to political decay and chaos or alternatively coups carried out by the often most institutionalized group, the military.[69] As a reflection of how the military during the Arab uprisings played a crucial role in a number of countries, though in quite different ways and has returned to centre stage in Arab politics, there has moreover been a renewed interest in the (Arab) "man on horseback". While this topic only gained limited attention in the years before the Arab uprisings based on the assumption that the military had returned to the barracks, the role of the military in Arab politics received much scholarly attention in the past.[70] Against this background, there have recently been a number of calls to revive the classic debate about civil-military relations in the Arab world, but also to reconsider and maybe revise the way we have previously approached the question about the military in politics. It has among others been suggested that it is necessary to pay more attention to the at times contradictory role of the military in state/nation building; to the different kinds of roles the military assumes in homogenous vs heterogeneous societies or in republican vs monarchical regimes; and to new manifestations of the classic issue about the "military/industrial complex" and the political economy of military rule.[71] A cluster of classic debates – and associated "classics" – related to the question about the political implications of incongruity between state and nation and the presence of sub- and supra-state identities has moreover received new attention. In view of the contested nature of national identity in some Arab countries, Dankwart Rustow has for instance been re-introduced as a reminder of how elections in a context without some sense of common nationhood may end up deepening existing cleavages and lead to fragmentation.[72] As a way of grasping how the self-immolation of a street vendor in a rather remote part of Tunisia could ignite a region-wide "Tunis-ami", influencing domestic politics in large parts of the Arab world, it is useful to recall Noble's famous metaphor about the Arab world as a "vast sound chamber", in which currents of thought and information circulate widely and enjoy resonance across state frontiers.[73] Kerr and Seale's classic discussions of Arab politics during the "Arab Cold War" in the 1950s and 1960s have in a similar way been re-launched as potentially useful analytical lenses for grasping the implications of the growing intertwinement of regional and local politics in weakened and therefore permeable states in what has been coined the "new Arab – or Middle East – Cold War".[74] The highly contested notion of political culture has also been revived as part of an attempt to account for whether, why, and how "traditional" forms of social organization – such as tribes and kinship networks, guild-like cliques, sects and religious communities – influence the dynamics of Arab politics.[75] Finally, the cluster of debates about the implications of inclusion/exclusion has received renewed interest. While the question about whether or not inclusion leads to moderation gained much attention in the early days of the Arab uprisings,[76] in particular since the Egyptian military coup in 2013, there has also been a renewed interest in the related classic issue about repression/radicalization and Islamist insurgency. In this debate frequent references have been made not only to Algeria in 1991 but also to 1950s Egypt, where Nasser's repression of the Muslim Brotherhood at the same time gave rise to Qutb'ian militancy and Hudaiby's quietism.[77]

On reflecting on our self-reflections

The Arab uprisings did not only come as a surprise to the rulers in the Arab world, but also to most observers of Arab politics. While the dramatic events first and foremost have impacted on large parts of the Arab world, they have also left their mark on scholarship about Arab politics. Most of the scholarly attention has been directed to the challenge of explaining and understanding the immediate and underlying causes of the uprisings, their nature, and very different trajectories around the Arab world, and to assess what consequences these dramatic events are going to have for future Arab politics. However, the Arab uprisings have also given rise to a more self-reflective debate regarding whether our assumptions and theoretical approaches to Arab politics have been proven inadequate and our reasoning flawed, and if some kind of rethink is necessary regarding how this is supposed to take place. The focus of this article has been on this specific part of the debate about the Arab uprisings. It has not only identified a vast array of specific positions to this more self-reflective *problematique* and shown how this debate has given rise to various forms of soul-searching, critiques, and rejoinders among the participants, it has also shown how these positions are not only related to different views on the nature and implications of the Arab uprisings (for example, will it lead to a "transition to democracy"; "transition to nowhere", "transition to somewhere"?), but also to different ways of framing the overall *problematique*. Thus, the article has identified three different kinds of "frames" and has shown how these are associated with very different ways of debating the analytical implications of the Arab uprisings. In this way, the article also serves as a reminder of the fact that the kind of answers you end up with depend upon how you are posing your questions – and for this reason it is useful now and then to reflect upon how we are reflecting.

Acknowledgements

I would like to thank Eric Davis, Michael Hudson, Mervat Hatem, Steven Heydemann, Raymond Hinnebusch, August Richard Norton, and anonymous reviewers for constructive comments and suggestions on various ideas discussed in this article.

Disclosure statement

No potential conflict of interest was reported by the author.

Notes

1. Cf. Gause, "Why Middle East Studies"; Pace and Cavatorta, "The Arab Uprisings"; Brynen et al., *Beyond the Arab Spring*; Aarts et al., *From Resilience to Revolt*; POMEPS, "Arab Uprisings"; Valbjørn and Volpi, "Revisiting Theories."
2. For a discussion of the purpose of different kinds of meta-studies see Zhao, "Metatheory"
3. For a detailed account of these two eras see Valbjørn and Bank, "Examining the 'Post' in Post-democratization."
4. Huntington, "The Third Wave."
5. Fukuyama, "The End of History?"
6. Hudson, "Democratization and the Problem of Legitimacy."
7. Bromley, "Middle East Exceptionalism," 328.
8. Norton, "The Future of Civil Society," 206.
9. Hudson, "After the Gulf War," 426.
10. Choucair-Vizoso, "Movement in Lieu of Change."
11. Albrecht and Schlumberger, "'Waiting for Godot.'"
12. Brumberg, "Liberalization Versus Democracy."
13. In Giuseppe Tomasi di Lampedusa's classic novel *The Leopard* on the changes in Sicilian life and society during the Risorgimento one of the leading characters, Tancredi, famously states that "if we want things to stay as they are, things will have to change." 40.
14. Heydemann, "Upgrading Authoritarianism."
15. Heydemann, "La question"; cf. Albrecht and Schlumberger, "Waiting for 'Godot'"; Anderson, "Searching Where the Light Shines."

16. Schlumberger, *Debating Arab Authoritarianism*.
17. Bank, "Die Renaissance."
18. Lucas, "Monarchial Authoritarianism"; Posusney and Angrist, *Authoritarianism in the Middle East*; Hinnebusch, "Authoritarian Persistence"; Lust-Okar, "Elections under Authoritarianism."
19. Valbjørn and Bank, "Examining the 'Post' in Post-democratization," 191. The notion "paradogma" comes from "paradigm" and "dogma" and refers to a situation where a certain paradigm in academia has almost reached the status of a dogma in the sense of a set of core principles or beliefs that are accepted uncritically and held stubbornly.
20. Ottaway et al., "Democracy," 1.
21. Heydemann, "Syria and the Future of Authoritarianism," 1.
22. For an account of various controversies related to the study of Middle East politics, including a number of Middle East "surprises" such as the outbreak of the civil war in Lebanon; the Iranian revolution and the following declaration of an Islamic republic; the Kuwait War; the rise and fall of the Oslo peace process; 9/11; and the 2003 Iraq War, see Lockman, "Contending Visions"; and Kramer, "Ivory Towers."
23. Goodwin, "Why We Were Surprised."
24. Part of this section draws on Valbjørn, "Upgrading Post-democratization Studies."
25. Gershman, "The Fourth Wave."
26. Masoud, "The Road"; Lobe, "Politologie."
27. Hudson, "Awakening."
28. Gause, "Why Middle East Studies."
29. Lynch, "After Egypt."
30. Storm, *Party Politics*.
31. Joffé, "The Arab Spring."
32. Grand, *Understanding Tahrir Square*.
33. Muasher, *The Second Arab Awakening*.
34. Heydemann and Leenders, "Authoritarian Learning."
35. Carothers, "Approach Analogies with Caution"; cf. Way, "Comparing the Arab Revolts."
36. For a comparison between Jordan 1989 and Jordan 2011 see Valbjørn, "The 2013 Parliamentary Elections."
37. Brownlee and Stacher, "Change of Leader."
38. Goldberg, "Mubarakism without Mubarak."
39. Bellin, "Lessons From the Jasmine and Nile Revolutions."
40. Way, "Comparing the Arab Revolts."
41. Heydemann, "Syria and the Future of Authoritarianism," 72.
42. Brownlee, *Democracy Prevention*, 171.
43. Hudson, "After the 'Arab Spring,'" 246.
44. Valbjørn, "The 2013 Parliamentary Elections."
45. Valbjørn, "Upgrading Post-democratization Studies," 31.
46. Brynen et al., *Beyond the Arab Spring*, 9.
47. Aarts et al., *From Resilience to Revolt*, 10.
48. See Hinnebusch "Authoritarian Upgrading"; Aarts et al., *From Resilience to Revolt*, 18–20; and Brynen et al., *Beyond the Arab Spring*, Ch. 7, among others.
49. Khatib and Lust, *Taking to the Streets*.
50. Ibid.
51. Aarts et al., *From Resilience to Revolt*, 40, Bayat, *Life as Politics*.
52. Stepan and Linz, "Democratization Theory."
53. Aarts et al., *From Resilience to Revolt*, Ch. 8.
54. Hudson, "After the Arab Spring," 242.
55. Valbjørn and Boserup, "Genpolitisering"; Valbjørn, "Upgrading Post-democratization Studies."

56. Cook, "Mubarak Still Rules"; Valbjørn, "The 2013 Parliamentary Elections."
57. Volpi, "Explaining (and Re-explaining)."
58. For example, Brynen et al., *Beyond the Arab Spring*; Volpi, "Explaining (and Re-explaining)"; Hudson, "After the 'Arab Spring.'"
59. Anderson, "Searching Where the Light Shines."
60. Ibid., 210.
61. Valbjørn and Bank, "Examining the 'Post' in Post-democratization," 191.
62. Anderson, "Searching Where the Light Shines," 210.
63. Ibid.
64. Valbjørn, "Upgrading Post-democratization Studies"; Valbjørn and Boserup, "Genpolitisering"; POMEPS, "Arab Uprisings," 10.
65. POMEPS, "Arab Uprisings"; Lynch, "After Egypt"; El-Ghobashy, "Politics by Other Means"; Ottaway, "Preventing Politics."
66. Skocpol, "Bringing the State Back In," 4; Migdal, *Strong Societies and Weak States*.
67. Davis, "The Breakup"; Miller, "Tribes with Flags"; Gaub and Pawlak, "Sykes-Picot and Syria"; Gause, "Beyond Sectarianism."
68. For classic contributions to this debate see Anderson, "The State in the Middle East"; Ayubi, *Over-Stating the Arab State*, Badie, "'State,' Legitimacy and Protest." For a recent example of how this classic debate about state/society relations has been related to the debate about the Arab uprisings see Hinnebusch, "Historical Sociology."
69. Huntington, *Political Order*; cf. Fukuyama, "Political Order"; Hinnebusch, "Historical Sociology."
70. For classic contributions see among others Haddad, *Revolutions and Military Rule*; Horowitz, *Middle East Politics*; Picard, "Arab Military in Politics," for an overview see Stansfield, "Political Life and the Military."
71. Cf. Sayigh, "Rethinking the Study"; Albrecht and Bishara, "Back on Horseback"; Barak, "The Middle East Security Sector and the Arab Revolts"; Gause, "Why Middle East Studies."
72. Rustow, "Transition to Democracy"; cf. Aarts et al., *From Resilience to Revolt*, 84.
73. Noble, "The Arab System"; cf. Valbjørn, "Upgrading Post-democratization Studies."
74. Kerr, *The Arab Cold War*; Seale, *The Struggle for Syria*; cf. Ryan, "The New Arab Cold War"; Lynch, "The Arab Cold War"; Gause, "Beyond Sectarianism."
75. Hudson, *Arab Politics*; cf. Patel, "An Opportunity to Revisit"; Brynen et al., "Ch. 5: Political Culture Revisited."
76. Schwedler, "Can Islamists Become Moderates?"
77. Anderson, "Lawless Government"; cf. Cook, "Return to the Bad Old Days."

References

Aarts, P., P. van Dijke, I. Kolman, J. Statema, and G. Dahhan. *From Resilience to Revolt – Making Sense of the Arab Spring*. Amsterdam: University of Amsterdam – Department of Political Science. WODC, 2012.

Albrecht, H., and D. Bishara. "Back on Horseback: The Military and Political Transformation in Egypt." *Middle East Law and Governance* 3, nos. 1–2 (2011): 13–23.

Albrecht, H., and O. Schlumberger. "'Waiting for Godot': Regime Change without Democratization in the Middle East." *International Political Science Review/Revue internationale de science politique* 25, no. 4 (2004): 371–392.

Anderson, L. "Lawless Government and Illegal Opposition: Reflections on the Middle East." *Journal of International Affairs* 40, no. 2 (1987a): 219–232.

Anderson, L. "The State in the Middle East and North Africa." *Comparative Politics* 20, no. 1 (1987b): 1–18.

Anderson, L. "Searching Where the Light Shines: Studying Democratization in the Middle East." *Annual Review of Political Science* 9, no. 1 (2006): 189–214.

Ayubi, N. *Overstating the Arab State – Politics and Society in the Middle East*. London: I.B. Tauris, 1995.

Badie, B. "'State,' Legitimacy and Protest in Islamic Culture." In *The State in Global Perspective*, edited by A. Kazancigil, 250–265. Aldershot: Gower, 1986.

Bank, A. "Die Renaissance des Autoritarismus. Erkenntnisse und Grenzen neuerer Beiträge der Comparative Politics und Nahostforschung." *Hamburg Review of Social Sciences* 4, no. 1 (2009): 10–41.

Barak, O. "The Middle East Security Sector and the Arab Revolts: A Theoretical and Conceptual Framework." In *Civil-Security Relations in the Middle East – The Role of the Military after the Arab Spring*, edited by B. Hansen and C. Jensen, New York: Routledge, forthcoming.

Bayat, A. *Life as Politics: How Ordinary People Change the Middle East*. Stanford, CA: Stanford University Press, 2010.

Bellin, E. "Lessons From the Jasmine and Nile Revolutions: Possibilities of Political Transformation in the Middle East?" *Middle East Brief – Brandeis University's Crown Center for Middle East Studies*, no. 50 (May 2011): 1–8.

Bromley, S. "Middle East Exceptionalism: Myth or Reality." In *Democratization*, edited by David Potter, David Goldblatt, Margaret Kiloh, and Paul Lewis, 321–343. Cambridge: Polity Press, 1997.

Brownlee, J. *Democracy Prevention: The Politics of the U.S.-Egyptian Alliance*. Cambridge: Cambridge University Press, 2012.

Brownlee, J., and J. Stacher. "Change of Leader, Continuity of System: Nascent Liberalization in Post-Mubarak Egypt." *Comparative Democratization* 9, no. 2 (2011): 1, 4–9.

Brumberg, D. "Liberalization versus Democracy – Understanding Arab Political Reform." *Carnegie Papers – Middle East Series*. 2003.

Brynen, R., P. Moore, B. F. Salloukh, and M.-J. Zahar. "Political Culture Revisited." In *Beyond the Arab Spring: Authoritarianism and Democratization in the Arab World*, edited by R. Brynen, P. Moore, B. F. Salloukh, and M.-J. Zahar, 95–116. Boulder, CO: Lynne Rienner, 2012.

Carothers, T. "Approach Analogies with Caution." *Alliance Magazine*, December 1, 2011.

Choucair-Vizoso, J. "Movement in Lieu of Change." In *Beyond the Facade – Political Reform in the Arab World*, edited by M. Ottaway and J. Choucair-Vizoso, 261–276. Washington, DC: Carnegie Endowment for International Peace, 2008.

Cook, S. "Mubarak Still Rules – The Bodies Pile Up in Cairo, But Nothing Has Changed." *Foreign Policy – Argument*. August 14, 2013a. http://www.foreignpolicy.com/articles/2013/08/14/why_hosni_mubarak_still_rules_egypt?page=full.

Cook, S. "Return to the Bad Old Days – Will Egypt's crackdown on the Muslim Brotherhood fan the embers of Islamic insurgency?". *Foreign Policy – Argument*. September 12, 2013b. http://www.foreignpolicy.com/articles/2013/09/12/return_to_the_bad_old_days_egypt_1990s.

Davis, E. "The Breakup of the Middle East State System – Fact or Fiction?" *The New Middle East*, October 26, 2012. http://new-middle-east.blogspot.dk/2012/10/the-breakup-of-middle-east-state-system.html.

El-Ghobashy, M. "Politics by Other Means – In Egypt, Street Protests Set the Agenda." *Boston Review* November/December (2011): 39–44.

Fukuyama, F. "The End of History?" *The National Interest* 16, no. Summer (1989): 3–18.

Fukuyama, F. "Political Order in Egypt." *The American Interest* 6, no. 5 (2011): 7–12.

Gaub, F., and P. Pawlak. "Sykes-Picot and Syria." *ISS Alert – European Union Institute for Security Studies*, no. 34 (October 2, 2013): 1–2.

Gause, F. G. "Why Middle East Studies Missed the Arab Spring – The Myth of Authoritarian Stability." *Foreign Affairs* 90, no. 4 (2011): 81–90.

Gause, F. G. "Beyond Sectarianism: The New Middle East Cold War." *Brookings Doha Center – Analysis Paper* No. 11, 2014.

Gershman, C. "The Fourth Wave." *The New Republic*. March 14, 2011. http://www.newrepublic.com/article/world/85143/middle-east-revolt-democratization.

Goldberg, E. "Mubarakism Without Mubarak – Why Egypt's Military Will Not Embrace Democracy." *Foreign Affairs – Snapshot*. February 11, 2011. http://www.foreignaffairs.com/articles/67416/ellis-goldberg/mubarakism-without-mubarak.

Goodwin, J. "Why We Were Surprised (Again) by the Arab Spring." *Swiss Political Science Review* 17, no. 4 (2011): 452–456.

Grand, S. R. *Understanding Tahrir Square – What Transitions Elsewhere Can Teach Us about the Prospects for Arab Democracy*. Washington, DC: Brookings Institution Press, 2014.

Haddad, G. *Revolutions and Military Rule in the Middle East*. New York: Robert Speller, 1973.

Heydemann, S. "La question de la démocratie dans les travaux sur le monde arabe." *Critique International* 17 no. 4 (2002): 54–62.

Heydemann, S. "Upgrading Authoritarianism in the Arab World." *Brookings Institution Saban Center Analysis Paper* No. 13, 2007.

Heydemann, S. "Syria and the Future of Authoritarianism." *Journal of Democracy* 24, no. 4 (2013): 59–73.

Heydemann, S., and R. Leenders. "Authoritarian Learning and Authoritarian Resilience: Regime Responses to the 'Arab Awakening.'" *Globalizations* 8, no. 5 (2011): 647–653.

Hinnebusch, R. "Authoritarian Persistence, Democratization Theory and the Middle East: An Overview and Critique." *Democratization* 13, no. 3 (2006): 373–395.

Hinnebusch, R. "Syria: From 'Authoritarian Upgrading' to Revolution?" *International Affairs* 88, no. 1 (2012): 95–113.

Hinnebusch, R. "Historical Sociology and the Arab Uprising." *Mediterranean Politics* 19, no. 1 (2014): 137–140.

Horowitz, J. C. *Middle East Politics: The Military Dimension*. New York: Praeger, 1969.

Hudson, M. C. *Arab Politics – The Search for Legitimacy*. New Haven, CT: Yale University Press, 1977.

Hudson, M. C. "Democratization and the Problem of Legitimacy in Middle East Politics – Presidential Address 1987." *MESA Bulletin* 22, no. 2 (1988): 157–171.

Hudson, M. C. "After the Gulf War: Prospects for Democratization in the Arab World." *Middle East Journal* 45, no. 3 (1991): 409–426.

Hudson, M. C. "Awakening, Cataclysm, or Just a Series of Events? Reflections on the Current Wave of Protest in the Arab World." *Jadaliyya Blog*. May 16, 2011. http://www.jadaliyya.com/pages/index/1601/awakening-cataclysm-or-just-a-series-of-events-ref.

Hudson, M. C. "After the 'Arab Spring': Emergent Democracy vs. Resurgent Authoritarianism." In *Modern Middle East Authoritarianism – Roots, Ramifications, and Crisis*, edited by N. Jebnoun, M. Kia, and M. Kirk, 242–255. London: Routledge, 2014.

Huntington, S. P. *Political Order in Changing Societies.* New Haven, CT: Yale University Press, 1968.
Huntington, S. P. *The Third Wave: Democratization in the Late Twentieth Century.* Norman: University of Oklahoma Press, 1991.
Joffé, G. "The Arab Spring in North Africa: Origins and Prospects." *The Journal of North African Studies* 16, no. 4 (2011): 507–532.
Kerr, M. *The Arab Cold War – 1958–1964 – A Study of Ideology in Politics.* London: Oxford University Press, 1965.
Khatib, L., and E. Lust, eds. *Taking to the Streets – The Transformation of Arab Activism.* Baltimore, MD: Johns Hopkins University Press, 2014.
Kramer, M. *Ivory Towers on Sand – The Failure of Middle Eastern Studies in America.* Washington, DC: Washington Institute for Near East Policy, 2001.
Lobe, A. "Politologie: Die Wissenschaft vom stabilen Orient." *Frankfurter Allgemeine Zeitung*, 24. März. 2011.
Lampedusa, Giuseppe Tomasi di. *The Leopard.* New York, NY: Pantheon Books, 1960.
Lockman, Z. *Contending Visions of the Middle East – The History and Politics of Orientalism.* Cambridge: Cambridge University Press, 2010.
Lucas, R. E. "Monarchical Authoritarianism: Survival and Political Liberalization in a Middle Eastern Regime Type." *International Journal of Middle East Studies* 36, no. 1 (2004): 103–119.
Lust-Okar, E. "Elections under Authoritarianism: Preliminary Lessons from Jordan." *Democratization* 13, no. 3 (2006): 456–471.
Lynch, M. "After Egypt: The Limits and Promise of Online Challenges to the Authoritarian Arab State." *Perspectives on Politics* 9, no. 2 (2011): 301–310.
Lynch, M. "The Arab Cold War." In *The Arab Uprising: The Unfinished Revolutions of the New Middle East*, 29–42. New York, NY: Public Affairs, 2012.
Masoud, Tarek. "The Upheavals in Egypt and Tunisia: The Road to (and from) Liberation Square." *Journal of Democracy* 22, no. 3 (2011): 20–34.
Migdal, J. S. *Strong Societies and Weak States: State-Society Relations and State Capabilities in the Third World.* Princeton, NJ: Princeton University Press, 1988.
Miller, A. "Tribes With Flags – How the Arab Spring has Exposed the Myth of Arab Statehood." *Foreign Policy.* February 27, 2013. http://www.foreignpolicy.com/articles/2013/02/27/tribes_with_flags_arab_spring_states?page=full.
Muasher, M. *The Second Arab Awakening.* New Haven, CT: Yale University Press, 2014.
Noble, P. "The Arab System: Pressures, Constraints, and Opportunities." In *The Foreign Policies of Arab States*, edited by B. Korany and A. E. H. Dessouki, 49–102. Boulder, CO: Westview, 1991.
Norton, A. R. "The Future of Civil Society in the Middle East." *Middle East Journal* 47, no. 2 (1993): 205–216.
Ottaway, M. "Preventing Politics in Egypt – Why Liberals Oppose the Constitution." *Foreign Affairs – Snapshot.* December 10, 2012. http://www.foreignaffairs.com/articles/138497/marina-ottaway/preventing-politics-in-egypt?page=show.
Ottaway, M. S., J. Schwedler, S. Telhami, and S. E. Ibrahim. "Democracy: Rising Tide or Mirage?" *Middle East Policy* 12, no. 2 (2005): 1–27.
Pace, M., and F. Cavatorta. "The Arab Uprisings in Theoretical Perspective – An Introduction." *Mediterranean Politics* 17, no. 2 (2012): 125–138.
Patel, D. S. "An Opportunity to Revisit the Political Culture Baby That Drowned in the Bathwater." In *Arab Uprisings – New Opportunities for Political Science*, edited by M. Lynch, 44–45. Washington, DC: POMEPS Briefings, 2012.
Picard, E. "Arab Military in Politics: From Revolutionary Plot to Authoritarian State." In *Beyond Coercion: The Durability of the Arab State*, edited by A. Dawisha and W. Zartman, 116–146. London: Croom Helm, 1988.

POMEPS. "Arab Uprisings – New Opportunities for Political Science." *POMEPS Briefings. No. 12.* 2012.
Posusney, M. P., and M. P. Angrist, eds. *Authoritarianism in the Middle East – Regimes and Resistance.* Boulder, CO: Lynne Rienner, 2005.
Rustow, D. "Transitions to Democracy: Toward a Dynamic Model." *Comparative Politics* 2, no. 3 (1970): 337–363.
Ryan, C. "The New Arab Cold War and the Struggle for Syria." *Middle East Report*, no. 262 (2012): 28–31.
Sayigh, Y. "Roundtable: Rethinking the Study of Middle East Militaries." *International Journal of Middle East Studies* 43, no. 3 (2011): 391–407.
Schlumberger, O. *Debating Arab Authoritarianism Dynamics and Durability in Nondemocratic Regimes.* Stanford, CA: Stanford University Press, 2007.
Schwedler, J. "Can Islamists Become Moderates?: Rethinking the Inclusion-Moderation Hypothesis." *World Politics* 63, no. 2 (2011): 347–376.
Seale, P. *The Struggle for Syria – A Study of Post-war Arab Politics 1945–1958.* Oxford: Oxford University Press, 1965.
Skocpol, T. "Bringing the State Back In: Strategies of Analysis in Current Research." In *Bringing the State Back In*, edited by P. Evans, D. Rueschemeyer, and T. Skocpol, 3–37. Cambridge: Cambridge University Press, 1985.
Stansfield, G. "Political Life and the Military." In *A Companion to the History of the Middle East*, edited by Y. Choueiri, 355–371. Oxford: Wiley-Blackwell, 2008.
Stepan, A., and J. Linz. "Democratization Theory and the 'Arab Spring.'" *Journal of Democracy* 24, no. 2 (2013): 15–30.
Storm, L. *Party Politics and the Prospects for Democracy in North Africa.* Boulder, CO: Lynne Rienner, 2014.
Valbjørn, M. "Upgrading Post-democratization Studies: Examining a Re-politicized Arab World in a Transition to Somewhere." *Middle East Critique* 21, no. 1 (2012): 25–35.
Valbjørn, M. "The 2013 Parliamentary Elections in Jordan: Three Stories and Some General Lessons." *Mediterranean Politics* 18, no. 2 (2013): 311–317.
Valbjørn, M., and A. Bank. "Examining the 'Post' in Post-democratization: The Future of Middle Eastern Political Rule Through Lenses of the Past." *Middle East Critique* 19, no. 3 (2010): 183–200.
Valbjørn, M., and R. A. Boserup. "Genpolitisering og post-demokratisering: Studiet af mellemøstlig politik i lyset af de arabiske revolter." *Politik* 15, no. 1 (2012): 43–51.
Valbjørn, M., and F. Volpi. "Revisiting Theories of Arab Politics in the Aftermath of the Arab Uprisings." *Mediterranean Politics* 19, no. 1 (2014): 134–36.
Volpi, F. "Explaining (and Re-explaining) Political Change in the Middle East during the Arab Spring: Trajectories of Democratization and of Authoritarianism in the Maghreb." *Democratization* 20, no. 6 (2013): 969–990.
Way, L. "Comparing the Arab Revolts: The Lessons of 1989." *Journal of Democracy* 22, no. 3 (2011): 13–23.
Zhao, S. "Metatheory, Metamethod, Meta-data-analysis: What, Why, and How?" *Sociological Perspectives* 34, no. 3 (1991): 377–390.

Social movements, protest movements and cross-ideological coalitions – the Arab uprisings re-appraised

Vincent Durac

School of Politics and International Relations, University College Dublin, Dublin, Ireland

This article explores the utility of social movement theory, reviewing conceptual developments and its application to Middle East cases before examining its relevance to the Arab uprisings. The initial youth-led new social movements were non-ideological, leaderless, and lacking in clear organizational structures. As the protest movements spread, they grew to encompass a diverse array of other movements and actors: The breadth and diversity of these coalitions made the successful achievement of their core demands for regime change possible. However, the persistence of ideological cleavages within them made agreement on the post-regime change political order near impossible.

Introduction

One of the most remarkable features of the uprisings that swept the Arab world in 2011 was the absence of political parties, Islamist movements, and established civil society organizations from the ranks of those protesting against incumbent regimes. From the earliest phases of the protest movements in Tunisia and elsewhere across the region, commentators noted their amorphous nature – youth-led, non-ideological, horizontal, leaderless movements which relied on non-traditional means of mobilization and transmission of their message. Perhaps not surprisingly, given the conceptual assonances involved, social movement theory (SMT), and, in particular, the concept of new social movements (NSMs), have been frequently invoked in subsequent academic analyses of these events.

In 2011, Dupont and Passy identified a number of issues that might be answered by drawing on elements of SMT.[1] These related to whether the protests were actually "unpredictable" and whether elements usually associated with the revolutionary process – pre-existing networks, power fragmentation, cross-class coalitions – were absent; whether they were sudden and spontaneous, or whether they had deep organizational roots; whether a transformation in people's consciousness took place which might explain why the protests took off. Finally, they note the importance, as identified in political opportunity theory of examining the state and the ruling elites that are challenged by protest movements. Alimi and Meyer also stress the significance of political opportunity structures in the "revolutionary wave of contention" while Volpi has suggested that we might begin by locating the revolts along a continuum of contentious politics "ranging from social activism to revolutionary change".[2]

Beyond the general invocations to the potential usefulness of SMT, it has been drawn on explicitly by a number of writers to explain aspects of the uprisings in Morocco, Egypt, Syria, and elsewhere. In their critique of the 20 February movement in Morocco, Hoffman and Konig propose that the concepts developed in social movement research provide obvious starting points for study of the popular mobilizations of the "Arab Spring".[3] In particular, they focus on the concept of "collective action frames". Frames serve as "discursive weapons" for social movements and for activists who "frame" or assign meaning to relevant events and conditions in ways that are intended to mobilize potential adherents, attract support, and demobilize opponents. This forms the basis for their analysis of the 20 February movement.

Beinin represents Egypt's uprising in terms of the pre-existence of "three largely parallel social movements" – the workers' movement; the oppositional urban middle classes, best exemplified by the Kefaya movement that emerged in 2004 and brought together Nasserists, Marxists, unaffiliated leftists, liberals, and some Islamists; and educated, middle-class youth whose political activity prior to 2011 took place largely through social media. The uprisings in Egypt and elsewhere, he argues, grew not out of civil society but from the "diverse social protest movements" that had developed over previous decades involving urban intelligentsia, disaffected youth, blue- and white-collar workers and professionals, and marginalized religious communities and regions.[4]

Leenders offers an analysis of the initial stages of the anti-regime uprising in Syria in explicitly social movement terms. He locates his approach within the work of social movement scholars who emphasize the role of social networks in their attempts to understand mobilization in the face of "seemingly insurmountable obstacles and collective action problems".[5] Drawing on the language of SMT, he suggests that, in place of changing political opportunity structures at the domestic level, it was events in Tunisia and Egypt that Syrians saw as also opening up an opportunity in their own country. His analysis focuses on the "dense personal networks" that characterize Dar'a where the initial protests took place. Leenders identified a number of such networks which "informed, motivated and enabled unprecedented mobilization and its spread in the context of radically altered perceptions of opportunities generated by the 'Arab Spring' in Tunisia and Egypt".[6]

Finally, Joffé analyses the uprisings in Egypt, Tunisia, and Libya in explicitly social movement terms. He argues that the "liberalized autocracies" of Egypt and

Tunisia, in ironic fashion, set up the conditions for their own demise by creating the space for the emergence of "precursor" movements which under the right circumstances would evolve into "movements of political contention". In Tunisia, the existence of traditions of autonomous expression, exemplified in the Union Génèrale Tunisienne du Travail (UGTT) and the Tunisian League of Human Rights, a strong tradition of constitutionalism and the marginalization of the army, meant that when Mohamed Bouazizi's self-immolation catalyzed public anger in so far as there were organizations ready and able "to create a powerful social movement out of popular disgust at regime corruption and repression and targeted at removing it".[7] In Egypt, Joffé suggests three strands of protest were in operation – similar to those identified by Beinin – which responded to the opportunity created by the removal of Ben Ali from power in Tunisia. However, he treats Libya as exceptional because it remained an uncompromising autocracy.[8]

This article will argue that while reliance on SMT undoubtedly offers insight into the uprisings and their aftermath, the limitations of any such reliance must be acknowledged. In particular, it must be recognized that what we see, as the uprisings developed from youth-led protests against autocratic rule across the Middle East North Africa (MENA) region to broad-based coalitions of social and political forces capable of forcing "regime change", is a transformation in the character of oppositional forces. This transformation is expressed in a shift from the initial youth-led movements that sparked the uprisings to what may better be understood as coalitions of social movements. This shift from social movements to coalitions of movements has had significant consequences for post-uprising political dynamics. The resulting "movements of movements" – composed of quite disparate actors – in most cases lacked organizational or ideological coherence and enjoyed no shared consensus on an alternative to the status quo, the demise of which they sought to bring about. Thus, having succeeded in their core objective of regime change, these movements were, because of their intrinsic incoherence and diversity, highly prone to fracturing, thus paving the way for others to take advantage of the political openings that their efforts had secured.

Social movement theory and the Middle East and North Africa

SMT has become one of the most influential elements in contemporary social science scholarship. Indeed, the ubiquity of the term leads Stammers to suggest there is limited consensus on how such a movement is distinguished from "other forms of human association".[9] Nor indeed is there consensus on how the concept may be defined.

In his influential and much-cited discussion, Diani proposes that social movements comprise three core elements. The first of these is informal interaction involving individuals, groups, and organizations. These networks, which may be very loose and dispersed in character or may be tightly clustered, provide for the circulation of essential resources for action as well as broader systems of meaning. The second core element is a shared set of beliefs and "a sense of belongingness". This collective identity is a matter of self- and external definition – actors must define themselves as part of a social movement and be seen as such by opponents and external observers.

> In this sense, collective identity plays an essential role in defining the boundaries of a social movement. Only those actors, sharing the same beliefs and sense of belongingness, can be considered as part of a social movement. However, collective identity does not imply homogeneity of ideas and orientations within social movement networks. A wide spectrum of different conceptions may be present and factional conflicts may arise at any time.[10]

Finally, Diani explores the issue of the locus of social movement activities and concludes that the spectrum of social movement organizations (SMO) is so wide and undifferentiated as to prevent any clear restriction of its boundaries. In conclusion, he offers a synthetic definition of the concept: "A social movement is a network of informal interactions between a plurality of individuals, groups and/or organizations, engaged in a political or cultural conflict, on the basis of a shared collective identity."[11]

Charles Tilly, one of the founding fathers of SMT, stresses the notion of "unity" in his definition of a social movement which places emphasis on the effective transmission of the message that its supporters are "worthy, unified, numerous and committed".[12] For Stammers, social movements are understood as collective actors comprising individuals who understand themselves to share some common interest and identify with one another "at least to some extent". Social movements, he suggests, are chiefly concerned with defending or changing at least some aspect of society and rely on mass mobilization, or the threat of it, as their main political sanction.[13]

While there is significant variation in the literature on the definition of a social movement, the notions of some degree of unity and mutual identification on the part of members are recurring themes. The range of definitional approaches to the concept of social movement is matched by the diversity of theoretical approaches. In their 1999 survey of the field, Della Porta and Diani identified four "dominant perspectives": "collective behavior", "resource mobilization", "political process", and "NSMs".[14] In a subsequent edition of the same work, they stressed the shift from movements of industrial society to new movements, which in turn reflected a shift in the scholarship away from reliance on Marxist frames of reference. The "new" social movement approach had two specific advantages. It placed actors at the centre of the stage once again, and captured "the innovative characteristics of movements which no longer defined themselves principally in relation to the system of production".[15]

In recent decades, there have been an increasing number of attempts to apply social movement concepts and theories to different aspects of political life in the Middle East and North Africa. Much, although not all, of this effort has focused on Islamic movements and Islamic political dynamics. In his 1997 study of the politics of "the informal people", Bayat examines the everyday practices of the urban poor – from squatting to collectively organizing to provide basic services, sometimes illegally, to the activities of informal street vendors. However, while noting the characteristics that these activities share with social movements, he argues that they constitute something different. Whereas social movements in general represent "a long-lasting and more or less structured collective action" aimed at social change, these activities are characterized by spontaneity, individualism, and intergroup competition. Furthermore, while these practices resemble both "new" and "old" social movements, they differ from both in significant ways. "Old" social movements were often mobilized by charismatic leaders, whereas informal urban activism in the Middle East is self-generating for the most part. And, while NSMs focus largely on identity and meaning, these activities are concerned primarily with action.[16]

Wiktorowicz proposes the extension of the insights of SMT to Islamic activism, arguing that whereas the majority of studies of Islamic activism tended to assume that a particular set of grievances, translated into religious idioms and symbols, leads to mobilization, SMT demonstrates that other factors are inextricably linked to the process of mobilization, including resource availability, framing resources, and shifts in opportunity structures.[17] In the same volume, Singerman argues that Islamic activism is not, as many have seen it, unique, but has elements in common with all social movements. The organizational structures, repertoires of contention, and collective identity of Islamic movements are similar to those of other social movements throughout the world.[18]

Bayat takes up a similar theme. He critiques the ways in which Islamism has been represented and proposed an analysis in terms of SMT. In spite of the fact that Islamist movements are "internally fluid, fragmented and differentiated", they nonetheless operate on the basis of "partially-shared" interests and values, which, together with frame alignment or consensus mobilization, represent common strategies of Islamist movements.[19]

More recently, the concept of "NSM" has been drawn upon to provide insight both into Islamic movements and their relationships with other actors. The concept of NSM has assumed particular significance in the context of the Arab uprisings, a point that will be returned to. Simsek, in his analysis of recent activist strands in Turkish political life (Islamist, feminist, Alevi, and Kurdish, respectively) and Sutton and Vertigans in their analysis of radical, transnational Islamism, also identify the concept of NSM as key.[20] Sutton and Vertigans isolate six key elements that stand out as commonly recognized features of NSM activity. NSMs are concerned with post-industrial and "postmaterial" politics. Their constituencies transcend the working class – they bring together "socially differentiated rainbow coalitions" that are not easily accounted for by older social movement perspectives "tied to materialist explanations". NSMs are non-hierarchical organizations – they are characterized by loose networks, anti-hierarchical structures, and participatory approaches to organization. They rely on the "symbolic direct actions" – adopting a non-violent approach to protest is symbolic of their attempts to bring about cultural change rather than attempting to take political power. In contrast to "old" social movements, NSMs are characterized by limited political ambitions, combining radical aims with reformist strategies and the interests of new middle-class groups with those of marginalized groups. Finally, NSMs work at creating "new identities though self-realization and the right to autonomy rather than the assimilation of their demands into mainstream politics".[21]

Abdelrahman offers an analysis of the increased cooperation between leftists, Nasserists, and Islamists in Egypt during the 2000s within the framework of NSMs. These three groups, none of which, as she acknowledges, is homogenous within itself, increasingly cooperated over a number of issues. Abdelrahman proposes a conceptual perspective on the new alliances that emerged. She draws on the concept of "network" to describe them. In this context, a network can include social movements but also non-governmental organizations (NGOs), professional unions, and the media. However, crucially, Abdelrahman focused on the persistent divisions between the three very different elements of regime opposition at this time, noting the adoption by individual movements within the network of the tactic of "cooperative differentiation", which consists of maintaining a public face of solidarity towards the network's objectives while differentiating themselves in communications with their constituencies. "This allows for diverse political groupings with different ideological leanings, class interests and long-term projects to work together."[22] She further argues that the burgeoning cooperation among regime opponents in Egypt demonstrated many of the characteristics of NSMs – consisting of "loose, informal decentralized groups whose members reject hierarchical structures and systems of authority characteristic of traditional political organizations. However, she distinguishes the "movement" in Egypt from others in so far as it was not a single issue movement but rather was concerned with objectives that ranged from lifting of the Emergency Law to the institutionalization of measures to promote democracy, and from ending Mubarak's rule to securing the resignation of the minister of the interior. To this end, she points out that the objective of cooperation between leftists and Islamists constituted informal coalition building. There was no intent to pursue "programmatic cooperation" or a "third way" – indeed there was an almost "unbridgeable" gap between the political programmes and ideologies of both sides.[23]

Abdelrahman's identification of a gap between the component elements of the opposition movement in pre-uprising Egypt anticipates the incoherence of the movements that subsequently drove the uprisings of 2011. While these fit the definition of NSM set out by Abdelrahman and others, the limitation of subsuming an ideologically diverse set of actors within the catch-all category of "social movement", as will be argued, is that it suggests a degree of coherence that may not exist beyond the most minimal level of a shared objective of opposition to the incumbent regime. In this context, the distinction made by Asef Bayat, in his seminal 1998 study of Iran and Egypt, is useful. Bayat argues that popular discontent, whatever its cause, may give rise to two types of mobilization. The first type, protest or insurrectionary movements, like Iran's revolutionary movement of 1978, aims solely to negate the existing order. The second, social movements, aim to alter the dominant arrangements but also attempt to build alternative institutions and value systems before a total change. He suggests that European socialist movements, Poland's Solidarity movement and some Islamic movements represent such a pattern. Such social movements tend to be more or less structured and require the "durable efforts" of a relatively large number of people to effect social change. They differ from "free-form collective action" such as riots or street demonstrations or from rigidly structured interest groups, which concern only their own members. They are also different from power-seeking political parties, small cliques such as secret discussion groups, or underground guerrilla organizations without mass support. But they may be connected to these kinds of activities, share many features with them, or even transform into one another. Crucially, Bayat also distinguishes social movements from revolutions, which are processes of pervasive, usually violent, and rapid change where political authority collapses and is replaced by contenders.

Protest movements, on the other hand, are usually transitory and do not last long. Either they succeed or they are suppressed, although in some instances they may transform themselves into a more structured and institutionalized social movement. Unlike protest movements or insurrections, which only negate the prevailing order, social movements typically construct alternative institutions and value systems such as structures for provision of credit, housing, welfare, or social protection. They may also give rise to "social and cultural sub-systems" that exist within, if sometimes in tension with, the prevailing order. This is not to say that they merely integrated or co-opted into the system. Instead of leading to sudden revolutionary transformation, these movements often both coexist and compete with the "dominant social arrangement".[24]

In the case of the Arab uprisings, both protest movements and social movements coexisted within the broader coalition of forces that came together to bring about change. This was key to their success, however unexpected. As Goldstone has noted, if a protest draws support from just one class or group, it is easier for the state to suppress that group as a disruptive element. If, however, support comes from a number of different groups, it is much more difficult for the state to confront. For this reason, almost all successful revolutions come about with the support of cross-class coalitions.[25] However, as Goldstone also points out, while cross-class coalitions are vital for the success of revolutions, what is even more important is how the continuing dynamics of the coalition affect its future trajectory. The key issue for an understanding of post-uprising political dynamics in the MENA region is not the fact that a diversity of social movements came together to bring about political change, rather it is the consequences of such diversity for the aftermath of that change.

Social movements, coalitions, and the Arab uprisings

A striking feature of the initial surge of protest across the MENA region in 2011 was the leaderless, horizontal, and largely non-ideological character of the movements at their centre. Particularly in Tunisia, Egypt, and Yemen, the uprisings were, in their earliest stages, driven by young people who had limited or no experience of established political parties or movements, who rejected formal organizational structures, mobilized online, and lacked a coherent or unifying ideology beyond a clear rejection of the status quo and incumbent regimes. The second important feature of those movements was the rapidity with which they expanded to embrace a broad diversity of actors. The coalitions that emerged from this were key to the fall of regimes across the region. However, they were also inherently unstable coalitions precisely because of the diversity that characterized them.

In Tunisia, as Aleya-Sghaier points out, young people were key protagonists in the initial phase of the uprising – "young, unemployed, or informal workers; students; civil servants; itinerant peddlers; and marginalized or excluded individuals". The young people in Tunisia came from different classes – from urban housing estates of major towns and cities but also, if to a lesser degree, the youth of the bourgeois areas were also actively involved.[26] However, very quickly a range of other actors joined the anti-regime movement. The UGTT, the trade union federation, which had been founded in 1946, and the leadership of which had developed close ties to the regime, shifted its position in response to regime violence against protesters. The leadership gradually joined the revolt while local and regional offices became centres for the revolutionaries. From an early stage, the Tunisian Bar Association declared its support for the uprising. The council of the Bar Association reflected a diversity of interests, from secularists and Islamists to members of the ruling party, Marxists, and Arab nationalists. The role of political parties in Tunisia was more ambivalent. Some were close to the then president, Ben Ali, while legal opposition political parties including the Progressive Democrat Party, the formerly communist Ettajdid, and the Forum for Democracy and Labour were openly critical of the regime. These criticized regime repression of the protests but did not join the uprising. However, banned parties such as the Communist Labour Party of Tunisia, the Maoist Al Watad, and a selection of Arab nationalist parties organized to oppose the regime without garnering significant influence over the young people who were the leading force in the uprising. Finally, when Ben Ali fled the country on 14 January, Islamists became active in the anti-regime movement.[27] As a result, almost every shade of political opinion in the country was ranged against the regime.

In Egypt, the group that triggered the protests that ultimately unseated Mubarak consisted of what Beinin describes as "the educated, middle-class 'Facebook' youth whose political activity prior to 2011 was organized mainly through social media".[28] The 6 April Youth Movement first emerged in 2008 when Esraa Abdel Fatteh established a Facebook page calling on Egyptians to stay at home on 6 April in support of workers in Mahalla al-Kubra who were planning to strike in support of their demand for a national minimum monthly wage. The page attracted 70,000 "likes" in a week. Abdel Fatteh subsequently established the 6 April Youth Movement with Ahmad Mahir and others. Wael Ghonim set up the "We are all Khaled Said" Facebook page in 2010, in memory of a young

Egyptian who was beaten to death by police in Alexandria. The page attracted 325,000 "likes". The co-administrator of the page, Abd al-Rahman Mansour, convinced Ghonim to permit it to be used to call for demonstrations on 25 January in collaboration with the 6 April movement, several other youth movements, and some small unrecognized parties. As in Tunisia, the early phase of the uprising in Egypt was notable for the absence of any significant role for the established opposition political parties or the Muslim Brotherhood.

However, youth movements were by no means the only actors involved in the uprising. Beinin identifies three "largely parallel Egyptian social movements" that pre-existed but fed into the events of 2011. These were the worker's movement, the oppositional urban middle-class, and the youth movement.[29] Abdelrahman offers a slightly different tripartite categorization. The first set of actors comprised the "pro-democracy movement" a loose network outside of formal political institutions and professional syndicates. This brought together professionals, students, political activists, the youth wings of political parties, and individuals from different backgrounds. These activists avoided hierarchical structures and rejected formal leadership, preferring temporary, flexible managing committees.[30] The second element feeding into the 2011 protests was labour mobilization. Abdelrahman refers to a strike by over two million workers that followed the enactment of the Unified Labour Law of 2003 as well as a number of later labour mobilizations. The role of the Egyptian labour movement in the uprisings is also discussed in some detail by Beinin. Finally, Abdelrahman discusses the more spontaneous "dispersed" protests by marginalized citizens that swept Egyptian streets. These were in response to the state's failure to provide minimal services and goods such as health care, electricity, running water, and affordable basic foodstuffs.[31]

As in Tunisia, the initial phase of protest was followed by the expansion of the anti-regime movement to embrace almost every sector of society. Youth protesters were joined by a diverse range of others, including the Youth of the Muslim Brotherhood, the Youth of Kifaya, young people of the Tomorrow Party, and young people of the Democratic Front Party. They were later joined by young people of the leftist Tagammu Party, the Nasserite Party, the Popular Movement for Democratic Change, young people of the Labour Party, young people of the Wafd Party, and the Front of Coptic Youth. The leadership of the Muslim Brotherhood responded to warnings from state security by issuing a statement that it would not formally participate in the demonstrations of 25 January, although its youth movement did so. However, its full participation followed on 28 January – the "Day of Rage" – when the Muslim Brotherhood mobilized large numbers of its followers to confront the brutality of the security forces. In total, the number of Egyptians who took part in the 18 days of protests before Mubarak left office has been estimated at 15 million.[32]

In Yemen, those who took to the streets in early 2011 to protest against the long-standing regime of Ali Abdullah Saleh were, as in Tunisia and Egypt, the young. The Yemeni uprising shared many characteristics with those of Tunisia and Egypt. On 11 February, after al-Jazeera broadcast the scenes from Cairo that followed Mubarak's departure from office, hundreds of Yemeni students, teachers, and political activists gathered in front of Sana'a University and began to chant in favour of political change in the country. The protest camp in Sana'a covered approximately a square mile at its peak in early May and housed over 10,000 people. Around half of these were young representatives of the country's pro-democracy movements, most of whom saw themselves as unaffiliated to any of the established political parties. In March 2011, they formed an umbrella group – the Civil Coalition of Revolutionary Youth – which brought together Yemen's four main youth organizations: the Alliance for the Youth's Revolution; the Alliance of the People's Youth Revolution; the Alliance of Youth and Students for a Peaceful Revolution; and the Coalition of Change Leaders. Like the youth protesters elsewhere in the region, while they cooperated among themselves and with others, they were reluctant to nominate leaders or to form political parties.[33]

In Yemen as elsewhere in the region, regime violence against the youth protesters altered the balance of the forces arrayed against the regime. Initially, the coalition of opposition parties, the Joint Meetings Party (JMP), adopted a cautious approach to unfolding events, offering to mediate between the protesters and the government. However, violent attacks on protesters led the JMP leadership to instruct its supporters to join the uprising. One result of this was greatly to add to the ideological diversity of the protest movement in Yemen. The JMP is a coalition of established political parties that includes highly disparate forces from the Yemeni Socialist Party (the former ruling party of the People's Democratic Republic of Yemen) to the Islamist *Islah* party as well as Arab nationalists and smaller Shia Zaydi parties.[34] The range of forces supporting the Yemeni uprising expanded further when key regime allies defected. By March 2011, these included General Ali Mohsen al-Ahmar. Ali Mohsen, a cousin of the president, and one of the most senior military figures in the country.[35] By this time also, the uprising was being supported by two regionally based movements that had posed a long-standing threat to the regime in Sana'a. The Houthi movement, a Zaydi[36] revivalist movement originating in Saada in northern Yemen, fought six wars with President Saleh's regime between 2004 and 2010. The Houthis announced their support for the uprising on the same day that the JMP withdrew from dialogue with the government. The Hirak emerged in 2007 as a vehicle for the expression of southern grievances against the central government in Sanaa. Initially, the Hirak sought redress of southern grievances in the context of the unitary state of Yemen but over time became increasingly secessionist in character.[37] As a result, by the summer of 2011 Saleh was opposed by all the major opposition parties, by defectors from his own party, by senior figures in the tribal confederation to which his family owed allegiance, by regional actors, as well as by the original youth movements who initiated the protests.

The protest movement in Libya bore some similarities with those elsewhere but quickly took a violent and regionally-based turn, largely in response to regime behaviour. Following events elsewhere in North Africa, a "Day of Rage" was planned for 17 February but protests were ignited in advance of this following the arrest in Benghazi two days earlier of a young human rights lawyer and activist, Fathi Terbil. When his supporters gathered outside the local police station they were fired upon by state security personnel. This in turn prompted thousands more to protest in towns and cities across the country.[38] As elsewhere, the protesters represented a broad cross-section of society united by the desire to see the end of the Gadhafi regime. However, young people were at the heart of the initial phase of the uprising. The 17 February Youth Movement was a key group uniting the revolutionary forces. Largely composed of young, urban, middle-class Libyans, most of whom had obtained a higher degree, the youth movement claimed to have around 100 civil society organizations under its umbrella. Its platform revolved around eliminating corruption and bringing the voice of the people into government.[39]

The Libyan protest movement expanded and rapidly altered in composition. Regime repression led to the defection of military conscripts as well as professionals and civil servants in almost every field. Deeb notes that regional governors, newspaper editors, prominent businessmen, university professors, teachers, lawyers, human rights activists, and women's associations all shifted their support to the revolt. More organized opposition groups also joined the forces massing against the regime.[40] These included a range of exiled groups of varying degrees of significance, tribal groups in Cyrenaica who had always resented Gadhafi's rule, as well as Islamist opposition – the Libyan Islamic Group, the Libyan Islamic Fighting Group, and others. Other smaller minority groups also became involved in the uprising – Berbers, Tebu, and Tuareg[41] – who the regime refused to recognize in the course of Arabization campaigns undertaken in previous years.[42] Writing before the death of Gadhafi, Genugten noted that the Libyan opposition was "an alliance of strange bedfellows built around a single purpose – the removal of Gadhafi" but with little agreement on how Libyan society should be organized when that had been achieved.[43]

The expansion of anti-regime protest movements in Tunisia, Egypt, Libya, and Yemen to encompass a wide range of actors, including youth, established and formerly proscribed opposition political parties, Islamist movements, as well as individuals and groups of all ideological orientations (and none) conforms almost precisely to the process of cross-class (and cross-ideological) coalition building which Goldstone identified as crucial to the success of revolutions. However, it also raises questions about the capacity of any such coalition to hold together in the aftermath of a change in regime.[44]

Anti-regime coalitions in the aftermath of regime change

The novel character of the protest movements of 2011 – leaderless, non-ideological, horizontally organized – enabled the mobilization of collective action in ways that had previously been impossible in repressive settings, in so far as both significantly escaped the control and repression of the authoritarian state.[45] However, these very characteristics also limited their potential to take advantage of the political openings that followed the demise of autocratic regimes. When, in Tunisia, Egypt, Yemen, and elsewhere, youth protesters were joined by established political parties of all ideological orientations, Islamists, lawyers, trade unionists, and others, the problems of structural as well as ideological incoherence were exacerbated.

As Goldstone observes, had the protests in Tunisia remained confined to rural townspeople or those in Egypt to the student and labour groups, then the state might more easily have suppressed them. It was when the protest movements grew to include workers, students, professionals, Islamists, rural and urban dwellers, in what he characterizes as "whole-society" opposition that the potential to overthrow the regime developed.[46] The difficulty with this, however, is that such coalitions rarely transform themselves into coherent social movements. In a "social movement process", according to Diani, there are more than networks of alliances and collaborations. Beyond shared material and symbolic resources, organizations that are part of a social movement will also identify each other as part of a broader collective actor that is not limited to any specific protest event or campaign. However, for the most part, when organizations come together to pursue a single common aim, it is on the basis of instrumental logic rather than shared common identity.[47]

In the case of the protest movements of 2011, it is clear, as Goldstone and others have pointed out, that only one objective united all participants – their opposition to the status quo. "What united these broad coalitions, more than economic grievances, discrimination, religion or nationalism was a shared enmity towards a hated dictator."[48] As to what might or should follow the demise of the regime, there was a considerable diversity of opinion ranging from the highly detailed to the utterly undeveloped. Furthermore, lacking even the minimal level of coherence, shared ideology, or shared collective identity, the protest movements were innately vulnerable to fracturing in the post-uprising period. This becomes clearer when political dynamics following the desired regime change has taken place are examined. This can be seen most clearly when the cases of Egypt and Tunisia are contrasted. In the Egyptian case, the persistence of critical differences between the constituent elements of the anti-regime movement meant that the oppositional coalition was incapable of taking advantage of the political opening that emerged with the fall of Mubarak. In the political vacuum that resulted, the established actors of the Muslim Brotherhood, the military, and remnants of the old regime contended for political benefit. In Tunisia, by contrast, a much deeper level of mutual identification and shared goals amongst key elements of the anti-regime movement made for a very different outcome.

In the Egyptian case, tensions within the anti-Mubarak movement were quick to emerge. Many of the anti-regime groups consciously worked outside formal political institutions. They were not only opposed to the regime but to the failed formal opposition of the Mubarak era such as political parties and professional syndicates. The protest movement was characterized by the absence of leaders, a specific programme, or a structure, it was not led by political parties but conducted by decentralized networks that relied on diffuse methods of communication, and it was driven not by a specific political agenda but by a more abstract "feeling of fatigue and weariness" with the predatory practices of the state, corruption, and arbitrariness, and the absence of any sense of collective purpose. The protest movement bridged social and ideological divides because it focused on what the protesters did not want (that is, Mubarak) rather than any positive agenda or set of demands.[49] Following the fall of Mubarak, some activists sought to form coalitions to coordinate the disparate groups occupying Tahrir Square in Cairo in order to prioritize demands and negotiate with the Supreme Council of the Armed Forces, which had taken control of the state. However, no broad-based alliance or representative organization emerged from this.[50]

The resignation of Mubarak was followed by an early split between the Muslim Brotherhood and its erstwhile allies in the "revolutionary" camp. The Muslim Brotherhood maintained channels of communication with the regime even as it mobilized its members to join the anti-Mubarak protests. When Mubarak resigned, the Muslim Brotherhood presented itself as an intermediary between the Supreme Council of the Armed Forces (SCAF) and the Egyptian people. Stein argues that for the Muslim Brotherhood the revolution offered an opportunity to institutionalize its de facto political presence "after years of precarious political co-existence with an authoritarian regime for which, rhetorically at least, Islamism represented an existential threat". As a result, it quickly shunned collaboration beyond the Islamist camp.[51] The post-Mubarak era was characterized by ever deepening polarization between the Muslim Brotherhood and more secular elements of the anti-regime movement. The constitutional referendum of 2012 became "an acrimonious tug of war" between the Islamists and secular forces. The Muslim Brotherhood and rival Islamist parties were victorious in the referendum and in subsequent parliamentary and presidential elections as well as a second constitutional referendum, leading to accusations that it had "hijacked" the revolution.[52] Ultimately, divisions between the Islamist and secular elements in the anti-regime protest movement culminated in the Tamarod movement of 2012/2013 which sought to replicate the anti-Mubarak movement, this time to unseat the elected Islamist President Morsi whose policies were viewed by many as Islamization by stealth. In the ensuing political instability in the country, the military intervened once more, to depose the president and inaugurate a new and increasingly authoritarian phase in Egyptian political life.

The post-Ben Ali transition process in Tunisia has followed a very different path. In October 2011, the country held its first ever free and fair multiparty elections to a National Constituent Assembly (NCA). The Islamist Ennahda party became the largest party with 90 seats out of a total of 217. After the elections, Ennahda entered into a coalition (the "Troika") with two secular leftist parties: Ettakatol and the Congress for the Republic. The mandate of the NCA was initially expected to last one year, in which time it would draft a constitution and an electoral framework. Its inability to do so saw the term of the assembly extend to two years as increasing political instability developed in the country, particularly in the form of tension between secularist and Islamist forces. After two years in power, the Ennahda-led government stepped down in January 2014 to be replaced by a government of "technocrats", the first instance of an Islamist-led government handing over power after the 2011 uprisings. A new constitution was agreed and parliamentary elections were held in October 2014, which saw Ennahda emerge as the second largest party behind a newcomer, the secularist, Nida Tounes, led by Beji Caid Essebsi who had served as foreign minister under Ben Ali.

The contrast with the outcome in Egypt could hardly be clearer. The dialogue process that saw the resignation of the Ennahda-led Troika was the result of an inclusive process brokered by an alliance of the UGTT, the employers union, the Tunisian Bar Association, and the Human Rights League. Kerrou attributes the success of the process to four key factors: the army's professional and apolitical status, lessons learned from Egypt, civil society's rallying behind the dialogue, and the conciliatory and decisive role played by political leaders. In particular, he suggests that the process succeeded because secular and Islamist political leaders agreed on the need for a negotiated consensual settlement. That the dialogue was successful was also due to the strength of the UGTT which, despite its leadership's close relations with the regime before the uprising, nonetheless remained the most powerful civil society organization in the country with one million members out of a total population of ten million people.[53] The shared consensus that emerged on the need for a consensus-based solution to the crisis in Tunisia that would preserve a transition to democracy is in striking contrast to the Egyptian situation.

However, the agreement that was brokered in January 2014 was not merely a factor of post-uprising political dynamics. In part, it was possible because of a much longer ideological reorientation that had shaped the development of the Islamic movement in Tunisia. This in turn is closely linked with the evolution of the political thinking of Ennahda leader Rachid al-Ghannouchi. In the late 1970s, the party subscribed to the notion of an "Islamic" state and the application of sharia. By the early 1980s, Ghannouchi had begun to rethink the nature of the state. This led to a change in Ennahda's position to one of support for the creation of a civil state in which references to religion are identity-based and not sources for public policy-making. The party also shifted its position on the issues of human rights and gender equality, such that the party claims to support the liberal personal status code that was introduced in Tunisia in the 1980s.[54] The result of this was that, in the course of negotiating the new constitution in January 2014, Ghannouchi was able to persuade his party to accept the removal of a reference to sharia as well as the abandonment of an article that referred to the "complementary" status of women to men.

But the rethinking of fundamental political positions was not confined to Ennahda, as secular activists reconsidered their views on cooperation with Islamism. The common experience of repression by the Ben Ali regime led some secularists to see political inclusion as key to Tunisia's future. The human rights activist, and subsequent interim president, Moncef Marzouki, argued that democracy could come to Tunisia only through agreement with Ennahda and not in spite of it.[55] In June 2003, representatives of the country's four major non-regime parties – Ennahda, Ettakatol, the Congress for the Republic, and the Progressive Democrats – signed an agreement in France that stipulated that any future elected government would have to be founded on the sovereignty of the people as the sole source or legitimacy; that the state, while showing respect for the people's identity and its Arab-Muslim values, would guarantee the liberty of beliefs to all. Furthermore, the parties demanded the full equality of women and men.[56]

Therefore, by the time of the uprising of 2011, the major opposition forces who comprised important elements of the anti-regime protest movement, had already arrived at a degree of consensus on the democratic and inclusive nature of post-Ben Ali Tunisia and on the need for continuing cross-ideological cooperation that quite simply never existed in the Egyptian case. As a result, when political crisis and widespread popular discontent beset the Islamist transitional government in 2013, it was possible to forge a consensus on the way forward that preserved the democratic transition in Tunisia.

Conclusion

The anti-regime social movements that drove the Arab uprisings underwent crucial transformations as they attracted ever-greater societal support. The initial youth-led NSMs were non-ideological, leaderless, and lacking in clear organizational structures. As the protest movements spread, they grew to encompass a diverse array of other movements and actors: political activists, opposition political parties, trade unions, lawyers, journalists and other professional groups, Islamist movements and parties, and, in some cases, regionally-based actors. Such diverse "movements of movements" were, however, able to agree only on minimal demands – the fall of the regime and the establishment of a new political order based on vague references to justice and dignity. The breadth and diversity of these coalitions made the successful achievement of their core demands for regime change possible. However, the persistence of ideological cleavages within them made agreement on the post-regime change political order near impossible.

When the autocrats departed in Egypt and Yemen the actors who initiated the protest movements were unable to seize the opportunities presented. In Egypt, the SCAF and the Muslim Brotherhood were able to draw on their vast organizational structures and power bases while the activists who occupied Tahrir Square proved incapable of offering a coherent alternative vision of the state. In the case of Yemen, apart from a few activists who were ideologically divided amongst themselves, the youth protesters had "no idea how to organize themselves or to draft a political programme".[57] This in turn permitted what Bayat characterizes as the "free-riders" to take advantage of the situation – the older established political parties, the Islamists who did have the organizational resources and, up to a point, the ideological coherence to present an alternative to the status quo, as well as remnants of the old regimes. In Egypt the Muslim Brotherhood effectively abandoned its erstwhile allies in the broad coalition that unseated Mubarak, quickly seeking an uneasy coexistence with the military, which ended with the coup of July 2013. In Yemen the post-Saleh order was dominated by a power-sharing coalition of the former ruling party, the General People's Congress, and a long-standing coalition of opposition parties, dominated by the Islamist Islah.

The exceptional case is that of Tunisia, where a process of mutual identification and toleration among the forces of opposition, as well as agreement on the shape of a post-Ben Ali order, was already under way almost a decade before the fall of the autocratic order in the country, only there did a more coherent anti-regime movement emerge. The capacity of opposition forces in Tunisia to overcome deep-seated ideological differences in the pursuit of shared aims distinguishes it from each of the other cases of the Arab uprisings to date. By contrast, the inability of the members of the movements that drove the uprisings in Egypt and Yemen to forge any consensus on the future shape of political life condemned them to fracturing and marginalization in the aftermath of the fall of the regime.

Disclosure statement

No potential conflict of interest was reported by the authors.

Notes

1. Dupont and Passy, "The Arab Spring."
2. Alimi and Meyer, "Seasons of Change," 478; Volpi, "Framing Political Revolutions," 155.
3. Hoffman and Konig, "Scratching the Democratic Façade," 3.
4. Beinin, "Civil Society, NGOs."
5. Leenders, "Social Movement Theory," 277.
6. Ibid., 277.
7. Joffé, "The Arab Spring in North Africa," 519.
8. Ibid., 517–521.
9. Stammers, *Human Rights and Social Movements*, 34.
10. Diani, "The Concept of a Social Movement," 9.
11. Ibid., 13.
12. Tilly, *Durable Inequality*, 213.
13. Stammers, "Social Movements and the Social Construction of Human Rights," 984.
14. Della Porta and Diani, *Social Movements* (1999).
15. Della Porta and Diani, *Social Movements* (2006), 9–10.
16. Bayat, "Un-civil Society," 57.
17. Wiktorowicz, *Islamic Activism*.
18. Singerman, "The Networked Worlds of Islamist Social Movements," 145.
19. Bayat, "Islamism and Social Movement Theory," 903.

20. Simsek, "New Social Movements in Turkey"; Sutton and Vertigans, "Islamic 'New Social Movements.'"
21. Sutton and Vertigans, "Islamic 'New Social Movements,'" 102–103.
22. Abdelrahman, "With the Islamists?," 40.
23. Ibid., 41.
24. Bayat, "Revolution without Movement, Movement without Revolution," 141.
25. Goldstone, "Cross-class Coalitions," 457.
26. Aleya-Sghaier, "The Tunisian Revolution," 39–40.
27. Ibid., 42–45.
28. Beinin, "Civil Society, NGOs," 402.
29. Ibid., 402.
30. Abdelrahman, "A Hierarchy of Struggles," 616.
31. Ibid., 616–617.
32. El-Din Shahin, "The Egyptian Revolution," 60–65.
33. Nevens, "Yemen's Youth Revolution," 26; Durac, "Protest Movements and Political Change," 165.
34. For more on the JMP, see Durac, "The Joint Meeting Parties."
35. Hill and Nonneman, "Yemen, Saudi Arabia and the Gulf States," 3.
36. Zaydism is a branch of Shia Islam that emerged from a ninth-century split in the community. The Zaydis claimed that Zaid ibn Ali was the fifth Imam while the majority of Shiites recognize Muhammad al-Baqir and his son Jafar al-Sadiq as the rightful heirs to the Imamate. The Zaydis founded a state in Yemen in 993 which survived until 1962.
37. Longley Alley, "Yemen's Multiple Crisis," 72.
38. Brahimi, "Libya's Revolution," 606.
39. Templehof and Omar, "Stakeholders of Libya's February 17 Revolution," 5.
40. Deeb, "The Arab Spring."
41. The Berber, Tuareg, and Tebu are minorities within Libya. The Berber are an Amazigh-speaking group concentrated in the north of the country; the Tuareg are composed of two groups – those who originally inhabited the Libyan-Algerian borderland and those who immigrated from Niger and Mali; the Tebu inhabit the eastern part of Fezzan in the east. The numbers of each are the subject of highly variable estimates since ethnic minorities were not registered in Libya under Gadhafi. For more, see Kohl, "Libya's 'Major Minorities.'"
42. International Crisis Group, "Making Sense of Libya"; Deeb, "The Arab Spring."
43. Genugten, "Libya after Gadhafi," 62.
44. Goldstone, "Cross-class Coalitions," 457.
45. Bellin, "Reconsidering the Robustness of Authoritarianism," 138.
46. Goldstone, "Cross-class Coalitions," 457–460.
47. Diani, "Social Movement Theory and Grassroots Coalitions."
48. Goldstone, "Cross-class Coalitions"; See also Genugten, "Libya after Gadhafi"; Al-Wazir, "'Youth' Inclusion in Yemen"; Roberts, "The Revolution that Wasn't."
49. International Crisis Group, "Egypt Victorious?," 19–20.
50. Abdelrahman, "In Praise of Organization," 580.
51. Stein, "Egypt's Fraught Transition," 51–52.
52. Gunning and Baron, *Why Occupy a Square?* 303–304.
53. Kerrou, "Tunisia's Historic Step."
54. Cavatorta and Meorne, "Moderation Through Exclusion," 860–861.
55. Ibid., 870.
56. Stepan, "Tunisia's Transition," 97.
57. Al-Sakkaf, "The Politicization of Yemen's Youth Revolution."

Bibliography

Abdelrahman, Maha. "'With the Islamists? – Sometimes. With the State? Never!' Cooperation between the Left and Islamists in Egypt." *British Journal of Middle Eastern Studies* 36, no. 1 (2009): 37–54.

Abdelrahman, Maha. "A Hierarchy of Struggles? The 'Economic' and the 'Political in Egypt's Revolution.'" *Review of African Political Economy* 39, no. 134 (2012): 614–628.

Abdelrahman, Maha. "In Praise of Organization: Egypt Between Activism and Revolution." *Development and Change* 44, no. 3 (2013): 569–585.

Aleya-Sghaier, Amira. "The Tunisian Revolution, the Revolution of Dignity." In *Revolution, Revolt and Reform in North Africa: The Arab Spring and Beyond*, edited by Ricardo Rene Laremont, 30–52. London: Routledge, 2014.

Alimi, Eitan Y., and David S. Meyer. "Season of Change: Arab Spring and Political Opportunities." *Swiss Political Science Review* 17, no. 4 (2011): 475–479.

Al-Sakkaf, Nadia. "The Politicization of Yemen's Youth Revolution." *Arab Reform Bulletin*, April 27, 2011. http://www.carnegieendowment.org/arb/?fa=show&article=43735

Al-Wazir, Atiaf. "'Youth' Inclusion in Yemen: A Necessary Element for Success of Political Transition." *Arab Reform Bulletin* 64 (2012). http://www.arab-reform.net/%E2%80%9Cyouth%E2%80%9D-inclusion-yemen-necessary-element-success-political-transition

Bayat, Asef. "Un-civil Society: The Politics of the 'Informal' People." *Third World Quarterly* 18, no. 1 (1997): 53–72.

Bayat, Asef. "Revolution without Movement, Movement without Revolution: Comparing Islamic Activism in Iran and Egypt." *Comparative Studies in Society and History* 40, no. 1 (1998): 136–169.

Bayat, Asef. "Islamism and Social Movement Theory." *Third World Quarterly* 26, no. 6 (2005): 891–908.

Beinin, Joel. "Civil Society, NGOs and Egypt's 2011 Popular Uprising." *The South Atlantic Quarterly* 113, no. 2 (2014): 396–406.

Bellin, Eva. "Reconsidering the Robustness of Authoritarianism in the Middle East: Lessons from the Arab Spring." *Comparative Politics* 44, no. 2 (2012): 127–149.

Brahimi, Alia. "Libya's Revolution." *Journal of North African Studies* 16, no. 4 (2011): 605–624.

Cavatorta, Francesco, and Fabio Meorne. "Moderation through Exclusion? The Journey of the Tunisian Ennahda from Fundamentalist to Conservative Party." *Democratization* 20, no. 5 (2013): 857–875.

Deeb, Mary-Jane. "The Arab Spring: Libya's Second Revolution." In *The Arab Spring: Change and Resistance in the Middle East*, edited by Mark Haas and David Lesch, 64–78. Boulder, CO: Westview Press, 2013.

Della Porta, Donatella, and Mario Diani. *Social Movements: An Introduction*. Oxford: Blackwell, 1999.

Della Porta, Donatella, and Mario Diani. *Social Movements: An Introduction*. Oxford: Blackwell, 2006.

Diani, Mario. "The Concept of a Social Movement." *The Sociological Review* 40, no. 1 (1992): 1–25.

Diani, Mario. "Social Movement Theory and Grassroots Coalitions in the Middle East." Paper presented to the ASA Annual Meeting, Boston, August 1–4, 2008.
Dupont, Cédric, and Florence Passy. "The Arab Spring or How to Explain those Revolutionary Episodes?" *Swiss Political Science Review* 17, no. 4 (2011): 447–451.
Durac, Vincent. "The Joint Meeting Parties and the Politics of Opposition in Yemen." *British Journal of Middle Eastern Studies* 38, no. 3 (2011): 343–365.
Durac, Vincent. "Protest Movements and Political Change: An Analysis of the 'Arab Uprisings'." *Journal of Contemporary African Studies* 31, no. 2 (2013): 175–193.
El-Din Shahin, Emad. "The Egyptian Revolution: The Power of Mass Mobilization and the Spirit of Tahrir Square." In *Revolution, Revolt and Reform in North Africa: The Arab Spring and Beyond*, edited by Ricardo Rene Laremont, 53–74. London: Routledge, 2014.
Genugten, Saskia. "Libya after Gadhafi." *Survival* 53, no. 3 (2011): 61–74.
Goldstone, Jack. "Cross-class Coalitions and the Making of the Arab Revolts of 2011." *Swiss Political Science Review* 17, no. 4 (2011): 457–462.
Gunning, Jeroen, and Ilan Zvi Baron. *Why Occupy A Square: People, Protests and Movements in the Egyptian Revolution*. London: Hurst, 2013.
Hill, Ginny, and Gerd Nonneman. "Yemen, Saudi Arabia and the Gulf States: Elite Politics, Street Protests and Regional Diplomacy." Chatham House Middle East and North Africa Programme Briefing Paper No. 2011/01, May (2011). http://www.chathamhouse.org/sites/default/files/19237_0511yemen_gulfbp.pdf
Hoffman, Anja, and Christoph Konig. "Scratching the Democratic Façade: Framing Strategies of the 20 February Movement." *Mediterranean Politics* 18, no. 1 (2013): 1–22.
ICG (International Crisis Group). "Popular Protest in North Africa and the Middle East (I): Egypt Victorious?" *Middle East and North Africa Report No. 101* (2011). http://www.crisisgroup.org/en/regions/middle-east-north-africa/egypt-syria-lebanon/egypt/101-popular-protest-in-north-africa-and-the-middle-east-i-egypt-victorious.aspx
ICG (International Crisis Group). "Popular Protest in North Africa and the Middle East (V): Making Sense of Libya." *Middle East and North Africa Report No. 107* (2011). http://www.crisisgroup.org/en/publication-type/media-releases/2011/making-sense-of-Libya.aspx
Joffé, George. "The Arab Spring in North Africa: Origins and Prospects." *Journal of North African Studies* 16, no. 4 (2011): 507–532.
Kerrou, Mohamed. "Tunisia's Historic Step Towards Democracy." *Carnegie Endowment for International Peace*, April 22, 2014. http://carnegieendowment.org/2014/04/17/tunisia-s-historic-step-toward-democracy/h8t0?reloadFlag=1
Kohl, Ines. "Libya's 'Major Minorities,' Berber, Tuareg and Tebu: Multiple Narratives of Citizenship, Language and Border Control." *Middle East Critique* 23, no. 4 (2014): 423–438.
Leenders, Reinoud. "Social Movement Theory and the Onset of the Popular Uprising in Syria." *Arab Studies Quarterly* 35, no. 3 (2013): 273–289.
Longley Alley, April. "Yemen's Multiple Crises." *Journal of Democracy* 21, no. 4 (2010): 72–86.
Nevens, Kate. "Yemen's Youth Revolution." In *The Arab Spring: Implications for British Policy*, 24–27. London: Conservative Middle East Council, 2011.
Roberts, Hugh. "The Revolution That Wasn't." *London Review of Books*, September 12, 2013. http://www.lrb.co.uk/v35/n17/hugh-roberts/the-revolution-that-wasn't
Simsek, Sefa. "New Social Movements in Turkey since 1980." *Turkish Studies* 5, no. 2 (2004): 111–139.
Singerman, Diane. "The Networked Worlds of Islamist Social Movements." In *Islamic Activism: A Social Movement Theory Approach*, edited by Quentin Wiktorowicz, 143–163. Bloomington: Indiana University Press, 2004.

Stammers, Neil. "Social Movements and the Social Construction of Human Rights." *Human Rights Quarterly* 21, no. 4 (1999): 980–1008.

Stammers, Neil. *Human Rights and Social Movements*. London: Pluto, 2009.

Stein, Ewan. "Revolution or Coup? Egypt's Fraught Transition." *Survival* 54, no. 4 (2012): 45–66.

Stepan, Alfred. "Tunisia's Transition and the Twin Tolerations." *Journal of Democracy* 23, no. 2 (2012): 89–103.

Sutton, Phillip W., and Stephen Vertigans. "Islamic 'New Social Movements'? Radical Islam, Al-Qa'ida and Social Movement Theory." *Mobilizations* 11, no. 1 (2006): 101–115.

Templehof, Susanne Tarkowski, and Manal Omar. "Stakeholders of Libya's February 17 Revolution." *United States Institute of Peace* (2011). http://www.usip.org/publications/stakeholders-of-libya-s-february-17-revolution

Tilly, Charles. *Durable Inequality*. Los Angeles: University of California Press, 1998.

Volpi, Frederic. "Framing Political Revolutions in the Aftermath of the Arab Uprisings." *Mediterranean Politics* 19, no. 4 (2014): 153–156.

Wiktorowicz, Quentin, ed. *Islamic Activism: A Social Movement Theory Approach*. Bloomington: Indiana University Press, 2004.

Fragmenting states, new regimes: militarized state violence and transition in the Middle East

Joshua Stacher

Department of Political Science, Kent State University, Kent, OH, USA

Scholars working in the transitology tradition assume that authoritarian breakdown leads to movement towards democratization after an initial period of uncertainty. If a transition falls short of democratization, there is an assumption that a return to authoritarian normalcy has transpired. Yet, whether one looks at Egypt, Libya, Syria, or Bahrain, the emergent trend is neither democratization, a return to the old authoritarian order, or a delayed transition. Rather, the weakening and fragmenting of regimes by popular mobilizations stimulated elites' militarization of the state apparatus and unprecedented levels of state violence against ordinary citizens in a process of regime re-making.

Introduction

When Tunisia's Zine al-Abidine Ben Ali boarded a plane for exile in January 2011, he became the first Arab leader unwillingly removed from power by popular mobilization. Tunisia's mobilization kicked off a wider regional process that touched other Arab countries. People in Egypt, Bahrain, Libya, Yemen, and Syria rose against regimes that had repressively governed for decades. As the literature on democratic transitions argued, diffusion was a contagious juggernaut for autocrats.[1] The pressure on existing autocracies suggested the older order was coming to an end. Scholars, pundits, and the media named the revolutionary wave the "Arab Spring", which implied better days lay ahead.[2] While everyone included a disclaimer that full democratization would be a long process, the analysis of events was imbued with tenets of modernization theory and references to the "Third Wave of Democratization".[3] Educated, middle-class opposition to outdated governing autocracies was expected to drive democratization.[4] Yet, no transition away from autocracy occurred, with the possible exception of Tunisia.[5]

Before 2011, scholars on the Arab world were forced into debates about the democratically resistant and exceptional politics of the Arab world.[6] In fact, beyond being the "least free" in the world, the Arab states were hardly mentioned in disciplinary conversations about more sophisticated hybrid regimes or competitive authoritarianism.[7] Then, nearly overnight, the cases of the Arab universe became the epicentre for studying transitions away from authoritarian rule.[8]

There is a large theoretical literature about transitions. These works cover aspects such as pacted transitions, the power of popular mobilization, and incremental democratization by elections.[9] Not only have they helped us understand the Arab cases, but the uprisings also expose the literature's blind spots. One problematic aspect of a transitions lens is that it suggests a temporary phase that leads either to democracy or a return to a pre-transitory state. Yet, in the Arab case, there has been neither a democratic transition nor a simple return to authoritarian pre-transitory politics.

The Arab uprisings' most visible product to date has been the militarization of politics and societies, seen in an expansion of state violence against the citizenry, producing a qualitative change in state-society relations. Popular mobilization broke down previously established governing practices and fragmented the state apparatus. In most cases, this invited those fragments that had both vested political interests and weapons (organized armies, militias, security forces) to expand their influence in this void. Rather than consent to a transition, counter-revolutionary agents conspired with transnational partners and capital to block popular empowerment by building new authoritarian regimes out of the remains of what had previously existed.[10] Capturing this process of social struggle – a fragmenting state that produces elites who militarize society by employing elevated levels of violence against their populations to forge new "regimes-in-formation" and reformulate state-society relations should become the central frame for scholarly analysis of the Arab uprisings.[11] This article's main purpose is theoretically to re-evaluate often assumed democratic transitions by throwing light on the grim area of state violence.

Theoretical approaches

The current repertoire of theories on transitions from authoritarian rule is inadequate for accurately representing the current political process in Arab states. These theories depict a sanitized version of events that sweeps away the dirty and often violent underside of political change.

To illustrate the type of linear analysis that transitology studies promotes, we only need to look as far as Stepan and Linz's application of it to the Arab cases in *Journal of Democracy*.[12] They view the Arab uprisings as authoritarian breakdown. The extent of movement towards democracy was seen to vary chiefly according to the degree of pre-uprising "sultanism" from which a country emerges. For example, the fall of the uber-sultanistic Qadhafi regime in Libya left a state that needs rebuilding from scratch. This makes democracy a distant prospect. Syria's dynastic regime made a pacted transition a slim prospect and, consequently, civil conflict rose as the existing regime dug in against its people. Semi-sultanistic Egypt has propelled the "military as institution" into the political drama but the Supreme Council of the Armed Forces' (SCAF) convening of elections suggested to them that, despite some reservations, Egypt could "break democratic" in the future.[13] Even though Ben Ali's Tunisia was also deeply sultanistic, the army intervened and exited, leaving political society a "relatively coherent and democratic alternative".[14] Thus, where one starts on the sultanism spectrum conditions what is immediately possible or how far a country has to go to reach democracy, with immediate outcomes labelled "authoritarian-democratic hybrids".[15] Linz and Stepan are not ready to declare regional democracy inevitable but they clearly indicate there will be no going back to "presidents for life".[16] And breakdown is assumed to usher in a more democratic form of politics than what existed prior to the uprisings. This passage illuminates their thinking:

> Recent historical events such as the fall of communism, the entry of ten former communist countries into the EU, the demise of military governments in Latin America, and the aspirations raised by Tahrir Square do not mean the "end of history" and the reign of full democracy. Yet in countries such as Egypt, they have fueled a growing sense of the dignity of the individual, of people as citizens rather than mere subjects, and of democratic practices as things that are normally expected. In this new world, passively accepting for sixty years in a row one military officer after another as Egypt's ruler is no longer possible.[17]

There are two weaknesses in this approach. While the authors emphasize that transitions are moments of uncertainty, they do not get beyond the still optimistic notion of transition (as a stage towards democracy) or account for the grim repression and violence in post-uprising states. Further, their main explanation for outcomes, the "sultanistic" starting point, seems to predetermine trajectories, to the neglect of post-uprising agency. While history matters greatly, it is the interaction of political actors with inherited institutions that primarily shapes trajectories. What they do not account for, in particular, is that trajectories depend on which parts of the *state* are activated and deactivated and, as I will argue, the capacity of security forces to recover the initiative and use violence in regime re-making is crucial.

More attention is given to agency in the literature on the Third Wave of democratization, which draws on the experiences of southern Europe and Latin America in the 1970s and 1980s. Canonical works by O'Donnell and Schmitter describe transitions as a process in which opposition movements use popular mobilization as leverage to extract concessions from power-holders.[18] This precipitates a coalition between reform-minded elements within the incumbent regime (or softliners) and opposition moderates that marginalizes hardliners in the regime and radicals in the opposition, thereby minimizing confrontation and violence. Pact-making, arrived at via negotiation, bargaining, and compromise over the rules of the political game, governs the transition to democracy.[19] While this stress on agency and the interaction of divided elites and masses is welcome, it does not explain why in the Arab case such pacts failed or failed to prevent massive violence.

In the next generation of "transitology" literature that emerged in response to the fall of dictatorships in post-communist Europe, there is less emphasis on elite pact-making and more on the impact of popular mobilization on what pact-making takes place. This literature, dubbed the "Fourth Wave of democracy and dictatorship" by scholars such as McFaul, revises the structural and institutional factors that allow some cases to break towards democracy while others retreat into autocratic rule or become mired in some type of purgatory, mixing democratic and authoritarian elements.[20] For McFaul, democratizing pacts occur when the opposition is in a stronger position to rewrite the political rules of the game than are surviving autocrats. As he claims, "If powerful democrats draft the rules, it does not matter what electoral system is adopted ... What matters most is the powerful are committed to the democratic project."[21] Bunce, who also works on post-communist regime transitions, agrees. She shows that the prior character of regimes and opposition histories matter to the relative bargaining power of incumbents and opposition, and that democratization demands a breakage with the past regime, not a bridge built from it. For Bunce, mass mobilization produces "a large opposition united in its rejection of the incumbent regime".[22] Without this, the outcome is a "compromised democracy". This literature is an advance in that it more explicitly combines structure and agency, and gives equal attention to elite pact-making and mass mobilization; but it still expects a full or partial transition to democracy and it cannot explain the fact that in the Arab cases millions of protestors mobilized but for very limited democratic gains. They might argue that the distribution of power between the incumbents and opposition were too uneven to produce a "democratic" transition; but in that case their expectation would be that transition is merely delayed or regresses. The past four years in the Arab world suggest that it is not regression or delay but a remaking of state-society relations that is entrained.

None of these approaches grasp the role of violence in shaping post uprising tangents. While political scientists have studied civil wars extensively, there is less work on the political violence that state elites deploy after authoritarian breakdown. Schmitter and Karl reminded us long ago that politics after authoritarian breakdown are usually not more "orderly, consensual, stable, or governable than the autocracies they replace".[23] Data exist showing that fewer people die in consolidated authoritarian regimes and functioning democracies than in between these poles. Helen Fein has called this the "More Murder in the Middle" (MMM) theory.[24] Her data reveal that "there will be more conflict mobilized and incentives for repression – i.e., worse violations for life integrity – as democracy is extended before it is fully institutionalized".[25] While Fein demonstrates the prevalence of violence, her data do not identify their sources – whether the state is killing its citizens, criminal gangs are claiming innocent lives in turf wars on the streets, or society is targeting the state. Nor does she address its effect on democratization prospects and still assumes the outcome is a transition to democracy.

Discussing violence in the politics of the Arab world has been noticeably absent considering the long-time everyday levels of repression, human rights abuses, and widespread incarceration. Yet, this gap is being addressed. For example, as Laleh Khalili points out, while some feel that focusing on violence in the Arab world advances clichés, prejudices, and stereotypes about the region, it is flawed to defer to this pressure because violence and "other forms of coercion" help replicate "institutions of state".[26] If researchers want to understand how state violence helps a weak state build, change, or replicate hierarchies, then it needs to be studied on its own terms. An illuminating example of this is Neep's work, which shows how violence forged state-making in French-occupied Syria.[27] This research joins Charles Tilly's work about how violence aids the process of state-building.[28] Yet, rather than state-building, it might be better conceptualized as regime-making – how elites and society struggle over the everyday practices and patterns whereby regimes establish the ability to govern. Thus, delving deeper into increased levels of violence and into who is perpetrating the violence is instructive for explaining what is politically occurring in the Arab world.

Grasping the role of state violence in the Arab uprisings

Residents and visitors to the Arab world witnessed "slow violence" as part of everyday life in the region before 2011.[29] This included deterring warnings such as plainclothes thugs or riot police selectively attacking protesters, security personnel and informers watching from street corners, activists receiving invitations from interior ministries, or internet videos surfacing of people being tortured in police stations.[30] Arbitrary and rotating imprisonment of activists pushing against the status quo was the political norm.[31] People living in these societies challenged such repression. Domestic groups and independent journalists bravely published reports about the quotidian abuses committed by the incumbent regimes. This type of slow violence became accepted, if despised, by many. In fact, some have shown that the repressive character of the region's authoritarian regimes encouraged parallel structures that helped people intentionally stay out of the state's way.[32]

Yet, the regime that permitted its security forces to kill activists was a rarity. While it could happen and security forces would not be held to account, it was a line not many regimes crossed willingly. The case of Khalid Sa'id is an example.[33] Two police officers got into an altercation with Sa'id in Alexandria's Sidi Gaber district in June 2010 and beat him to death in the stairwell of a building. The pictures taken at the morgue show his disfigured face with lacerations, broken facial bones, and extensive bruises. This galvanized Egyptians, who circulated the morgue's pictures. Marches commemorating his death took place in major Egyptian cities as activists established the "We are all Khalid Sa'id" Facebook page. The outrage at the death of a single person, who was probably killed accidently, is instructive because of the contrast to the levels of violence the Arab world experienced just six months later.

The Arab uprisings ushered in the most violent period of state-society relations in the history of the contemporary region. Sustained popular mobilization pressured or cracked the edifice of authoritarian ruling coalitions, the state apparatus, and ruling regime practices. This pressure, in some cases, merely reshuffled who belonged to or led the ruling coalition but usually did not break the ruling class that staffed the apparatus and enforced order. Rather than bend towards the popular will and open up the politics as citizen mobilization demanded, the surviving elites militarized and reconfigured regimes from parts of what previously existed. In some other cases the collapse of regimes put the state itself at risk and left a vacuum in which authority became contested. Both outcomes obstructed democratization but did not mean a return to the days of pre-revolutionary authoritarianism. Rather, it was regime-making. This requires political engineering and state violence becomes one chief tool still available to weakened state apparatuses – that have lost, for example, much of their previous co-optative capacity. Where sustained mobilizations occurred, state elites conducted informal dirty wars against their people. Entrenched state elites or elites that assumed control of fragmenting states unleashed the repressive arm of the states to end popular mobilization as a prelude to devising new governing practices between rulers and ruled.

These trajectories flip the transition paradigm on its head. Rather than regime softliners and opposition moderates winning the day, regime hardliners block, obfuscate, and delay democratization, often using violence against society. This tends to split the opposition and discredit the so-called moderates while so-called opposition radicals are empowered, become intransigent, and respond to the new regime with counter-violence, setting off a spiral of violence between the hardline elements in both state and society. This leads to a militarization of states as armies and security forces re-enter the halls of governance. The return of military and security specialists to the centre of power leads to escalated levels of state violence – including both body counts and other types of violence like military courts for civilians, employing third-country mercenaries, and highly coercive crowd-control policing. Depicting this historical struggle in this manner tempers overly optimistic expectations encouraged by the transition framework, and re-directs attention to the role of state violence, which has become the most prominent factor shaping political development in the uprising states. Politics in so-called Arab transitions has been dangerous precisely because surviving elites never allowed popular demands to be realized in emancipatory ends.

Some might argue that in addition to state violence other forms of violence have emerged as a result of the Arab uprisings, such as sectarian conflict, elevated levels of sectarian awareness, and terrorist acts against states by extremists groups. This is not up for dispute. However, rather than resort to a "cycles of violence" frame, I wish to place the emphasis on which side is better armed and capable of inflicting the most damage. While car bombs that target security forces and may kill innocent bystanders are deplorable, a military operation, the use of air power, or organized military-style clearances of public squares always result in the deaths of more people than the former. State violence is disproportionately violent compared to other forms.

Cases from the Arab uprisings

The Arab uprising countries have followed diverse paths explained, in significant part, by variations in the role of violence and of state specialists in violence. Tunisia remains the cautiously optimistic case. The fact that its military was small and traditionally apolitical proved to be an advantage in the post-Ben Ali era.[34] The absence of military officers inserting themselves or their institution into politics forced the emergent civilian politicians to compromise among themselves. Although some political assassinations occurred, incremental civilian negotiations over the rules of the game kept the deployment of state violence to a minimum.[35] Tunisia is proving to be the exception to the rule of increased state violence because the small military restrained itself.[36]

If Tunisia suggests hope, Syria reveals the nightmare. Shortly after President al-Asad claimed that the country was immune to an uprising, protests began in the southern border town of Der'a. The protests spread around the country and Syria became engulfed in a civil war. The regime did not split under the pressure, nor sacrifice the president and his cronies to save itself, calculating that this would open up a power vacuum that could lead to the state unravelling.[37] The disparate opposition forces seemed destined to lose as parts of major cities such as Homs and Aleppo were razed by military force. The weaker the state becomes, the more the remaining elites violently militarize the conflict against the people. As Haddad argued, "The Syrian tragedy is increasingly more about the fall of Syria(ans) than the fall of the Syrian regime."[38]

Civilian institutions that regulated the authoritarian bargain that Hafez al-Asad brokered are disappearing. Entities like the massive ruling B'ath party seemingly receded into the background as the multiple security branches and the Armed Forces stepped to the forefront. These "violence specialists", as Tilly calls them, do what they are trained to do. Allegations that the state has used chemical weapons against its opponents as well as frequently conducting air strikes on armed militias in the north are now common. The United Nations has stopped updating a death count in Syria's civil war because the numbers have become too unreliable but claim over 100,000 had died by July 2013.[39] Tens of thousands of others are detained and subjected to torture. Furthermore, the state's violence has led to parts of the country slipping out of regime control because the militarization of the opposition raised the costs for the over-stretched military of re-establishing control of all parts of the state's territory. The regime decided to concentrate its forces in its most vital core areas. The situation in Syria has led to the proliferation of transnational extremist groups, a war economy that incentivizes the continuance of the conflict, and the worst refugee crisis since the Rwandan genocide in 1994.[40]

Whatever governing structures eventually emerge from this conflict, the old B'athist state designed by Hafez al-Asad is gone. Any group that eventually maintains or assumes control of the weak state will be focused on state re-building. New relational practices between those who govern and the people will be essential after militarization tapers off. There is no transition in Syria, only state fragmentation and violence.

Between the extreme cases of Tunisia and Syria are located other cases that have produced militarizing state power in varying degrees. Libya bore witness to an internationally sponsored military intervention that led to the lynching of long-time leader Muammer Qadhafi. While some governments and analysts held out hope following Libya's 2012 election, most now accept that the fall of Qaddafi's brutal regime has taken the state down with it.[41] In the words of one reporter, Libya is "coming undone". As Fahim reports, "In the absence of a strong government, a monstrous shadow state was emerging, centred on the power of militias made up of men who fought Colonel Qaddafi and never put down their arms."[42] There is no central authority in Libya, only multiplying militias, factionalized violence, and political incoherence. The removal of a dictator and the collapse of the state left an arena where militarization and violence will be the *lingua franca* that is likely to propel the next Libyan leader to power. Then, assuming a coherent state is even possible, those elites will have to re-start the state-building and regime-making process.

Bahrain represents another instance where popular mobilization has produced an increase in state violence as well as militarization against society. In the wake of Egypt's revolutionary wave, Bahrainis rallied to appeal to their Emir to renegotiate the ruling bargain. Unwilling and unable to concede to the crowds, and backed by its nervous Saudi patron, Bahraini security forces fired on the protestors, stopped doctors from treating the wounded, and imprisoned those pushing for change. As of the beginning of 2014, 164 had died and around 3000 been injured. The ruling establishment also invited the Gulf Cooperation Council (GCC) across the causeway that connects the country to Saudi Arabia to bolster its repressive capacity. Shaykh Hamid ibn Isa Al-Khalifa even ordered the main gathering spot of the demonstrators, the Pearl Roundabout, destroyed in 2011 so that it could not become a symbol for change. Although there have been international attempts to mediate between the protesters and the state, the minority-Sunni Bahraini establishment has used the issue of sectarianism to divide the opposition and tarnish what began as a nationalist movement for more rights.[43] The army continues to be deployed around the small island, where checkpoints give citizens the feeling that they are under occupation by their own government. Activists say they live in the "kingdom of tear gas" because of the seemingly endless supply the state uses and imports from the United States and other states.[44] Furthermore, to ensure a sectarian tinge to the uprising, state elites employ mercenaries from Sunni states to target and police the Shia majority.[45] The militarization of the Bahraini uprising – like the other cases – reveals the state's inability to politically convince its citizens. The major consequence of the uprising has been an uptick in state violence, political imprisonment, policing, and repression of people rather than a march towards emancipation.

There is probably no better case than Egypt to demonstrate that state violence – not democratic transitions through pacts or elections – is where researchers should spend their efforts. On 25 January 2011 protesters took to the streets and collided with the seemingly immovable force of their state. After 18 days of street battles, presidential speeches, and international policy recalibrations, Hosni Mubarak stepped down as president after nearly 30 years.[46] Egypt's uprisings reorganized the ruling coalition and facilitated the military's re-entry into national politics.[47] Organized around the SCAF, Field Marshall Hussein al-Tantawi took control of the country and promised a quick transition to civilian rule. Instead, SCAF more deeply embedded itself into politics, protected the military's economic holdings, led a coup d'état against an elected civilian president, and ultimately produced a president, Field Marshall 'Abd al-Fattah al-Sisi, who was elected in May 2014.

The military-led transition also oversaw the greatest expansion of state violence against Egyptians in contemporary history.[48] Whether one looks to measures such as the use of military courts against civilians or an increase in body counts, Egyptians experienced an explosion of state violence following the mobilization that dislodged Mubarak.[49] This was no simple period of uncertainty followed by a failed transition towards democracy. Rather, from the start, the senior generals of the Egyptian Armed Forces implemented a policy that used systematic state violence against a restive population wanting change.[50]

SCAF resorted to state violence because the state apparatus had fragmented and Mubarak-era governing practices collapsed. Generals, who were caught off guard by the mobilization and found themselves catapulted into the driver's seat of the state, proved unwilling or unable to incorporate the demands of the protests. In moving against Mubarak they dumped parts of the regime in order to salvage the rest. They used the Muslim Brothers as tools to help demobilize the population. SCAF tried to use elections to channel a type of popular political participation between February 2011 and June 2012. The goal was to get protesters off the streets and into formal governing structures and processes while the generals manipulated the transition to protect themselves. When their attempts to calm the population's restiveness failed, they resorted to violence to dampen down popular mobilization. Thousands were injured and hundreds killed over the 17 months of SCAF's rule. Between March and June 2011, electric prods were used against activists and females subjected to army-sanctioned virginity tests in the Egyptian National Museum. In June, over 500 protestors were injured when security forces clashed with families of 25 January martyrs outside the Balloon Theatre in Cairo.[51] In October 2011, the violence qualitatively escalated when the military killed 28 protesters at Cairo's Maspero television building.[52] Security forces killed another 41 (and injured over 1000) in the Mohamed Mahmoud Street battles the week before parliamentary elections.[53] Nineteen protesters died (750 injured) at the hands of the military at the Cabinet Offices sit-in in January 2012,[54] and another 15 were killed in protests near the Interior Ministry in February

2012.[55] Twelve more were killed at a Defence Ministry sit-in between April and May 2012.[56] Security forces killed another 48 protesters while injuring over 800 in Port Said protests after alleged rioters at a football match were acquitted in January 2013.[57] Others died when citizens battled one another while the security forces were either absent or deliberately unresponsive. After instigators started a riot at a football match citizen-on-citizen violence left 79 dead and over 1000 injured in Port Said in February 2011.[58] The Brotherhood's supporters attacked protesters after Morsi's constitutional declaration, leaving another nine dead at the presidential palace.[59] There were also lynching murders of four Shias in a Giza village in June 2013.[60]

In the aftermath of al-Sisi's coup in July 2013, state violence changed again, from defensive to offensive. Morsi's removal signified that the pact between the military and the Muslim Brothers and the utility of procedurally fair elections were not enough to contain popular mobilization. One of the ways that the army directly participated in creating an environment conducive for a coup against Morsi, the dehumanization of the Brotherhood, and popular acceptance for the use of state violence against the group was through the vehicle of Tamarod. Tamarod was a group that emerged with the support of military intelligence and the police as well as funding by a business tycoon. They purportedly collected 22 million signatures demanding Morsi call for early elections. They also led calls for the demonstrations that were used by the military to remove Morsi from power. Thus, the generals overthrew Morsi but only after manipulating public discontent over his presidency.

Once Morsi was relieved as president, his illegal detention prompted protests from his supporters. At one such protest, near the republican guard headquarters in July, security services supported by the military used sharpshooters and opened fire in the early hours of the day, killing 51 people.[61] This violent re-assertion of the state was legitimized through a propaganda campaign hailing a state-led war against terrorism. Relying on 30 years of international and domestic discourse about autocratic Islamist "intentions" and exaggerating the exclusivist tendencies of Morsi's presidency, the target of this "counter-terrorist" offensive was identified as the anti-coup coalition, which was staging large pro-Morsi sit-ins at Rabaa and Nahda squares. The media railed against the secretive and nefarious Brothers as Egyptian pilots skywrote black and red flags and hearts above the crowds in Tahrir and sweet shops in posh parts of Cairo began selling cupcakes with al-Sisi's picture on them.

Having laid this groundwork, al-Sisi appealed to people to rise up and give the state a mandate to combat terrorism. This secured, through the work of military-supported Tamarod, SCAF thwarted an American and European plan to resolve rising tensions politically and unleashed overwhelming violence to force a political outcome.[62] Seventy were killed when security forces opened fire at a sit-in at Rabaa Square.[63] Then, on the morning of 14 August, the security forces pounced, leaving between 800 and 1000 dead in Rabaa Square.[64] Images of corpses and areas on fire were circulated to signal that the Brotherhood was no longer permitted to resist entrenching military rule. Arrests of national, governorate, and district leaders followed, to ensure that the Brotherhood would cease to exist as a semi-opposition party waiting in the wings to threaten the regime again in the near term. State violence at that point was not a merely an option for SCAF, it was a necessity, as part of a two-pronged strategy to dismember and break the Brotherhood's nationally organized networks.

State violence changed again in the wake of al-Sisi's political ascendance.[65] It is now far more lethal than at any point in Egypt since the 1952 Free Officers movement. The state's fist is no longer seeking to preserve an existing system against resistance; rather, state elites are using organized violence to formalize a new narrower ruling coalition and to break their opponents, to proactively restructure Egypt's political arena and reregulate state-societal relationships. As Andrea Teti has argued, "the repressive wave aimed at the Brotherhood was *useful* to the 'deep state'".[66] In effect, state violence is being used to create a new regime.

Thus, state violence becomes a window onto the relative strength of the state. When a regime is in equilibrium with its society, violence is selective and deployed when politics fails. It is also limited. When the state apparatus has been rapidly weakened or under threat, state violence is deployed on a massive scale to smash resistance to the new regime in formation.

Conclusions

Viewed through the prism of the transitions literature, the Arab uprisings appear violent because they are unsettled moments of uncertainty. These are not, however, democratizing cases. They are also not moving along a spectrum of varying degrees of lessening or deepening authoritarianism. The process is more intricate but it can be theoretically explained.

There has been tremendous political change in the region since the mobilizations began in December 2010. Yet, it has mostly fragmented the older order and in Syria, Libya, Egypt, Tunisia, and Bahrain has changed the way politics is practiced. While the cases travel diverse paths, the overwhelming majority have brought with them increased state violence that has militarized the governing apparatus. This is not a transitional moment of uncertainty. It is deliberate political engineering by elites who are directing violence against their citizens in order to maintain some part of the existing regime or create a new regime on the ashes on the older order.

Transitology misleads and disguises the reasons for the increase in state violence. By thinking about changing regime practices, we gain a better understanding of the historic process of struggle unfolding in the Arab world. Elites are deploying state violence against those pushing for more freedoms, better economic prospects, and more social justice. This popular mobilization may still one day result in democratization but for now scholarly efforts are better directed at developing more concise theories of militarizing state violence if we are to accurately portray contemporary Arab politics. While the transition literature may have acknowledged the possibility of increased violence after the fall of a long-time incumbent, scholars have seen it as a mere detour on the road to democratization. In not sourcing the expansion of counter-revolutionary violence they are prevented from understanding its role, as a new form of regime re-formation.

Notes

1. Brinks and Coppedge, "Diffusion is No Illusion."
2. Calling these moments a "Spring" has European origins. The revolutions of 1848 were called the "Springtime of the People." Marc Lynch claims credit for naming the 2011 protests the Arab Spring. See Lynch, *The Arab Uprising*, 9.
3. Huntington, *The Third Wave*. It is not surprising that journal articles and issues started to directly reference Huntington's canonical text. For example, *Current History* called its November 2011 issue "Democracy's Next Wave." The *Journal of Democracy's* October 2013 issue focused on "Tracking the 'Arab Spring.'"
4. Fukuyama, "Middle-Class Revolution"; Fukuyama, "Political Order in Egypt."
5. Tunisia is different than the other cases for a number of reasons. First, its military actually sided with the population against the executive and domestic security forces. Yet, the military did not step into the void and try to govern. It returned the system to civilian rule where fits and starts continue to move the country into the best case of a transition from authoritarian rule. See Anderson, "Demystifying the Arab Spring." Also, Henry and Springborg, "A Tunisian Solution."
6. Waterbury, "Democracy without Democrats?"; Stepan with Robertson, "An 'Arab' More than 'Muslim' Electoral Gap."
7. Levitsky and Way, *Competitive Authoritarianism*.
8. Lust, "Why Now?"
9. O'Donnell, Schmitter, and Whitehead, *Transitions*; Bunce, "Rethinking Recent Democratization"; Linberg, *Democratization by Elections*, 1–21.
10. Jones, "Saudi Arabia"; Brownlee, "The Transitional Challenge."
11. I employ "regime" in ways that Charles Tilly defined it. As he argues, "Once we have identified a government, we can search around that government for organized political actors that sometimes interact with the government. The whole set of interactions with each other and with the government constitutes a political regime." Tilly, *The Politics of Collective Violence*, 28–29.
12. Stepan and Linz, "Democratization Theory."
13. Ibid., 22.
14. Ibid., 29.
15. Ibid, 20.
16. Ibid., 29.
17. Ibid., 21.
18. O'Donnell, Schmitter, and Whitehead, *Transitions*, 26–28.
19. Ibid.
20. McFaul, "The Fourth Wave."
21. Ibid., 225.
22. Bunce, "Rethinking Recent Democratization," 172.
23. Schmitter and Karl, "What Democracy Is," 85.
24. Fein, "More Murder in the Middle," 170–191.
25. Ibid., 170.
26. Khalili, "Thinking About Violence," 791.
27. Neep, "Occupying Syria."
28. Tilly, "War Making."

29. Nixon, *Slow Violence*, uses "slow violence" to mean everyday violations such as environmental pollution to constitute a type of violence that society accepts because it is not as visible as a violent event such as a school shooting. Yet, over time, slow violence is perhaps more deadly to a society than spectacular events that people stop to notice. Yet, "slow violence" can also be limited everyday accepted levels of repression that physically maim or inflict psychological damage but do not necessarily result in actual or immediate death.
30. During field research in the spring and summer of 2005, for example, I personally witnessed Kifaya protesters in Egypt being beaten and sexually assaulted by security forces or those employed by them. In Syria during April 2004, dissident lawyer Anwar al-Bunni showed me a formal invitation that he received from state security that requested he come to the directorate to talk to them about his activism. In 2006, a video appeared on YouTube of a taxi driver named Emad al-Kabir being sodomized in an Egyptian police station. The purpose of its release was to humiliate the victim.
31. Just in my own research experience, I watched nearly all of my Syrian opposition contacts spend time in prison. In particular, those jailed included Anwar al-Bunni, Michel Kilo, and Haitham al-Maleh. In Egypt, most of the leadership contacts I had while researching Egypt's Muslim Brothers had spent time in jail.
32. Singerman, *Avenues of Participation*; also Bayat, *Life as Politics*, 43–64.
33. Ali, "Saeeds of Revolution."
34. Henry and Springborg, "A Tunisian Solution."
35. Most notably, Chokri Belaid was assassinated in February 2013 and Mohamed Brahmi was killed in July 2013.
36. Tunisia's Armed Forces comprises around 48,000 people. They have 84 tanks, 25 patrol boats, and 27 combat planes. By comparison, Egypt's armed forces include 468,000 active soldiers. Its Air Force has over 1300 combat planes and the Egyptian Army has more tanks than the rest of sub-Saharan Africa and Latin America combined. See Marshall, "Egypt's Other Revolution."
37. Stacher, *Adaptable Autocrats*, 12–18.
38. Haddad, "As Syria Free-Falls."
39. Heilprin, "UN Decides to Stop Updating Syria Death Toll."
40. As of July 2013, there were over two million Syrians living in neighbouring countries including Lebanon, Jordan, Turkey, Iraq, and Israel. Nearly 6000 people a day leave the country. Another four to six million are internally displaced. See Davis and Taylor, "Syrian Refugees."
41. Hilsum, *Sandstorm*, 99–116.
42. Fahim, "Still Torn by Factional Fighting."
43. Matthiesen, *Sectarian Gulf*.
44. Carlstrom, "In the Kingdom of Tear Gas."
45. Kafai and Shehabi, "The Struggle for Information."
46. El-Ghobasy, "The Praxis."
47. Stacher, *Adaptable Autocrats*, 5–12.
48. Stacher, "Deeper Militarism in Egypt."
49. Stacher, "Egypt Transformed by State Violence."
50. There is some debate about whether Egypt's generals intentionally pursued this policy of military take-over from the beginning or not. It is unknowable but the best estimate is that SCAF was caught off guard by the Egyptian uprising.
51. "Health Ministry: 590 Injured."
52. Carr, "Why is Maspero Different?"
53. "Clashes Erupt Again in Mohamed Mahmoud Street."
54. "Details Emerge Over Latest Cabinet Attack."
55. Fahmy and Lee, "Anger Flares."

56. Werr and Awad, "Army Imposes Curfew."
57. "January Death Tool in Egypt's Port Said Reaches 48."
58. Fahmy and Lee, "Anger Flares."
59. Hussein, "Egyptian Protestors."
60. Al-Tawy, "Egypt's Islamists."
61. Kingsley, "Killing in Cairo."
62. Kirkpatrick, Baker, and Gordon, "American Hopes."
63. Saleh and Robinson, "With Dozens Dead."
64. Abi-Habib and El-Mergawi, "Hundreds Dead."
65. For the best analysis of the increase in deaths, see Egyptian Initiative for Personal Rights, "The Weeks of Killing."
66. Teti, "The Function of Violence."

Bibliography

Abi-Habib, Maria, and Leila El-Mergawi. "Hundreds Dead in Egypt Crackdown." *Wall Street Journal*, August 15, 2013. http://online.wsj.com/article/SB10001424127887324823804579011880172936694.html

Ali, Amro. "Saeeds of Revolution: De-Mythologizing Khaled Saeed." *Jadaliyya*, June 5, 2012. http://www.jadaliyya.com/pages/index/5845/saeeds-of-revolution_de-mythologizing-khaled-saeed

Al-Tawy, Ayat. "Egypt's Islamists Under Fire Over Shia Mob Killings." *Ahram Online*, June 24, 2013. http://english.ahram.org.eg/News/74821.aspx

Anderson, Lisa. "Demystifying the Arab Spring." *Foreign Affairs*, May/June, 2011.

Bayat, Asef. *Life as Politics: How Ordinary People Change the Middle East*. Stanford, CA: Stanford University Press, 2009.

Brinks, Daniel, and Michael Coppedge. "Diffusion is No Illusion: Neighbor Emulation in the Third Wave of Democracy." *Comparative Political Studies* 39, no. 4 (2006): 463–489.

Brownlee, Jason. "The Transitional Challenge to Arab Freedom." *Current History* 110, no. 739 (2011): 317–323.

Bunce, Valerie. "Rethinking Recent Democratization: Lessons from the Postcommunist Experience." *World Politics* 55 (2003): 167–192.

Carlstrom, Gregg. "In the Kingdom of Tear Gas." *Middle East Report*, April 13, 2012. http://www.merip.org/mero/mero041312

Carr, Sarah. "Why is Maspero Different?" *Mada Masr*, October 10, 2013. http://www.madamasr.com/sections/politics/why-maspero-different

"Clashes Erupt Again in Mohamed Mahmoud Street." *Ahram Online*, November 21, 2011. http://english.ahram.org.eg/NewsContent/1/64/27121/Egypt/Politics-/Clashes-erupt-again-in-Mohamed-Mahmoud-Street.aspx

Davis, Rochelle, and Abbie Taylor. "Syrian Refugees in Jordan and Lebanon: A Snapshot from Summer 2013." (Summer 2013): http://ccas.georgetown.edu/document/1242799693627/Syrian+Refugee+Report+Sept+2013.pdf

"Details Emerge Over Latest Cabinet Attack." *Ahram Online*, December 16, 2011. http://english.ahram.org.eg/NewsContent/1/64/29483/Egypt/Politics-/Details-emerge-over-latest-cabinet-attack.aspx

Egyptian Initiative for Personal Rights. "The Weeks of Killing: State Violence, Communal Fighting, & Sectarian Attacks in the Summer of 2013." June 2014. http://eipr.org/sites/default/files/reports/pdf/weeks_of_killing_en.pdf

El-Ghobasy, Mona. "The Praxis of the Egyptian Revolution." *Middle East Report* 258 (Spring 2011): 2–13.

Fahim, Kareem. "Still Torn by Factional Fighting, Post-Revolt Libya is Coming Undone." *New York Times*, July 27, 2014. http://www.nytimes.com/2014/07/28/world/africa/fighting-for-control-of-airport-in-tripoli-post-revolt-libya-is-coming-undone-us-embassy-evacuating-staff.html?hp&action=click&pgtype=Homepage&version=HpSumSmallMedia&module=second-column-region&region=top-news&WT.nav=top-news&_r=0

Fahmy, Mohamed Fadel, and Ian Lee. "Anger Flares in Egypt After 79 Die in Soccer Riot." *CNN*, February 2, 2012. http://edition.cnn.com/2012/02/02/world/africa/egypt-soccer-deaths/index.html?hpt=hp_t1

Fein, Helen. "More Murder in the Middle: Life-Integrity Violations and Democracy in the World, 1987." *Human Rights Quarterly* 17, no. 1 (1995): 170–191.

Fukuyama, Francis. "Political Order in Egypt." *The American Interest*, May 1, 2011. http://www.the-american-interest.com/articles/2011/05/01/political-order-in-egypt/

Fukuyama, Francis. "The Middle-Class Revolution." *The Wall Street Journal*, June 28, 2013. http://online.wsj.com/news/articles/SB10001424127887323873904578571472700348086

Haddad, Bassam. "As Syria Free-Falls ... A Return to Basics (Part 1)." *Jadaliyya*, August 31, 2012. http://www.jadaliyya.com/pages/index/7147/as-syria-free-falls-.-.-.-a-return-to-the-basics-(

"Health Ministry: 590 Injured in Tahrir and Balloon Theatre Clashes." *Egypt Independent*, June 29, 2011. http://www.egyptindependent.com/news/health-ministry-590-injured-tahrir-and-balloon-theater-clashes

Heilprin, John. "UN Decides to Stop Updating Syria Death Toll." *AP*, January 7, 2014. http://bigstory.ap.org/article/un-decides-stop-updating-syria-death-toll

Henry, Clement M., and Robert Springborg. "A Tunisian Solution for Egypt's Military." *Foreign Affairs*, February 21, 2011. http://www.foreignaffairs.com/articles/67475/clement-m-henry-and-robert-springborg/a-tunisian-solution-for-egypts-military

Hilsum, Lindsey. *Sandstorm: Libya in the Time of Revolution*. New York: Penguin Books, 2012.

Huntington, Samuel P. *The Third Wave: Democratization in the Late 20th Century*. Norman: University of Oklahoma Press, 1993.

Hussein, Abdel-Rahman. "Egyptian Protesters Claim They Were Tortured by Muslim Brotherhood." *Guardian*, December 12, 2012. http://www.theguardian.com/world/2012/dec/12/egyptian-protesters-tortured-muslim-brotherhood

"January Death Tool in Egypt's Port Said Reaches 48." *Ahram Online*, March 16, 2013. http://english.ahram.org.eg/NewsContent/1/64/67005/Egypt/Politics-/January-death-toll-in-Egypts-Port-Said-reaches-.aspx

Jones, Toby Craig. "Saudi Arabia Versus the Arab Spring." *Raritan* 31, no. 2 (2011): 43–59.

Kafai, Nazgol, and Ala'a Shehabi. "The Struggle for Information: Revelations on Mercenaries, Sectarian Agitation and Demographic Engineering in Bahrain." *Jadaliyya*, May 29, 2014. http://www.jadaliyya.com/pages/index/17912/the-struggle-for-information_revelations-on-mercen

Khalili, Laleh. "Thinking about Violence." *International Journal of Middle East Studies* 45, no. 4 (2013): 791–794.

Kingsley, Patrick. "Killing in Cairo: The Full Story of the Republican Guards Club Shooting." *Guardian*, July 18, 2013. http://www.theguardian.com/world/interactive/2013/jul/18/cairo-republican-guard-shooting-full-story?google_editors_picks=true#part-one

Kirkpatrick, David, Peter Baker, and Michael Gordon. "How American Hopes for a Deal in Egypt were Undercut." *New York Times*, August 17, 2013. http://www.nytimes.com/

2013/08/18/world/middleeast/pressure-by-us-failed-to-sway-egypts-leaders.html?page wanted=all&_r=0
Levitsky, Steven, and Lucan A. Way. *Competitive Authoritarianism: Hybrid Regimes After the Cold War*. Cambridge: Cambridge University Press, 2010.
Linberg Steffan I. ed. *Democratization by Elections: A New Mode of Transition*. Baltimore, MD: Johns Hopkins University Press, 2009.
Lust, Ellen. "Why Now? Micro Transitions and the Arab Uprisings." *The Monkey Cage*, October 24, 2011. http://themonkeycage.org/wp-content/uploads/2011/10/Ellen_Lust_final.pdf
Lynch, Marc. *The Arab Uprising: The Unfinished Revolutions of the New Middle East*. New York: Public Affairs, 2012.
Marshall, Shana. "Egypt's Other Revolution: Modernizing the Military Industrial Complex." *Jadaliyya*, February 10, 2012. http://www.jadaliyya.com/pages/index/4311/egypts-other-revolution_modernizing-the-military-i
Matthiesen, Toby. *Sectarian Gulf: Bahrain, Saudi Arabia, and the Arab Spring that Wasn't*. Stanford, CA: Stanford University Press, 2013.
McFaul, Michael. "The Fourth Wave of Democracy and Dictatorship: Noncooperative Transitions in the Postcommunist World." *World Politics* 54 (January 2002): 212–244.
Neep, Daniel. *Occupying Syria under the French Mandate: Insurgency, Space and State Formation*. Cambridge: Cambridge University Press, 2012.
Nixon, Rob. *Slow Violence and the Environmentalism of the Poor*. Cambridge, MA: Harvard University Press, 2011.
O'Donnell, Guillermo, Philippe Schmitter, and Laurence Whitehead. *Transitions from Authoritarian Rule, Volume 4: Tentative Conclusions about Uncertain Democracies*. Baltimore, MD: Johns Hopkins University Press, 1986.
Saleh, Yasmine, and Matt Robinson. "With Dozens Dead, US Tells Egypt to Pull 'Back from the Brink'." *Reuters*, July 27, 2013. http://www.reuters.com/article/2013/07/27/us-egypt-protests-idUSBRE96O11Z20130727
Schmitter, Philippe, and Terry Lynn Karl. "What Democracy Is . . . And Is Not." *Journal of Democracy* 2, no. 3 (1991): 75–88.
Singerman, Diane. *Avenues of Participation: Family, Politics, and Networks in Urban Quarters of Cairo*. Princeton, NJ: Princeton University Press, 1996.
Stacher, Joshua. *Adaptable Autocrats: Regime Power in Egypt and Syria*. Stanford, CA: Stanford University Press, 2012.
Stacher. "Deeper Militarism in Egypt." *Middle East Institute Transitions Project*, September 16, 2013. http://www.mei.edu/content/deeper-militarism-egypt
Stacher. "Egypt Transformed by State Violence." *New Left Project*, September 18, 2013. http://www.newleftproject.org/index.php/site/article_comments/egypt_transformed_by_state_violence
Stepan, Alfred, and Juan J. Linz. "Democratization Theory and The 'Arab Spring'." *Journal of Democracy* 24, no. 2 (2013): 15–30.
Stepan, Alfred, with Graeme B. Robertson. "An 'Arab' More than 'Muslim' Electoral Gap." *Journal of Democracy* 14, no. 3 (2003): 30–44.
Teti, Andrea. "The Function of Violence in Egypt." *Open Democracy*, August 22, 2013. http://www.opendemocracy.net/andrea-teti/function-of-violence-in-egypt
Tilly, Charles. "War Making and State Making as Organized Crime." In *Bringing the State Back In*, edited by Rueschemeyer Evans and Skocpol, 169–187. Cambridge: Cambridge University Press, 1985.
Tilly, Charles. *The Politics of Collective Violence*. Cambridge: Cambridge University Press, 2003.

Waterbury, John. "Democracy Without Democrats?: The Potential for Political Liberalization in the Middle East." In *Democracy with Democrats*, edited by Ghassan Salame, 23–46. London: I.B. Tauris, 1994.

Werr, Patrick, and Marwa Awad. "Army Imposes Curfew in Cairo District After Clashes." *Reuters*, May 4, 2012. http://www.reuters.com/article/2012/05/04/us-egypt-protest-idUSBRE8430P520120504

Islamism and the state after the Arab uprisings: Between people power and state power

Frédéric Volpi[a] and Ewan Stein[b]

[a]*School of International Relations, University of St Andrews, St Andrews, UK;* [b]*Politics and International Relations, School of Social and Political Science, University of Edinburgh, Edinburgh, UK*

This paper examines the trajectories of different Islamist trends in the light of the Arab uprisings. It proposes a distinction between statist and non-statist Islamism to help understand the multiplicity of interactions between Islamists and the state, particularly after 2011. It is outlined how statist Islamists (Islamist parties principally) can contribute to the stabilization and democratization of the state when their interactions with other social and political actors facilitate consensus building in national politics. By contrast when these interactions are conflictual, it has a detrimental impact on both the statist Islamists, and the possibility of democratic politics at the national level. Non statist-Islamists (from quietist salafi to armed jihadi) who prioritize the religious community over national politics are directly impacted by the interactions between statist Islamists and the state, and generally tend to benefit from the failure to build a consensus over democratic national politics. Far more than nationally-grounded statist Islamists, non-statist Islamists shape and are shaped by the regional dynamics on the Arab uprisings and the international and transnational relations between the different countries and conflict areas of the Middle East. The Arab uprisings and their aftermath reshaped pre-existing national and international dynamics of confrontation and collaboration between Islamists and the state, and between statist and non-statists Islamists, for better (Tunisia) and for worse (Egypt).

1. Introduction: Islamism, the state and socio-historical changes[1]

For a brief moment during the 2011 Arab uprisings, Islamism seemed to have become somewhat irrelevant. A year later, with the electoral gains made by many Islamists movements in the newly democratic atmosphere that then characterized the region, they appeared to be back on top of (and dictating) the political agenda. At the time of writing (early 2015), the wheel has turned again and neither democratic- nor Islamist-oriented institutional evolutions seem to be making headway.

A large (perhaps the largest) part of the apparent difficulty in delineating the Islamist factor relates to identifying and explaining political Islam/Islamism. Whatever Islamism may be – and the perspectives that we will be proposing in the following are analytical distinctions, not the "real face" of Islamism – the generic representations of the phenomenon that tend to dominate the political debate are commonly formatted to fit pre-existing explanations of political and institutional behaviour.[2] Beyond pointing out that political Islam has many faces,[3] we contend that making analytical distinctions within political Islam to reflect broader path dependencies is crucial to understanding the role, and fate, of Islamism during and after the Arab uprisings. Specifically, the many faces of Islamism reflect the different models of state governance that have predominated in the Middle East region (and beyond) over the years. This is particularly the case for those Islamists that we categorize as "statist" to emphasize the close connection between national structures of governance and the strategies of activists in their particular socio-cultural and socio-economic circumstances. It is those statist Islamists that, due to their aspirations to acquire state power, have been most obviously affected by regime change, reform, or hardening during the Arab uprisings.

Islamism is evidently not always best defined by its relationship with the state. For "non-statist" Islamists, the uprisings and their aftermath hold a different significance, even though they are affected by the changes in the relationship between the state and statist Islamists. We distinguish non-statist Islamists by the primacy they accord to their relationship to the community instead of the state. This very broad category includes quietist grassroots movements inspired by salafism as well as violent transnational jihadi organizations, although important distinctions exist between them. Whether they seek to avoid politics altogether or have a vision of a political community not bound to the modern nation state, these groups compete with statist Islamists for the Islamic high ground, thereby indirectly shaping national political landscapes. Crucially, these modalities of Islamist activism do not always correspond neatly to divisions between groups but can coexist within the same organization: the Muslim Brotherhood, for example, has strong statist and non-statist orientations, although the former commonly structures the latter. Conversely, following the Arab uprisings, traditionally non-statist salafi formations engaged in state-level politics (most notably the Egyptian Nour Party).

In the following, we present an analytical perspective on the evolution of the relationship between Islamists and the state grounded on this distinction between two path-dependent configurations of contemporary Islamism. In section 2 below, we discuss how forms of governance and developmentalism influenced political Islam in the preceding decades. Then in section 3 we focus more specifically on the dynamics of statist Islamism in the context of these political evolutions before, during and since the Arab uprisings. Section 4 follows the same approach to elucidate non-statist modalities of Islamist activism. In section 5 we offer some explanations for the differential outcomes, particularly between Egypt and Tunisia, in the wake of the uprisings.

2. Islamism and evolving models of governance and development

Seen from the vantage point of the politics of the nation-state, the evolution and diversification of Islamism reflects trajectories of state formation and socio-economic development in the Middle East and the rest of the developing world. In debates of the 1960s and 1970s dominated by modernization theory and class analysis, Islamism hardly featured in political analyses of Middle Eastern and other Muslim-majority developing countries. When it was considered, it tended to be dismissed as a rear-guard battle from traditional social forces heading for the dustbin of history.[4] State-builders focussed on developing strong institutions and a modern socio-economic system, generally inspired by liberal or socialist models. The modernist and authoritarian-populist Nasser regime had crushed the Egyptian Muslim Brotherhood, by then the leading Islamist movement in the region, in the second half of the 1950s. But the Nasserite model, widely assumed to exemplify the shape of things to come in the region, lasted barely a couple of decades. By the mid-1970s, Arab-socialism was falling apart in most of the region, while "anachronistic" regimes such as those of Saudi Arabia and the Gulf States were beginning to promote a rather different developmental pathway allying economic modernism with patrimonial rule and religious legitimation strategies.

In the 1980s, in the wake of the Iranian revolution, Islamism was deemed to be concerned primarily with the establishment of an "Islamic state". It was viewed, in part, as a kind of nationalist and revolutionary movement seeking to capture the institutions of the state to implement top-down its preferred new social order, just like other such movements from the left and the right had done previously throughout the region. In practice, the growing autonomy and internal fracturing of Islamist movements in the 1980s owed much to the Islamic revolution. The Muslim Brotherhood mostly applauded the revolution and saw it as evidence that Islamism could succeed in taking state power.[5] Salafis, on the other hand, opposed it on principle and condemned Khomeinism on sectarian grounds. Arab regimes were able to withstand the challenge, in part because of their coercive resources, and in part because the mainstream Islamist movements at the time calculated that they lacked the societal base to spark an Iranian-style revolution.[6] The failure of the jihad in Egypt to launch a large-scale popular insurrection in the wake of President Sadat's assassination in 1981 suggested to many Islamist activists that Arab societies were not ready for an Islamic revolution. When revolutionary Islamism failed by and large to be replicated outside Iran, the challenge to the state posed by political Islam was deemed by some scholars to have missed.

With the increasingly evident failure of state modernism and developmentalism, and the growing influence of the Saudi model, dependent on oil rents, Arab states entered a phase of "post-populism".[7] This was reinforced in the 1980s and 1990s by the spread of neo-liberalism to the region under pressure from the International Monetary Fund. Post-populism represented a means whereby authoritarian regimes could strengthen themselves even as they abandoned the old populist social contract, by diversifying their constituencies and diluting potential political opposition from civil society. This entailed combinations of increased dependence on external sources of revenue (or "rents"), limited political opening and some "outsourcing" of governance to non-state actors such as Islamist charities. From the perspective of regimes, Islamism also served the broader purposes of neoliberal reform to the extent that it fostered self-help strategies on the part of local populations, providing not only spiritual services, but also educational, medical and financial support.

The post-populist turn towards neoliberalism created new domestic environments for social and political activism. Islamist movements made headway in society because they proposed a model of religious solidarity that responded, and adapted, to the downscaling of the role of the state throughout the region. As democratizing discourse entered the region after 1990, some Islamists movements portrayed their new involvement in electoral politics as a means of nurturing a "good" Muslim society (and as such an endeavour which could be intellectually reconciled with their ideological emphasis on God's sovereignty).

In parallel, however, post-populist regimes adopted more sophisticated versions of "divide and rule" by which they sought to control rising Islamism, particularly through provoking or exploiting "culture wars"[8] between Islamist and secular actors. Absent the interest aggregation and mediation function of democracy, competition in civil and political society was played out on the terrain of morality and identity, with the cultural sphere (that is influence over education, media and cultural production) being the only one to which authoritarian regimes devolved any substantial power. This had the effect of depoliticising public discourse as a whole in many Middle Eastern countries and strengthening movements, like Islamism, that prioritized culture and identity.[9]

The "culture wars" waged by Islamist activists against secular civil society, and *vice versa*, militated against unified oppositions to regimes in many Arab states. The Islamist movement itself was divided along many lines from the 1980s, including between those that favoured accommodation with the regime and participation in pseudo-democratic politics (the Muslim Brotherhood and other Islamist parties), those that sought disengagement from state-level politics altogether (salafis) and those who sought to impose their vision of an Islamic order via the violent overthrow of the existing social and political system (jihadists).[10] Within each of these categories, furthermore, differences over strategy existed. Nevertheless, during the 1990s Islamism grew to constitute the principal (if not sole) viable alternative to secular authoritarianism in much of the region, a reality that was emphasized but not invented by regimes that sought to frighten the western democracies into keeping them in power.

After 11 September 2001, analyses inspired by the "war on terror" tended to categorize Islamist movements primarily in relation to their use of violent rhetoric or practices, overlooking the different articulations and trajectories of Islamism.[11] However, as Francois Burgat indicates, over-emphasis on one type of violent Islamism overshadowed other forms of Islamist activism.[12] Using violence as the main distinction among Islamic movements obscures important structural similarities and overlaps between jihadi and salafi groups, in particular their shared ambivalence toward state-level politics and attempt to operate beyond or in defiance of the state. Shifts in state-society relations did not affect them in the same way as they did those Islamists that sought state power. The focus on Islamist violence parallel to the increased focus of the international community on "hard" security issues was matched by a "hardening" of the Middle Eastern states and a political discourse dominated by securitization. Keen to tap into the external support offered under the rubric of the "war on terror", regimes cracked down on violent and non-violent Islamist opposition alike.

The 2011 Arab uprisings marked another re-articulation of the relationship between the state and Islamism. The process of regional "state weakening", which arguably began with the external shock of the US invasion of Iraq and toppling of Saddam Hussein in 2003,[13] continued with regime changes in Libya and Yemen, as well as the civil war in Syria. The weakening of state power in all these cases vastly increased the salience of non-statist salafi and jihadi movements. In Egypt and Tunisia, the Arab uprisings fundamentally challenged the "cronyistic" development strategies pursued by the Mubarak and Ben Ali regimes. In neither case, however, did the Islamist beneficiaries of these uprisings offer compelling alternatives to this economic model. Ennahda in Tunisia – and the political class as a whole – remained vulnerable to bottom-up pressure from the marginalized (*muhammishin*), who looked to salafism as a more promising vehicle for social inclusion.[14] The Muslim Brotherhood in Egypt was pushed aside by the military after a lacklustre year in power which, if it did not disprove the claim that "Islam is the solution", cast doubt on the capacity of Islamism's oldest movement to implement it. Political discourse there reverted to familiar "war on terror" territory, as the state relied more than ever on virtually unchecked coercive power to deal with the "Islamist threat".

3. Islamist variations

In the following section, we track the evolution of statist and non-statist Islamist activism in the region in light of changing state dynamics. We do not claim that these trends encapsulate the entire complexity of contemporary Islamic activism or that the substantive differences we identify will necessarily retain their significance for all time. Our orientation toward national state institutions as our focal point is a heuristic device enabling us to map the contemporary patterns of interaction between Middle East regimes and Islamist activism and understand how specific trajectories of state and Islamist governance can come together to either strengthen or weaken a polity.

3.1. Statist Islamism

For some scholars "political Islam" refers to those groups and movements that actively engage with the state and national-level politics, unlike "fundamentalism", which eschews formal politics and focuses on the social sphere.[15] Recognizing that "the political" extends deeper than the state level, and also acknowledging the well-established conceptual problems with the term "fundamentalism",[16] we use the term "statist Islamism" to refer to institutionalized participation in the politics of the nation state. This variant of Islamism is exemplified by the Muslim Brotherhood, although it has outgrown the Brotherhood as an organization. The model of political action and the ideological programme elaborated by Hasan al-Banna, and more recently by Yusuf al-Qaradawi, Rached Ghannouchi and others, have been highly influential and embraced and adapted across the Middle East: actors like Ennahda in Tunisia, the Saudi "Sahwa" movement, or Islah in Yemen, have Brotherhood roots or links. Ideologically, this current has come closest to reconciling Islamic doctrines, and the sharia as the source of all legislation, with liberal forms of democracy. Socially, it has grown within the middle classes in the Arab world and is intrinsically connected with the expansion of education, urbanization and other facets of "development" in the region over the course of the twentieth century.[17]

In the main, statist Islamists have not been revolutionaries in the sense of seeking to overturn the existing social order. Their Islamism, rather, evolved as a reformist discourse through which often lower-middle class activists could connect with a broader popular constituency and challenge the claims of the (usually more secularized) establishment to speak for the nation. They also appealed to the aspirations and fears of dissatisfied middle classes, which, generally speaking, sought the improvement, rather than destruction, of existing systems. Islamism's claims were thus advanced not on the basis of challenging social hierarchies or the economic model, but in terms of an attack on corruption, moral laxity and neglect of religion, all of which, in their view, produced the socio-economic ills of the community. The economic problems were to be solved not by a drastically new system of governance or redistribution of wealth but by elites' recognising and acting upon their obligations to Islam and sharia.

Statist Islamism evolved in line with shifts in models of state governance and, concomitantly, forms of societal activism. The Muslim Brotherhood in Egypt, and elsewhere, had often been "moderate" to the extent it was willing – where permitted – to work within existing systems and broadly accepted the centrality of the nation-state as the locus of political identity.[18] Hasan al-Banna had rejected party politics as divisive and elitist, in line with the rest of the nationalist movement in Egypt at the time. Brotherhood intellectuals such as Sayyid Qutb and Muhammad al-Ghazzali supported nationalization and developed ideas reconciling socialism with Islam in ways that reflected and helped inform the official ideology that was Nasserism. Following the limited political opening under Sadat, more "liberal" democratic ideas and practices were incorporated into the movement – in contrast to other components of the resurgent Islamist movement that shunned or confronted the state.

"Moderation" was a growing trend among Islamist groups through the 1980s and 1990s. This corresponded to a time of partial political liberalization across the region. The Egyptian Muslim Brotherhood entered elections for the first time in 1984. In Algeria, the sudden and ill-structured political liberalization of the late 1980s enable the Islamic Salvation Front to mobilize voters and to become the leading political party of the ill-fated Algerian democratic transition (which ended in the 1992 military coup). In Tunisia, Ennahda slowly made gains throughout the 1980s during periods of political liberalization that culminated in their participation to the 1989 parliamentary elections; a short-lived opening that would prove inconsequential as President Ben Ali entrenched his power by closing down the political field in the ensuing years. In Jordan, the local branch of the Muslim brotherhood would eventually gain the approval of the monarchy to form a political party, the Islamic Action Front, in 1992. In Morocco, faced with the unwillingness of the main Islamist movement of the country al-Adl wa-Ihsane to formally recognize a monarchic system of governance, the Moroccan King, Hassan II, facilitated the entry into politics of another Islamist formation in 1996. This party, which would later become the Party of Justice and Development, was allowed to participate in formal politics because it was willing to recognize the legitimacy of the monarchy.

Over time, the possibility of aggregating demands for political inclusion increased as those movements "moderated" their ideological programmes as a result of political learning and strategic adaptation to a partially free political environment.[19] In the three decades or so prior to the Arab uprisings, Islamist groups had softened core ideological goals (such as the establishment of an Islamic state) and instead embraced norms related to human rights and democracy. There was, however, a "ceiling" beyond which Islamist movements would not moderate.[20] Although the high-profile activities of Muslim Brotherhood parliamentarians and the ideological innovations of "New Islamists"[21] contrasted markedly with the image of Islamism as a revolutionary, counter-system, force, this *wasatiyya*, or centrist, trend was by no means dominant within Islamism as a whole. Not only was it contested from within the Brotherhood and like-minded groups, producing internal tensions and schisms, but it was also rejected outright by grassroots movements, most notably salafis. The non-statist trends inside and outside the Muslim Brotherhood thus structured, to a great extent, the political horizons of the statist ones. Nonetheless, ideological and behavioural moderation enabled Islamists to sell their programmes to more secular-leaning constituencies as well as to a sceptical, if not Islamophobic, outside world.

3.2. *Non-statist Islamism*

Non-statist Islamism is not so much "apolitical" as it is "infra-political": local-level organizational, preaching and charitable activity. Grassroots activism is central to political Islam as a whole, as local networks help to structure support for, and seek to constitute, an Islamic society. While *da'wa* (proselytising) has taken many forms over time, contemporary grassroots Islamism tends toward a conservative interpretation of the "fundamentals" of Islam – a trend most evident in salafism. Islamist parties across the region have tended to emerge from and link with networks of charitable associations and other grassroots institutions. Salafism, which may be the most important grassroots Islamist phenomenon of recent decades, encourages a focus on the community rather than the state. Although it tends to be ultra-conservative, with an ideal society inspired by teachings and practices from the time of the prophet, salafis' articulation with traditional Muslim customs is not as straightforward as it might seem. The ease with which salafi actors can find their public in Muslim communities depends on their ability to insert their theological approach into the pre-existing religious practices of the local community.[22]

The ability and willingness of the state to cater for marginal groups diminished considerably from the late 1970s in the context of economic restructuring. As populist-authoritarian regimes metamorphosed into post-populist ones, large sections of society were forced to rely on self-help strategies, kinship networks and other "informal" mechanisms to compensate for exclusion at the national level. Grassroots Islamism operated alongside, or sometimes in place of, such existing support mechanisms. Salafis tend to promote an ascetic lifestyle and consider consumerism to be a distraction from religious duties. Such perspectives appeal to disenfranchised youth for whom consumerism may not be an available option.

Salafi and jihadi movements across the region are also directly influenced by political changes initiated at regime level. Salafis' avoidance of formal political engagement has benefited them at the grassroots level, sometimes with the approval of the state authorities. Indeed, salafis have benefited from the intolerance of regimes towards statist Islamists and jihadists. Although salafis have not completely escaped state repression, particularly post-9/11, because regimes have finite resources at their disposal they have tended to concentrate their repressive strategies on politicized and armed Islamists. In allowing or facilitating the expansion of Islamist grassroots infrastructure, regimes signalled their limited capacity to govern peripheral, rural or "informal" urban areas. This has left by default, and sometimes by design, the social field more open for salafis. Many regimes have sought to channel activists from politically active and militant Islamism toward a less overtly threatening salafism. In Egypt, the contemporary salafi movement originated (like the Muslim Brotherhood and the jihadis) in the student movement of the 1970s, and developed as a "safe" alternative to these two movements through the 1990s.[23] In Algeria, after the banning of the Islamic Salvation Front and the armed confrontation with Islamist guerrillas in the 1990s, the military-backed regime was content with the growth of salafism as an alternative to both political and armed activism.[24] Yet, even if many grassroots activists, for principled or pragmatic reasons, eschew politics, their activism has played a role as part of a broader Islamist movement in building constituencies for Islamist parties.[25]

So called jihadis, advocates of the establishment of an Islamic order through the use of violence, have been a persistent trend in Arab politics in recent decades. Typically they endorse jihad in furtherance of an idealized Islamic community on ideological/theological grounds, although some also turn to violence in response to the attempts by the state to repress other forms of Islamic activism, which, as highlighted by Hafez, make armed struggle a meaningful strategic choice for these organizations.[26] Even if leaders of jihadist groups may come from relatively well-off backgrounds (with Osama bin Laden and Ayman al-Zawahiri being good cases in point), violent activism commonly takes place among marginalized or dislocated communities. Jihadis generally emphasize a warrior ethos that shuns material possessions and rewards. They emerge particularly where the authority and legitimacy of the state are contested, absent or have been undermined and generally represent by-products of uneven, stalled, or indeed reversed, processes of state formation, as well as of the transnational flows of ideas and people encouraged by globalization.

Jihadi movements of the 1980s and 1990s generally failed to capture state power due to the superior military capabilities of the incumbent authoritarian regimes – for example, the Algerian civil conflict of the 1990s – as well as their inability to mobilize large constituencies favouring radical change. As the security capabilities of Arab regimes increased, national-based Islamist guerrilla movements increasingly turned toward more transnational forms of action to compensate for a lack of domestic success.[27] The trajectory of the Armed Islamic Group (GIA) in Algeria, which reinvented itself as the Salafist Group for Preaching and Combat, and finally as Al Qaeda in the Islamic Maghreb (AQIM) illustrates well this trend. Overall, jihadi failures in the face of coercive states have led to the concentration of violent Islamism in places where central coercive power is weak. The migration of Al Qaeda in the Arabic Peninsula (AQAP) from Saudi Arabia to Yemen is one example. The further weakening of state power in Yemen, as well as in Libya, Syria and Iraq, has correspondingly opened up opportunities for renewed violent activism in these countries.

4. Islamism following regime change: explaining differential outcomes

In seeking to understand Islamism's ongoing relationship with the state, it is important not to focus solely on the impact of "regime change" (or failure, or resilience). Beyond the immediate significance of regime change or revolutions, the uprisings opened up new possibilities in the general evolution of the state structure and mode of governance across the region. It is more useful to view the transformations in countries like Egypt, Tunisia, Libya and Yemen – as well as Syria, Iraq, Morocco and other countries where regimes remained in place – as part of a continuum of political change that impacted the short- and medium-term prospects of Islamism.

4.1. Statist Islam and the uprisings

Statist Islamism can, generally speaking, claim credit for the expansion of the political sphere in the Arab world, as a potential driver of democratization. In some cases, Islamists showed themselves to be highly adept at building structures of mass inclusion in authoritarian settings in which elite circulation was absent (Egypt). In others, this political effort could only take place after the fall of authoritarianism (Tunisia).

The uprisings of 2011 directly challenged the legitimacy of authoritarian regimes. They also challenged statist Islamism. They were able to mobilize significant numbers of people around slogans not related to religion or identity, something that struck at the heart of the "culture wars" framework that had served to neutralize dissent for decades. Hopes were high that societal unity would carry the day. In mobilizing on political and economic issues directly (bread, justice, freedom) protesters challenged all parties, but especially Islamists, to explicitly link their culture and identity claims to concrete plans for political and economic renewal. While statist Islamists can build political parties with substantial popular appeal, these dynamics are only supportive of democratization processes when they become institutionalized. Beyond the revolutionary moment of 2011 the challenge for the countries of the Arab uprisings is to institutionalize both the increased level of elites' circulation and the increased level of mass inclusion resulting from the revolution in order to make them sustainable in the longer term.

What the experiences of the Arab uprisings illustrate is that outcomes were as much the result of the choices made during and in the aftermath of the uprisings as they were of longer term path dependencies. Islamists faced key challenges in using the new opportunities to establish their presence in the post-uprisings political space. First, statist Islamism was diversifying, and particularly in Egypt the Muslim Brotherhood no longer had the political field to itself. Due in part to the process of estrangement that had taken place within the Islamist firmament from the 1980s, however, the new engagement did not take place in a way that coherently linked statist and grassroots challenges together. What has been termed "political" or "democratic" salafism, as embodied by Egypt's Nour Party, was shunned by many within the broader salafi sphere.[28] This contributed to the intra-salafi fracturing that became apparent following the ouster of President Morsi into those in the statist sphere that continued to support Morsi as a legitimate leader and those that endorsed the military takeover (or who chose to leave the national politics once more). Secondly, Islamists also struggled to win the support of protest movements that saw them as "hijackers" of the revolutions – a factor encouraged both by the evident deal-making that was occurring between the old regimes and Islamists (particularly in Egypt and Yemen) as well as by many Islamists' "accommodationist" track records. The longstanding antipathy between Islamist and secular actors (part of authoritarian divide and rule strategies) outlasted the overthrow of dictators. At the same time, statist Islamists struggled to consolidate and expand grassroots support for a political path fraught with compromises that seemed to fly in the face of long-cherished Islamist values. The contrasts between Egypt and Tunisia illustrate some of the principal factors that determined whether statist Islamists could effectively use the opportunity provided by the uprisings.

4.1.1. Egypt

While the fall of the Mubarak regime opened the door to a reconfigured political sphere, the political class as a whole (Islamist and non-Islamist) failed in the crucial transition period – due to a range of domestic and international factors – to realize a constitutional framework that would guarantee elite circulation. The Egyptian case is indicative of the vicious circle that a struggle for power at the top of the state, and legacies of authoritarian rule that precluded cooperation in civil society, can create. The actions of the statist Islamists (especially Muslim Brotherhood), of the military institution and of the elites from the former regime (particularly in the judiciary) prevented the routinization of multiparty and electoral politics.

For one, the contending political actors failed sufficiently to bridge the numerous divides that had segmented Egyptian politics over the previous decades. Even though the Muslim Brotherhood commanded a substantial following, as evidenced by the electoral performance of its political offshoot, the Freedom and Justice Party (FJP) and Morsi's (albeit narrow) victory, it failed to translate this support into deal-making on a constitutional framework. On the one hand, owing to legacies of mistrust from the Mubarak period, the Brotherhood and most other Islamist forces were unable to sustain an alliance with secular political parties or the revolutionary youth. On the other hand, despite early attempts to demonstrate its willingness to work with the existing coercive structures of the state (as represented by the Supreme Council of the Armed Forces), the Brotherhood failed to convince the military and security apparatus that it was a reliable political partner.

The inability of the contending political forces to find mutually acceptable "rules of the game" meant that growing popular opposition to Brotherhood rule did not spur further democratization and was instead directed toward the "exceptional" measure of a military coup in the absence of working institutionalized processes to mediate between contending interests. The high level of mass inclusion that occurred during the uprisings was then temporarily institutionalized via a "neo-populism" centring on the personality cult of Abd al-Fatah al-Sisi and the prestige of the military,[29] rather than being linked to the principle of a rotation of elites. The resurgent military regime in Egypt has destroyed the Muslim Brotherhood's ability to connect with its constituencies and hence function as a vehicle for inclusion – even a parallel one – as it had in the past. The Brotherhood has weathered repression from the regime before, but as Saad Eddine Ibrahim recently pointed out, the 30 June "Revolution" that precipitated a military coup four days later was the first time the Brotherhood had faced a mass popular rebellion.[30] The sheer scale of this uprising, exaggerated as it may have been, seriously damaged the Brotherhood's image as a popular movement in the region and hence as a conduit for democratization. The new Sisi regime in Egypt has its founding solidly grounded in a myth of popular sovereignty represented by the popular uprising of 30 June. Large numbers of secular intellectuals support the eradication of the Muslim Brotherhood even if they do not support the retrenchment of military-led authoritarianism in Egypt. In this respect, the Egyptian trajectory can be presented as a case of tentative return to the old culture wars encouraged by the new military regime.

Islamists were not mainstreamed as conservative parties in an institutional framework that guaranteed a regular rotation of political elites and Islamism's capacity to act as a vehicle for mass inclusion was so undermined that even if some form of elite circulation is established it will likely assume a "decorative" form (façade democracy, pseudo-democracy), lacking a meaningful democratic connection with the electorate. The potential of the Muslim Brotherhood and political Salafis to become handmaidens of democratization was lost.

4.1.2. Tunisia

A democratizing Arab state can be seen as a direct institutional outcome of the 2011 Arab uprisings in only one case, that of Tunisia. Rather than facilitating a return to authoritarian rule (either directly by taking advantage of their political success or indirectly by inciting their opponents to grab power for themselves) or undermining the capabilities of the state institutions, the Islamists of Ennahda contributed to the stability of the post-revolutionary democratic institutions and practices. The normalization of statist Islamism is tightly imbricated into the process of consolidation of multiparty democracy in the country.

As significant as the actual revolutionary uprising and foundational elections of 2011 were the processes of democratic consolidation that occurred subsequently (or in parallel). In this period the Islamists of Ennahda governed in coalition with leftist parties, and struck deals over the constitution and the holding of new elections with the main secularist forces of the country. Ennahda chose to tone down Islamist ideological claims and appeal to middle class voters via their general conservative outlook and "good governance" programme. This downgrading of the ideological claims of statist Islamism in a "democratizing" institutional context is best illustrated by the agreement reached on the new constitution with secularized parties, which resulted in the absence of direct references to the sharia in the text of the constitution. By making concessions on the constitutional framework and on their utilization of executive power, Ennahda facilitated the acceptance by social and political actors across pre-existing ideological divides of a democratic model in which most political parties estimate that losses today can be compensated by gains in the future.

The mainstreaming of Ennahda is also exemplified by the decision of the Ennahda-led government to hand over executive power to a technocratic government that was more acceptable to the opposition a year ahead of planned parliamentary and presidential elections. In the 2014 parliamentary elections, Ennahda came in second position, thus illustrating the "normality" of an institutionalized Islamist party in a functioning multiparty democracy characterized by a rotation of elites. Rather than seeking to have an immediate impact on the state institutions and state governance, statist Islamists in Tunisia have prioritized becoming an entrenched, mainstream party with a say in public and political life regardless of whether they are in opposition or in government. From an agent-centric perspective, it could thus be said that the strategies of the key actors of the Tunisian transition were conducive to a consolidation of democracy. But for Ennahda and its secular rivals to deepen their support bases and ward off the threat of "culture wars", the daunting task of narrowing socio-economic inequalities must be tackled. In such a case, statist Islamists move from purely cultural and moral claims as their main source of legitimation and become a party grounded on socio-economic policies that are drafted to appeal to a non-ideologically defined electorate.

4.2. Non-Statist Islamism and the uprisings

The post-2011 trajectories of salafis and jihadis in the countries of the Arab uprisings are also tied to both the general political evolution of the different states, and in particular to the success and failures of their statist Islamist rivals. However because jihadi actors do not primarily have a state-centric agenda, their local engagement varies according to circumstances, from the deterritorialized mode of action of Al Qaeda in the Islamic Maghreb[31] to the centralized control of the Islamic State of Iraq and Syria (ISIS).

Regionally, two main post-uprisings developments strengthened the jihadi trend, which was briefly deemed to fall into irrelevance at the time of the uprisings. First, the multiplication of civil conflicts and the reduction of state capacity (Syria, Iraq, Libya, Mali, Yemen) has increased the number of locations and of potential recruits for armed jihadism. Jihadi operations moved to those areas where armed resistance against the state seemed possible, legitimate and effective. Thus at the beginning of 2012, pre-existing jihadi networks in North Africa, particularly AQIM, redirected their efforts southwards towards Mali to join the challenge to the Malian state led by returning Tuareg from Libya. In the North African context, the disorganization of the security apparatuses of the old authoritarian regimes allowed them to operate more freely.[32] Similarly, in Syria, Al Qaeda-supported Iraqi networks redeployed themselves on the Syrian battlefield to oppose Asad's government (and more secularized rebel groups) by creating the al-Nusra front.

In conflict zones like Syria and Iraq, salafis and jihadis are more directly creating structures of popular inclusion – albeit on a divisive sectarian basis – as the state institutions are unable or unwilling to do so. This is indicative of the continued weakness of the state post-uprisings (despite it being "hard" and "fierce")[33] as well as the limited abilities of the statist Islamist parties to incorporate mass constituencies in such circumstances. There is evidently a causal relation between the ongoing violent confrontation between authoritarian state elites and statist Islamists and the reduced ability of both to address satisfactorily issues of mass inclusion.

When it is in control of territories, jihadism has proven to be an effective, and fairly economical, ideological and legal resource for groups seeking to enforce obedience and conformity among fragmented or traumatized communities, such as in the case of state weakening or collapse. The appeal of the jihadi model may relate to its simplicity and the ease by which it may be "rolled out" in different contexts.[34] Even if the leaderships of groups like the Islamic State and Ansar al-Sharia (both in its Yemeni and Libyan declinations) are not "organic" to the populations they seek to rule, they can garner consent by striking deals with (i.e. "buying off") tribal and other local authorities, appealing to disaffected Sunni youth and enforcing a recognizable – even if not welcomed – legal regime. The case of ISIS illustrates the evolution from infra-politics to the transnational politics of jihadism when the constraints of state control are relaxed. The organization is primarily concerned with, on the one hand, the micro-management of societal issues through religious regulations and, on the other, sustaining its capabilities to wage transnational warfare against opponents of their creed.

The transnational dimension of jihadi activism has also been strengthened by a particular regional combination of successes and failures of democratization after the Arab uprisings. The failure of democratization and the failure, apart from in Tunisia, of statist Islamism of the Muslim Brotherhood "brand", amidst the Syrian conflict and the Egyptian military coup have ensured the continuing relevance of a jihadi ideological discourse, which had been threatened when it appeared Islamist movements could gain power democratically. In 2014, with the rebirth of ISIS and the sectarian conflict in Iraq and Syria, the ideological attractiveness of jihadi discourses may also have increased.

The transnational and regional dimension of jihadism in connection with the post-Arab uprisings conflict goes well beyond the countries of the Arab uprisings themselves. In addition to the circulation of jihadists within the Arab world, "foreign fighters" are increasingly drawn from Muslim populations based in Europe.[35] Such dynamics, which are actively promoted by jihadi movements, illustrate that they are not solely the product of failures of democratization in the Arab world but reflect wider problems of social and political inclusion and alienation.

This means that states not currently in the throes of civil war will not necessarily escape jihadist or salafi activism. Across the region the salafi trend continues to act as a refuge for political (or armed) activism in the countries of the region for different reasons in both democratizing and non-democratizing countries. In Egypt the increase in repression and political blockage following the military coup has inexorably pushed would-be political activists back into either pious withdrawal or, for some, violence. In Tunisia, the rapid rise of Ansar al-Sharia in a context where an Islamist-led government was in charge of the country illustrated the dissatisfaction of many of the actors of the revolution (particularly the unemployed urban youth) with the slow pace of change and the pragmatic political approach taken by Ennahda. Thus, even in a context of strengthening and democratizing state institutions – that is in "successful" democratic transitions – the uneasy process of turning revolutionary citizens into "well-behaved" voters ensures that those constituencies that still feel excluded and/or unhappy from the dominant political consensus can find alternative avenues of inclusion via non-statist Islamist movements.

5. Conclusion

The different embodiments of Islamism in the region, their successes and their failures, track the rise and fall of different models of governance far more than they follow the fate of particular regimes. It is the degree and nature of transformation in state-society relations, through the formal and practical positioning of Islamist parties, that directly influence the evolution of post-uprisings Islamism. As O'Donnell and Schmitter already noted regarding the democratic transitions of the 1980s, the plasticity of identities is a crucial component of the political process during such transitional periods.[36] Because of historical trajectories, some Islamists movements faced a more arduous task than others in reinventing themselves and in contributing to an overall transformation of the political ethos in the post-uprisings situations. Thus Ennahda in Tunisia, with its well-considered reformist approach, its non-conflictual relations with a weakly politicized military, and organizational superiority over an emerging salafi movement was better placed than the Muslim Brotherhood in Egypt (or in heavily militarized and fragmented Libya and Yemen). This does not necessarily mean that the former was bound to succeed and the latter bound to fail, but rather that the strategies devised by each actor were crucial in tipping their countries towards or away from democratic consolidation. When, as in Tunisia, Islamist parties participate in a working multiparty system, accompanied by an increase in civil liberties, they can contribute to democratic consolidation, stability and enhanced state governance. Where Islamist movements are violently excluded, as in Egypt after the 2013 military coup and the ban on the Muslim Brotherhood, the opposite results.

Notes

1. The authors would like to thank the Arts and Humanities Research Council for facilitating the research for this article through their support of the research network People Power versus State Power of the Centre for the Advanced Study of the Arab World.
2. Volpi, *Political Islam Observed*.
3. Ayoob, *The Many Faces of Political Islam*.
4. Lockman, *Contending Visions*.
5. Abdelnasser, "Islamic Organizations in Egypt."
6. Bayat, "Revolution without Movement."
7. Hinnebusch, *Egyptian Politics under Sadat*.
8. Mehrez, *Egypt's Culture Wars*.
9. Shambayati, "The Rentier State."
10. Stein, "An Uncivil Partnership."
11. Ahmed, *The Thistle and the Drone*.
12. Burgat, *Islamism in the Shadow*.
13. Gause III, *Beyond Sectarianism*.

14. Torelli et al., "Salafism in Tunisia."
15. Roy, *Failure of Political Islam.*
16. Zubaida, *Islam, the People.*
17. Mitchell, *Society of the Muslim Brothers*; Lia, *Society of the Muslim Brothers*; Wickham, *Muslim Brotherhood.*
18. Teitelbaum, "Muslim Brotherhood in Syria"; Brownlee, "Muslim Brothers."
19. Anani, *Al-Ikhwan Al-Muslimun*; Schwedler, "Can Islamists Become Moderates?"; El-Ghobashy, "Metamorphosis of the Egyptian Muslim."
20. Wickham, "Path to Moderation."
21. Baker, *Islam without Fear.*
22. Bonnefoy, *Salafism in Yemen.*
23. Abd al-Al, "Al-Da'wa Al-Salafiyya"; Tammam, *Tasalluf Al-Ikhwan.*
24. Boubekeur, *Salafism and Radical Politics.*
25. Clark, "Social Movement Theory."
26. Hafez, *Why Muslims Rebel.*
27. Gerges, *Far Enemy.*
28. Naqib, "Al-Salafiya."
29. Sayigh, *Taking Egypt Back.*
30. Ibrahim, "*khusuf al-Islam al-Siyasi.*"
31. Filiu, *Al-Qaeda.*
32. Wehrey, "Libya's Revolution."
33. Ayubi, *Over-Stating the Arab State.*
34. Hudson et al., "Drone Warfare."
35. Hegghammer, "Should I Stay."
36. O'Donnell and Schmitter, *Transitions from Authoritarian Rule.*

References

Abd al-Al, Ali. "Al-Da'wa Al-Salafiyya Bi-Al-Iskandriyya . . . al-Nash'a Al-Ta'rikhiya Wa-Aham Al-Malamih [al-Da'wa Al-Salafiyya in Alexandria: Historical Growth and Key Features]." April 30 2011. http://ali-abdelal.maktoobblog.com/

Abdelnasser, Walid Mahmoud. "Islamic Organizations in Egypt and the Iranian Revolution of 1979: The Experience of the First Few Years." *Arab Studies Quarterly* 19, no. 2 (1997): 25–39.

Ahmed, Akbar S. *The Thistle and the Drone: How America's War on Terror Became a Global War on Tribal Islam*. Washington, DC: Brookings Institution Press, 2013.

Anani, Khalil al-. *Al-Ikhwan Al-Muslimun Fi Misr: Shaykhukha Turasi' Al-Zaman [The Muslim Brotherhood in Egypt: Gerontocracy against Time]*. Cairo: Dar al-Shuruq al-Dawaliya, 2007.

Ayoob, Mohammed. *The Many Faces of Political Islam: Religion and Politics in the Muslim World*. Ann Arbor: University of Michigan Press, 2009.

Ayubi, Nazih N. *Over-Stating the Arab State: Politics and Society in the Middle East*. London: I. B. Tauris, 1995.

Baker, Raymond William. *Islam without Fear: Egypt and the New Islamists*. Cambridge: Harvard University Press, 2006.

Bayat, Asef. "Revolution without Movement, Movement without Revolution: Comparing Islamic Activism in Iran and Egypt." *Comparative Studies in Society and History* 40, no. 1 (1998): 136–169.

Bonnefoy, Laurent. *Salafism in Yemen: Transnationalism and Religious Identity*. New York: Oxford University Press USA, 2012.

Boubekeur, Amel. *Salafism and Radical Politics in Postconflict Algeria*. Carnegie Papers no. 11, 2008. Middle East Center: Carnegie Endowment for International Peace.

Brownlee, Jason. "The Muslim Brothers: Egypt's Most Influential Pressure Group." *History Compass* 8, no. 5 (2010): 419–430.

Burgat, François. *Islamism in the Shadow of Al-Qaeda*. Trans P. Hutchinson. Austin: University of Texas Press, 2010.

Clark, Janine. "Social Movement Theory and Patron-Clientalism: Islamic Social Institutions and the Middle Class in Egypt, Jordan and Yemen." *Comparative Political Studies* 37, no. 8 (2004): 941–968.

El-Ghobashy, Mona. "The Metamorphosis of the Egyptian Muslim Brothers." *International Journal of Middle East Studies* 37, no. 3 (2005): 373–395.

Filiu, Jean-Pierre. *Al-Qaeda in the Islamic Maghreb: Algerian Challenge or Global Threat?*. Carnegie Papers, November 2009. Carnegie Endowment for International Peace.

Gause III, F. Gregory. *Beyond Sectarianism: The New Middle East Cold War*. Brookings Doha Center Analysis Paper no.11, 2014. Brookings Doha Center.

Gerges, Fawaz A. *The Far Enemy: Why Jihad Went Global*. Cambridge: Cambridge University Press, 2005.

Hafez, Mohammed M. *Why Muslims Rebel: Repression and Resistance in the Islamic World*. Boulder: Lynne Rienner, 2004.

Hegghammer, Thomas. "Should I Stay or Should I Go? Explaining Variations in Western Jihadis' Choice between Domestic and Foreign Fighting." *American Political Science Review* 107, no. 1 (2013): 1–15.

Hinnebusch, Raymond. *Egyptian Politics under Sadat: The Post-Populist Development of an Authoritarian-Modernizing State*. Boulder: Lynne Rienner, 1988.

Hudson, Leila, Colin S. Owens, and David J. Callen. "Drone Warfare in Yemen: Fostering Emirates through Counterterrorism?." *Middle East Policy* 19, no. 3 (2012): 142–156.

Ibrahim, Saad al-Din. "*khusuf al-Islam al-Siyasi: al-Ikhwan al-Muslimun namudhajan* [The eclipse of political Islam: the case of the Muslim Brotherhood]." *Majallat Al-Dimuqratiya [journal]*. 55, (July 2014): 34–48.

Lia, Brynjar. *The Society of the Muslim Brothers in Egypt: The Rise of an Islamic Mass Movement 1928–1942*. Reading: Ithaca Press, 1998.

Lockman, Zachary. *Contending Visions of the Middle East: The History and Politics of Orientalism*. Cambridge: Cambridge University Press, 2004.

Mehrez, Samia. *Egypt's Culture Wars: Politics and Practice*. New York: Routledge, 2008.

Mitchell, Richard P. *The Society of the Muslim Brothers*. New York: Oxford University Press USA, 1993.

Mubarak, Hisham. *Al-Irhabiyun Qadimun! Dirasa Muqarana Bayna Mawqif Alkhwan Al-Muslimoon Wa Gama'at Al-Gihad Min Qadiat Al-Unf 1938–1994 [The Terrorists Are Coming: A Comparative Study Between the Positions of the Muslim Brothers and the Jihad Groups on Violence 1938–1994]*. Cairo: Kitab al-Mahrusa, 1995.

Naqib, Ahmad Abd al-Rahman. "Al-Salafiya ... wa-Al-Salafiyun ... wa-Intikhabat Al-Ri'asa [Salafism, Salafists and the Presidential Elections]." *Ahmad Al-Naqib: Mawqi' Al-Basirah*. April 2012. http://www.albasira.net/cms/play.php?catsmktba=7987

O'Donnell, Guillermo, and Philippe C. Schmitter. *Transitions from Authoritarian Rule: Tentative Conclusions about Uncertain Democracies*. Baltimore: John Hopkins University Press, 1986.

Roy, Olivier. *The Failure of Political Islam*. Trans. C. Volk. Cambridge: Harvard University Press, 1994.

Sayigh, Yazid. "Taking Egypt Back to the First Republic." *Carnegie Endowment for International Peace*, February 6, 2014. http://carnegieendowment.org/2014/02/06/taking-egypt-back-to-first-republic/h09 g

Schwedler, Jillian. "Can Islamists Become Moderates? Rethinking the Inclusion-Moderation Hypothesis." *World Politics* 63, no. 2 (2011): 347–376.

Shambayati, Hootan. "The Rentier State, Interest Groups, and the Paradox of Autonomy: State and Business in Turkey and Iran." *Comparative Politics* 26, no. 3 (1994): 307–331.

Stein, Ewan. "An Uncivil Partnership: Egypt's Jama'a Islamiyya and the State after the Jihad." *Third World Quarterly* 32, no. 5 (2011): 863–881.

Tammam, Husam. *Tasalluf Al-Ikhwan: Takul Al-Utruha Al-Ikhwaniyya Wa-Su'ud Al-Salafiyya Fi Jama'at Al-Ikhwan Al-Muslimin [the Salafisation of the Brothers: The Erosion of the Brotherhood's Venture and the Rise of Salafism in the the Muslim Brotherhood Group]*. Alexandria: Maktabat al-Iskandriyya, Wahdat al-Dirasat al-Mustaqbaliyya, 2010.

Teitelbaum, Joshua. "The Muslim Brotherhood in Syria, 1945–1958: Founding, Social Origins, Ideology." *Middle East Journal* 65, no. 2 (2011): 213–233.

Torelli, Stephano, Fabio Merone, and Francesco Cavatorta. "Salafism in Tunisia: Challenges and Opportunities for Democratization." *Middle East Policy* 19, no. 4 (2012): 140–154.

Volpi, Frédéric. *Political Islam Observed: Disciplinary Perspectives*. New York: Oxford University Press USA, 2010.

Wehrey, Frederic. "Libya's Revolution at Two Years: Perils and Achievements." *Mediterranean Politics* 18, no. 1 (2013): 112–118.

Wickham, Carrie Rosefsky. "The Path to Moderation: Strategy and Learning in the Formation of Egypt's Wasat Party." *Comparative Politics* 36, no. 2 (2004): 205–228.

Wickham, Carrie Rosefsky. *Muslim Brotherhood Evolution of an Islamist Movement*. Princeton: Princeton University Press, 2013.

Zubaida, Sami. *Islam, the People and the State: Political Ideas and Movements in the Middle East*. London: I.B.Tauris, 1993.

Class forces, transition and the Arab uprisings: a comparison of Tunisia, Egypt and Syria

Jamie Allinson

Department of Politics and International Relations, University of Westminster, London, UK

This article intervenes into an ongoing debate on authoritarian regimes in the Arab world following the uprisings of 2011, in particular addressing the perceived failure of those uprisings to bring about "transition" to liberal democratic models. Drawing upon the method of comparative historical sociology used in seminal analyses of democratization and dictatorship in Europe, Asia and the Americas, the article seeks to explain the varying trajectories of the Arab Uprising states in terms of several structural factors, namely the balance of class forces, the relative autonomy of the state and the geo-political context. The article provides an empirical comparison of the cases of Egypt, Tunisia and Syria as points on a continuum of outcomes following the Arab uprising. The article mounts a critique of the absence of class analysis in mainstream transition theory and hypothesises instead an important role for workers' movements in bringing about even basic elements of liberal democracy. The empirical comparison is shown to support this hypothesis, demonstrating that in Tunisia, the state where the worker's movement was strongest a constitutional settlement has been reached while Syria, the state with the weakest and least independent workers' movement has descended into counter-revolution and civil war: the case of Egypt lying between these two poles.

The prevailing perception of the uprisings that swept the Arab world in late 2010 and early 2011 is that they have failed to bring about a long-awaited transition to liberal democracy in the region. The question has shifted from whether the so-called "Arab spring" overturns accepted wisdoms about the Middle East to "why did the 'Arab Spring' yield so modest a harvest?"[1] Posing the question in this way returns the study of comparative politics in the Arab world to the *status quo ante* the uprisings: a debate alternating between searching for faint signs of "democratic transition" on the one hand, and the attempt to understand an apparently resilient authoritarianism on the other.[2]

The intervention of democratization theorists into this long-running debate stresses political cultural explanations for the failure of democratic transition, such as the Sultanistic character of pre-uprising regimes, the role of religion in public life[3] or the lack of trust, rooted in authoritarian inheritances that obstructed negotiated transitions.[4] In this article I argue that although the case may be made that the Arab revolutions have "failed" – a necessarily shaky conclusion given the historic depth of these events – the transition theorists have overlooked an established pattern of agency in previous instances of "democratic transition". This is the phenomenon, documented by Rueschemeyer, Stephens and Stephens,[5] of the centrality of the working class, and in particular organized labour, to winning the minimal guarantees of civil rights and fairly elected representative government that transition theorists consider the essence of democracy.

This flaw, I argue, is not an accidental oversight but rather derives from the implicit assumption of, as Andrea Teti puts it, the "democratization framework's taxonomical end point – liberal democracy".[6] Treating the Arab revolutions as discreet events after which a "transition" to this variety of democracy can successfully be negotiated amongst elites, renders the institutional set-up and timing of this process the most important factor: ruling out then, the political economy analysis of the respective social bases of the actors, an analysis present in the previous work of democratization theorists.[7] This focus on process leads assumed division between "secular liberals" or "secular democrats" and Islamists (whose democratic credentials are always in question) at the expense of any other division in the societies in question, to the extent that very notion of class and political economy literally disappears from the analysis. Where structures of political economy do appear, they are largely the familiar ones of the rentier state.[8]

The transition approach thus misses the role of the working class, and the strong correlation between the strength of labour movements and the winning of minimal democratic rights in the region. I argue, drawing on the framework of Rueschemeyer et al.'s *Capitalist Development and Democracy*, that a comparison of Egypt, Syria and Tunisia on the basis of three "clusters of power – the balance of class forces, the degree of state autonomy, and the geopolitical conjuncture – demonstrates this correlation.[9] In keeping with the theme of this special issue, the historical sociology of state tangents and their impact on democratization, I seek through this comparison to demonstrate that a large part of the variation in the dynamics and results of the Arab uprisings matches the degree of mobilization, organization and consciousness of workers and their participation in the revolutions.

The paper proceeds in three parts. First I present a critique of the absence of the role of popular classes in democratic transition theory. Second, I outline the alternative posed to these underpinnings of approaches by the work of Rueschemeyer et al., and their method of comparing the respective power clusters of class forces, state autonomy, and geopolitical relations. In the third and final section I present a comparative narrative of the Tunisian, Egyptian and Syrian revolutionary processes, demonstrating that the cases with the highest degree of independent working class organization have achieved the most in terms of representative elections and constitutional freedoms, albeit with a danger of co-optation by the "deep state" most evident in Egypt.

Democratic transition theory: a critique

If Arab states are in the midst of a "transition", failed or otherwise, to what endpoint are they moving from their prior condition? The endpoints generally adopted in democratization studies[10] share a common core: essentially liberal, free market, Western democracy of the Euro-American type. Democracy thus means a process by which an electorate based on universal suffrage approves the circulation of governing elites. The power of these elites is notionally circumscribed both in terms of what they can do (guaranteed freedom of association, speech, etc.) and the sphere in which they can do it (there is to be no *prima facie* interference in the operative power relationships of the economy, for example).

Democratization for transition theorists results from negotiation between old and new elites to produce new institutions on the above model: mass protests, strikes reflecting economic discontent, may form a crucial variable, but they are refracted through the agency of elite actors.[11] Indeed, the prolonging of the popular insurgency characteristic of the "breakthrough" phase of democratization into the "consolidation" phase may itself threaten the transition itself – a concern evident, for example, in some of the democratization analyses of Egypt that see the diversion of popular energies away from "mass uprising" and into electoral campaigning as a *prima facie* good.[12]

The central variable for transition theorists then becomes the process of negotiation in which soft-liners in regime and opposition marginalize hardliners on both sides.'[13] Applied to the Arab cases, democratic transition theorists see the roots in particular of Egypt's failure to emerge as a liberal democracy as lying in the authoritarian inheritance of all actors: whether in the insufficient moderation of the Egyptian Muslim Brotherhood by comparison with the Tunisian Nahda, for example;[14] the opacity of the Supreme Council of the Armed Forces (SCAF) and its preservation of prerogatives over significant parts of the state and the economy; or the continued willingness of the opposition continually to engage in street protest.[15] In Syria, Stepan and Linz ascribe – with good reason – the ferocity of the state's response to what they describe as its "Sultanistic" nature, binding together the ruling core through (rational) fear of the drastic consequences of their fall from power in the context of sectarian division.[16] The lack of trust between actors, or of effective institutions or correctly timed juridical and electoral processes, explain the failure to achieve the limited liberal democracy assumed to have been demanded by those "secular liberals" who constituted the protest movements.[17]

What are the consequences for democratic transition theory of this engagement with the Arab uprisings? Existing critiques focus on its patchy empirical record, or the frequent failures of expected processes of transition to unfold as expected.[18] Most "transition" states, Carothers argued, were not on their way to democracy but rather occupied an intermediate position of "feckless pluralism or dominant power politics".[19] The "stages" of transition were absent in most cases, elections were often a shallow, mechanical exercise and the inherited cultural, economic and institutional – most of all state weakness – legacies were vitally important.[20] Although recent work by democratic transition theorists displays a much greater sensitivity to the fragility of the (assumed) process of transition, they still tend to reduce the actors involved to a schematic triad: the old regime, the Islamists and "secular liberals". This last group, it is implied, represent a middle-class, Westernizing influence and formed the core of the uprisings. They explain the "modest harvest" by reference to the insufficient degree of mutual toleration or the lack of a liberal democratic, trust-building attitude amongst these actors in the transition process.[21]

What is needed is a critique at a deeper level: in the conception of the agency behind the uprisings, and the lack of a historical sociology of that agency. Moreover, empirical evidence tends to dispute the transition paradigm's concentration on the above "triad" to the neglect of the popular classes. It is difficult to gauge the arguments of democratization theorists on the class character of the Arab world, because the concept appears only rarely in the literature. The word "Islamist" appears 12 times in Alfred Stepan's article on Tunisia and "secularism" seven: while "trade union" features once and "labour", "worker" and *Union Générale Tunisienne du Travail*" (UGTT) not at all, despite the centrality of that organization to the fall of Ben Ali.[22] In the special issue of the *Journal of Democracy* (2013) on the modest outcomes of the Arab uprisings: references to class are absent, except in the presumption that the protestors represented the "secular middle class". The only social cleavages that appear consistently in democratization analyses of the Arab uprisings relate to religious identity, whether to do with the sect to which one belongs, the degree of observance or the role allotted to religious sources of legitimacy in the political order. This perspective not only erases the actual dynamics of the uprising, it also leaves behind resources in historical sociology that can be fruitfully used to understand the present outcomes of the Arab uprisings.

Historical sociology of democratization and the role of the labour movement

The flaws of the democratic transition approach can be remedied with recourse to a different tradition in the study of democracy. With roots in the work of Guillermo O'Donnell[23] and even further back to Barrington Moore's seminal study, *The Social Origins of Dictatorship and Democracy* (1966), the political economy approach to the emergence of regime types takes a longer and broader view, linking the concerns of democratization, historical sociology and state tangents. Of particular relevance here is the body of work, such as Geoff Eley's *Forging*

Democracy (2002) and Rueschemeyer et al. *Capitalist Development and Democracy* (1992) stressing the role of labour movements and the political left in winning basic democratic rights.[24]

While Rueschemeyer et al. in particular adopt the same definition of procedural, formal liberal democracy as that used by transition theorists,[25] seeking to explain the outcome and persistence of polyarchy, in Dahl's sense,[26] they criticize transition approaches focus on immediate processes rather than on the long-term evolution of power relations that lies behind them.[27] Instead, they offer the argument that democracy is an outcome of balances of class power and class coalitions. In particular three clusters of power relations are central to the analysis: the balance between class forces and class coalitions, the relative autonomy of the state and "civil society", and "transnational power relations".[28]

The large cross-case comparison in *Capitalist Development and Democracy* found the following regularities. First, the most consistent force pushing for democracy was the urban working class, except for cases where a charismatic authoritarian leader was able to incorporate this layer: this finding matched the expectations of Rueschemeyer et al., given that the working class both has an interest in general inclusion of the lower social strata to which it belongs, and the mobilizational capacity effectively to demand that inclusion.[29] The autonomy of working class organization was thus a key factor in the successful emergence of democratic reform. The most consistently anti-democratic class was the landed upper class, fearing the loss of reservoirs of cheap labour. A coalition of landlords and bourgeoisie that perceived democracy as a threat to their interests was an especially potent anti-democratic force.[30] The middle class – in the sense of salaried professionals, shopkeepers and other intermediate strata – played an ambiguous role, supporting their own inclusion but hesitant about extending political rights to those below them: they formed fodder for alliances either with the working class or the upper classes.[31] Independent peasants in small-holding countries were a mobilizing factor for democracy while agricultural labourers tended to ally with urban workers.[32]

Two further clusters of power are found relevant to the analysis of the balance of class forces and class alliances. These are interconnected in the form of "transnational power relations" and the relative autonomy of the state. Geopolitical and economic dependency, Rueschmeyer et al. find, has a negative effect on the development of democracy partly due to the direct effect of foreign interference, aid to boost the repressive power of the military and so on, and partly because of the resulting patterns of economic development that hinder the emergence and organization of strong labour movements.[33] As regards the autonomy of the state apparatus, too autonomous a state presses down on the "dense civil society", particularly in the labour movement, which is necessary for democratic gains to be won. A state that is not autonomous enough, however, will likely to be under the control of largely anti-democratic elements from the landowners and *haute bourgeoisie*.[34]

Across their historical comparison, Rueschemeyer et al. find that the correlation between capitalist development and democracy is not due to capitalism per se – still less the patrimony of a heroic bourgeoisie – but to the struggles engendered within capitalism: capitalist development produces and empowers the working class, the most consistently pro-democratic force, while weakening the most-consistently anti-democratic force of large landowners.[35] In a finding germane to the Arab world, Rueschemeyer et al. found that characteristics of late or uneven development have a strong effect on this pattern: working classes in the global south as a general rule being smaller, less organized and less differentiated from broader urban masses than in the capitalist core.[36] This recognition is particularly appropriate in discussing the Arab states, whose economies do not resemble those of the classical European cases. As Rueschemeyer, Stevens and Stevens demonstrate, and the analysis below supports, it is precisely the differential and uneven nature of capitalist development that provides for the foundation of the different outcomes of transition processes. This is still capitalist development, albeit in uneven and combined form. Most Arab states lack the large and cohesive working classes that produced European labour movements and social-democratic parties but they all depend on some mix of resource extraction (for the global capitalist economy), the sale of goods or services produced by free employees (whether by state or private firms) or transfer payments from patron states in the core capitalist regions. It is these variations in the nature of capitalist development and their consequences for class formation that Rueschemeyer et al. capture in their argument that in:

> late developing countries, the relative size of the urban working class is typically smaller because of uneven, "enclave" development and because of the related stronger growth of the tertiary sector ... [meaning] that alliances across class boundaries become critically important for the advance of democracy.[37]

Yet, in focusing on a class analysis, does the approach of Rueschemeyer et al. not risk missing dynamics specific to the political arena? Particularly in Arab states, cross-class identities and ideologies appear to have more salience: does class analysis not neglect these? The first point to note is that almost all transition accounts do have a distorted and incomplete class analysis of the Arab uprisings: identifying the uprisings with an entity called the "secular Westernised middle class", or its youth, counter-posed, not to another class but to an ideological current, Islamism. An explicit class analysis that can then be empirically investigated is a necessary corrective. Second, one must distinguish between levels of analysis: between the political arena, the events and interactions of which are of course contingent, and the collectivities upon which those interactions are based. Sectarian heterogeneity in Syria, to take perhaps the toughest challenge to class analysis, is not an inherent natural characteristic: it is a socially constructed collectivity produced and reproduced through access to the state and the political economy that it oversees. This is not to say that sectarian identification is not a significant – at the time of writing the most significant – factor in Syrian politics, but that there is a basis in political economy for this salience. One may usefully distinguish between:

"(1) the class structure grounded in the organization of production and modified by patterns of mobility and interaction, (2) the ideas and attitudes of the members of a class, and (3) the determination and pursuit of collective goals through organized action on behalf of a class".[38] The first will always be present; the second and third vary, with the extent of sectarian identity or cross-class ideology important elements in that variation.

How then does this approach aid in answering the question: "why did the Arab spring produce so modest a harvest?" It does so by directing our attention, with some caveats, to the three inter-related levels of the balance of class forces and class alliances: the degree of state, or more often regime, autonomy within a wider political economy of capital accumulation, and the interpenetration of regional and global geopolitical competition. As demonstrated below, analysis of three cases most representative of the continuum of outcomes of the Arab uprisings, a strong confirmation of the class model emerges. In summary, Tunisia, site of the earliest uprising and of the strongest labour movement participation within it, resembles most closely the ideal of constitutionally limited representative government, or bourgeois democracy. Syria, with both the weakest (recent) record of labour organization and consequent low level of working-class participation in the uprising, has entered a path of convulsive violence seized by civil war, multi-lateral foreign intervention and the rise of a contender to the state itself in the guises of *Da"esh*, the Islamic State in Iraq and the Levant. Egypt lies somewhere between these poles: a popular uprising with significant labour participation, followed by the return of a military regime that co-opted part of the leadership of the fledgling independent union movement.

Comparative case study (1): Tunisia

Tunisia is usually seen as closest to the model of democratic transition used in mainstream analyses. Although arguably still far from the demands of "bread, freedom and national dignity", Tunisia has achieved a negotiated constitution.[39] Although slow in reaching this outcome – marked also by confrontations between the Islamists, the Left, and political fragments of the *ancien régime* – the popularly elected Constituent Assembly produced broad guarantees of the procedural democracy sought after in democratic transition theory.[40]

What are the class interests, class fractions and alliances of classes at play in the Tunisian case? At the outset, we immediately encounter a divergence from classic European or Latin American cases, the absence of class of large landholders reliant on labour-repressive agriculture, whom Rueschemeyer et al. see as the most consistently anti-democratic force, particularly when allied to an urban manufacturing bourgeoisie and a militarist state. These classic marriages of "iron and rye" have never characterized the ruling classes of the Arab states. Instead, the 1950s and 1960s were characterized by the rise of nationalist-minded middle-ranking military officers in a context of wider social turmoil, who established authoritarian populist regimes that embarked on some version of "passive revolution" or "revolution from above": breaking the power of large-landholders (in some cases colonists), enacting redistributive measures in favour of the middle peasantry and expropriating the urban merchant bourgeoisie (often from minority communities) in order to establish a state-led national capitalism.[41] The ruling classes against whom the Arab uprisings were directed were thus not the holdovers of a previous mode of production, but the comparatively recent mutations of a previous social settlement. Tunisia, unusually, was the site of relatively large-scale colonization by European settlers, who controlled around a fifth of the arable land.[42] Land was redistributed to Tunisians albeit gradually: large holdings did develop but, as discussed below, these were outgrowths of an existing capitalist class rather than labour-repressive grandees.[43]

By the 1980s, in common with the rest of the region, a new Tunisian leadership (under Zine Abidine Ben Ali) turned to a neo-liberal model, especially following an International Monetary Fund restructuring plan imposed in 1987.[44] It is this generation of a new private and state bourgeoisie that was (and remains even now) the predominant class in Tunisia as elsewhere.[45] Neoliberal policies of privatization and greater market involvement implied not a retreat of the state but rather its recasting.[46] Thus, in Tunisia a core ruling group around Ben Ali – and particularly his wife Leila Trabelsi – accumulated enormous wealth through the state, a relationship that radiated out and down through both the state apparatus and the new capitalists close to it.[47] Linked to a circuit of largely European capital,[48] this class fraction derived its surplus partly from state licensing and property speculation and was linked to large agricultural producers: but agriculture as an export-industry rather than large labour-repressive estates.[49]

At this point, the second two clusters of power discussed in *Capitalist Development and Democracy* come into play. For Rueschemeyer et al., the degree of state autonomy from anti-democratic class forces is crucial for the emergence of constitutional democracy – both autonomy from economically dominant classes, and from a particular family core of the ruling group (with the opposite usually referred to as "Sultanism" or patrimonialism in the broader literature).[50] In this respect, the Tunisian state was recognisably very responsive to the needs of capital, ensconced within its ruling committees,[51] while the ruling family was nonetheless much more separable from the broader interests of this class. Once the UGTT strikes became general, threatening the economy with collapse, the Ben Ali-Trabelsi clan were jettisoned. The armed forces were unwilling to continue the repression after the inflaming of the popular movement by the early violent state response, reflecting the independence of the high command.[52] This tight web of state, class and familial interest locked out the Islamist bourgeoisie and petty bourgeoisie, who articulated their discontent in a universalist language of "justice".[53]

Rueschemeyer et al.'s third cluster, that of the geopolitical constellations of power, may also be disaggregated along two axes: one of these being the deep structural effects of uneven development on the balance of class forces and the other being the conjunctural geopolitical interests at play. In the Tunisian case, unlike Egypt and to an even greater extent Syria, the latter were almost completely concentrated in one relationship: with the former colonial power, France – by extension the European Union and the USA. Ben Ali's repressive *laïciste* regime was considered an important ally in the "war on terror" and Tunisia formed the lynchpin of trans-Mediterranean trade agreements.[54] French support in money and materiel had long sustained the Ben Ali regime, until the very eve of the uprising.[55] The assumption that Western influence promotes democracy is undermined by the empirical evidence in this case.[56] Nonetheless, the absence of inter-state rivalry over the Tunisian revolution allowed a greater space for popular initiatives to push the process forward: a luxury not afforded to Syrians, for example.

What of the organized labour force identified by Rueschemeyer et al. as the most consistently democratic force? Outside of Aden, the Tunisian General Union of Workers (UGTT) played the most significant role in anti-colonial struggle of any Arab state.[57] Being an organization of significant social weight, the UGTT is of course no monolith: with deep divisions in attitude to the old regime and its remnants, for example, between rank and file members and the upper apparatus. In the post-independence period, the UGTT was co-opted into the Bourguibist regime. Even then, the UGTT did retain a degree of independence, reflecting the density of its rank and file organization. There were major struggles between workers and the regime in 1978 and 1983–1984; the outcome of the latter being a weakening of the UGTT.[58] The organization persisted, however, and contained within it many activists independent of the regime-linked leadership with experience in significant class struggle, and in particular a major strike at the Gafsa mine. This was to become crucial in the 2010–2011 uprising. The UGTT was, of course, not the sole actor in the Tunisian revolution: the motive force came from a heterogeneous revolutionary subject on the streets. However, it would be almost impossible to find another organization – not even the Islamist Nahda party, which was relatively marginal at the beginning of the revolt – that played as consistently significant a role as the UGTT. In this aspect Tunisia did indeed differ starkly from the other cases. Indeed, it was networks of UGTT activists that spread the uprising from the impoverished interior to the main cities, and organized the strike wave that finally put paid to Ben Ali's rule.[59]

How did the role of the organized working class then affect the "transition" period in Tunisia? First, pressure from the lower ranks of the UGTT was significant in forcing a more thorough purge of the ruling party, the *Rassemblement Constitutionnel Démocratique* (RCD) (forcing the resignation of the union's ministers in the first post-Ben Ali cabinet), by comparison to Egypt where the cadres of the ruling National Democratic Party (NDP) resurfaced in another guise. The union also lead the protests that won the commitment to an elected National Constituent Assembly in October 2011.[60] Thirdly, when in these elections, the Islamist Ennahda won a plurality and governed as part of a "troika" with the social democratic Takatol and liberal Congress for the Republic, unleashing a tripartite struggle among the Islamists (rooted in a fraction of the upper bourgeoisie, and with very wide cadres of petty bourgeois support), the remnants of the old regime, and the popular revolutionary movements, the union federation in Tunisia, unlike in Egypt, was the undeniable core of the latter. As Ennahda came into government, and the class struggles that had ignited the uprising continued (for example giving rise to mass strikes in towns such as Kesserine and Siliana), the hostility between the workers' movement and associated leftist parties, and the Islamists sharpened, particularly following the assassination of Leftist politicians by presumed Islamists. Fourth, however, the UGTT leadership, along with the employers' organization and others played a mediating role in a "national dialogue" that brought about the conclusion of the constitution, the "technocratic" government under former industry minister Mehdi Joma'a and the promise of further parliamentary and presidential elections on the constitutional basis.[61] Workers, therefore, played the decisive role in setting Tunisia on the road to democratic transition.

Comparative case study (2): Egypt

At the time of writing (early 2015), Egyptian politics seems to have returned to a more highly repressive version of the *status quo ante* of 25 January 2011, with a heavier dose of nostalgia for the high water mark of Egyptian power in the 1950s and 1960s. Lacking the developmental resources or redistributive policies of that time, the success of this austerity Nasserism cannot be vouchsafed. Nonetheless, as described below, this discourse has had a significant effect in binding parts of the independent labour movement to the state. How did Egypt's "transition" – never a propitious undertaking so long as the deep structures of the regime remained intact, if damaged – reach this bind? A flawed process definitely played a part, but the Egyptian trajectory reaches much further back.

As in Tunisia, by 2011 in Egypt, the locus of class differentiation had become urban rather than agrarian: after years of contradictory land reform initiatives, the countryside was dominated by property speculators and agro-capitalists rather than agrarian magnates dependent on semi-servile labour.[62] Who then composed the ruling class – those with most to lose – of Egypt in 2011? Again, the Egyptian case presents a fuller development of the Tunisian: an interlocking core of state-licensed and connected capital and the repressive state apparatus following more than three decades of *infitah*.[63] As well as the core group of *nouveaux riches*, Egypt's private sector was long-standing enough to produce a business class not directly imbricated with the Mubarak family, but who closely identified with state when it was under threat.[64] Second, the Egyptian military itself had become a bourgeoisie-in-arms, controlling vast stretches (estimates varying between 10 and 40%) of the economy.[65]

The final group, as in Tunisia, was the Islamist bourgeoisie. Largely excluded from the patronage of the regime, these pious industrialists developed their own commercial networks reaching deep down into local neighbourhoods and attracting the petit bourgeois who had long formed the core of Islamist support.[66] Of course, the appeal of Islamist ideology (in Brotherhood or Salafist form) spreads beyond a specific class, as does any ideology. To describe the Brotherhood as a bourgeois force with petit bourgeois and mass support does not mean a perfect congruity between these classes and the organization: it refers to the orientation of the group, the structural class position of its leading members and the class impact of the political economy envisaged by its ideology. On all these measures, the Brotherhood can reasonably be considered a bourgeois force, with a middle class periphery. Its leading members are themselves wealthy entrepreneurs and it derives its funding from donations (and external states) rather than from organized labour.[67] It orients its political work on commercial organizations and professional syndicates. Its electoral support amongst the urban poor is based on a passive relationship: ideological identification, to be sure, but also influence won by charitable services. Its stance on economic issues envisages a market economy, "just" wages ensured by scriptural sanction rather than worker self-organization and the removal of impediments to the fair operation of the market.[68] All ideologies contain some element of cross-class appeal – they would not be ideologies if they did not – but they do so in order to identify broader layers with an organization that has definite class content.

The history of the Egyptian revolution can thus to some extent be read through the fortunes of these class fractions: the military capitalists removing the Mubarak clique when it became clear the mass uprising against them threatened wider interests. This was to become crucial when the mass protests of the 18 days coalesced with a strike wave that penetrated the military enterprises themselves on the 10–11 February 2011: at this point, as in Tunisia, the military simply rid themselves of Mubarak. The resulting rule of the Supreme Council of the Armed Forces presented as "transition" what was actually a road-map to the restoration of the deep state.[69] The military and Islamists briefly converged around their shared animosity of Gamal Mubarak's crony capitalist faction, only later to split, leading to the exclusion of the Islamists.

In relation to the geopolitical conjuncture, where Tunisia saw a largely unidirectional relationship, Egypt – a far larger and more important state – was subject to a largely one-way influence at the global level and intra-Gulf competition at the regional level. Since Sadat's turn away from Soviet influence in the 1970s, the US had formed the major sponsor of the regime and in particular the Egyptian military. This relationship remained in place after the "18 Days". The US government's call for an "orderly transition" (to Mubarak's appointed deputy Omar Soleiman) undoubtedly signalled that Mubarak had become a liability.[70] The Obama administration showed a brief interest in the Muslim Brotherhood as a force for stability,[71] only to decline to use the word "coup" or strongly condemn the renewed repression after 30 June 2013. At the regional level, the intervention of Gulf oil states into the post-Egyptian revolutionary scene was much more competitive. In broad-brush strokes, Qatar funded and supported the Muslim Brotherhood, while the Saudis backed either Salafi groups as a counterweight to its rivals' influence, or retained their relationship with the Egyptian military.[72] This aspect confirms a further hypothesis of Rueschemeyer et al.: the influx of resources flowed not to the labour movement or subaltern classes but to other class forces. The flow of external resources thus empowered the authoritarian military and the Muslim Brotherhood, squeezing out the original revolutionary forces of the uprising.

What of the role of those subaltern classes, and in particular the working class in the Egyptian revolution? Although numerically large, Egypt's formally employed and organized working class is still a minority compared to the informal sector and those in "vulnerable employment".[73] From the Free Officers' coup until the strike wave that preceded the revolution, Egyptian unions were state-controlled.[74] Yet, more than 1.7 million workers took part in more than 1900 strikes and other protests (in the absence of free unions) between 2004 and 2008.[75] It was this strike wave that began to weaken the barrier of fear, prefiguring the revolution of 2011. A new independent organization emerged: the Egyptian Independent Trade Union Federation (EITUF), which was to play a significant role both before and after the fall of Mubarak. It was, to be sure, massive demonstrations that (at least temporarily) broke the power of the police apparatus, rather than strikes, although workers were present on them. However, the final days of Mubarak's reign, the 10–11 February marked a huge increase in strike activity. A general strike called on Wednesday 9 February spread quickly even to the military production facilities: at this point, the core ruling apparatus decided to dispense with Mubarak and declare the rule of the Supreme Council of the Armed Forces. The level of labour actually increased after this. There were 1400 recorded collective labour actions in 2011, 1969 in 2012, and 2400 in the first quarter of 2013.[76]

Yet what did not occur was the much anticipated "passing-over" of workers' struggles into a general challenge to the state. The uprising of the "18 days", and of the succeeding 18 months, did not destroy the deep state. The movement against Morsi was much more contradictory, including both those who wanted to extend the revolution and those who sought to roll it back. The workers movement did not become an indispensable central actor but remained caught in the struggle between the deep state and the (business-oriented) Muslim Brotherhood.

In part this outcome was the result of the predominant set of politics and institutional heritage of the workers' movement. The movement remained divided and dominated the old regime unions controlling the pension funds and other institutional sources of power. The dominant political element was committed to the side of the state against the Muslim Brotherhood, a hangover of nationalist corporatism. Thus Kamal abu Eita, leader of EITUF became the first minister of labour in the post-coup government.[77] Hamdeen Sabahi, standard-bearer of the nationalist Left, and winner of a fifth of the vote in the 2012 presidential election, supported the coup of the 3rd of July 2013.

The key force that Rueschemeyer et al. identify as winning minimal democratic reforms was thus in Egypt hampered by its institutional legacy, and by the predominant politics of attachment to the state. Yet might there have been even deeper reasons behind the social character of the Egyptian revolution: urban and popular, involving workers and strikes, but not a *workers' revolution* as such?

Mention has already been made of the vast rural-urban migration that Egypt experienced as a result of policies of "accumulation by dispossession" on the land: a set of policies replicated in urban areas also.[78] The expanding urban and peri-urban population were not, for the most part, moving to steady waged employment in organized workplaces, but to semi-, under- and unemployment. Indeed, much of the pre-revolutionary strike wave was directed against policies of deregulation, privatization and "precarization".[79]

In the context of a strong, independent and politically-oriented trade union movement a revolutionary subject of this sort could end up winning minimal democratic demands, as in Tunisia. A difficult balance prevailed: the necessary conditions being that the labour movement and its allies are strong enough to be threatening, but equally that the leadership of that movement is willing to reduce its demands to a degree that will not threaten the privileged strata. For all its efforts, the Egyptian workers' movement did not reach this level, leaving the revolution in a more high-stakes position: either to crack open the deep state and establish some other institutions of rule (presumably to the detriment of the bourgeoisie clustered around that state) or retreat in the face of the return of its return. In the end, Egypt took the latter path.

Comparative case study (3): Syria

Syria lies at the other end of the continuum from Tunisia. At the time of writing, the unyielding counter-revolution of the Assad regime looked close to triumph: or at least to transforming the revolution into a conflict with its Sunni chauvinist enemies, and in some cases former clients, such as the Islamic State in Iraq and the Levant.[80] The origins of this divergence are usually sought in the history of religious and linguistic divisions in Syria, and the accompanying vulnerability of the state to external interference: these are certainly important factors, but as I seek to demonstrate below, they intersect with and operate on the terrain of political economy. Sectarian identity is vital to understanding the Syrian crisis, but it is not an *a priori* variable that precedes processes of political economy and authoritarian state-building: it acquires meaning and salience through those processes.

The history of the Syrian regime and its ruling economic interests presents broadly similar story to that of Egypt, Tunisia and other formerly radical republics. As in Tunisia and Egypt, the large landlords and urban notables were dispossessed in the 1960s: the mobilization of poor peasants merging with the more urban Ba'ath during this period.[81] What made its trajectory somewhat different was that whereas Egypt and Tunisia made decisive turns to the West and market policies in the late 1970s, Hafez Al-Assad's "corrective movement" was directed against the Ba'ath Left but was accompanied by far less overt marketization.[82] The neoliberal moment in Syria came later, its tentative beginnings in the last years of Assad *pere*, then accelerated under Bashar.[83]

A result, intersecting with the dynamics (and instrumental use) of sectarian identification has been a Syrian bourgeoisie especially stratified by its access to the state.[84] Bassem Haddad refers to these as "the new economic elite" (in both state and private varieties), the old bourgeoisie, and the independent businesspeople.[85] The former group is, unsurprisingly, largely Alawite, and where not identical to the political and military leadership of the state, stands in solidarity with it. Although Bassem Haddad describes this as a state elite, it must also be recognized that to perhaps an even greater degree than other dictatorial clans, the Assads (and the Makhloufs) acquired an enormous slice of the country's wealth through covert privatization programmes. Rami Makhlouf, Hafez' brother-in-law, has been reported to control 60% of Syria's economic activity.[86] Even if this is an overestimate, it is certain that Makhlouf controls significant sectors of the liberalized Syrian economy, such as mobile telephone networks that became a target for protests in the early days of the revolution.[87]

Within the "new economic elite" there are both inner and outer layers. The outer sections of regime-linked capital, as opposed to the old merchant families, established themselves in the high period of Syrian *dirigisme* in the 1970s and 1980s and moved with the times, becoming private businessmen as the economy was neoliberalized.[88] This group is more widely spread and less directly connected to the ruling family.[89] Religious minorities feature but there are also representatives of the Sunni majority. However, their reliance on closeness to the regime ensures their loyalty.

The Syrian old bourgeoisie began as urban merchants and remain concentrated in textiles and internal trade.[90] Largely, if not exclusively, Sunni, this group and its periphery formed the backbone of opposition to Ba'athist radicalism in the 1960s.[91] A non-aggression pact of sorts prevailed afterwards between an Alawite state elite on the one hand and a Sunni economic elite on the other – albeit with the distrust between the two hampering further neoliberalisation.[92] The attitude of the old bourgeoisie to the Syrian revolution seems to have been one of wary vacillation.

As in the previous two cases, class formation at the top of Syrian society is tied into both the degree of autonomy of the state and geopolitical relations. In Syria the connection of state, regime and family (and therefore also sect) was the closest of all our examples.[93] The hard core of securocrats and connected businessmen were drawn from the same community, in a relationship that then cascaded down through the state apparatus. This structure is often ascribed to sectarianism, but the relationship can be said to work the other way: Hafez al-Assad carefully constructed the sharp edge of the state so that his clientele, most often kin and co-religionists, controlled the key positions.[94] Fear of the resentment provoked by this perceived privilege among the Sunni majority would serve to bind the minorities, and particularly the Alawites, to the ruling core even as they suffered the same political repression as other Syrians.[95] This strategy has proved extremely successful.

The pre-2011 Syrian state was of course not a purely Alawite preserve. However, it formed a kind of escape pod for the ruling core: as the uprising spread, the hardliners sloughed off the less loyal parts of the armed forces in particular – some of which went on to become the Free Syrian Army – until only the tougher sectarian nucleus was left.[96] This had the result of shoring up Bashar al-Assad, but also of causing the fracture and retreat of the state itself from many parts of the country.

These dynamics were linked to Rueschemeyer et al.'s final power cluster: the geopolitical conjuncture. Syria experienced particularly severe competition from both the regional and global levels, as the uprising intersected with regional and global new cold wars. Russia, Iran and Iraq backed the Assad regime to the hilt: Saudi Arabia and Qatar fought out their rivalry with each other in the battlefields and halls of the opposition, while sharing an enemy in Iran. The Western powers maintained a rhetorical commitment to the overthrow of Assad – much as he had maintained a rhetorical commitment to anti-imperialism – while remaining wary of dispensing weaponry. This external involvement also increased the sectarian threat to the uprising, as the regime retreated ever more to its non-Sunni rump, with the hardest fighting done by Iraqi and Lebanese Shia militias trained by Iranian Revolutionary Guards.[97] Likewise, Gulf funding flowed to the more conservative Sunni elements.[98] The most isolated and underfunded forces were those who had begun the uprising under the banner of a democratic and secular Syria.

The array of internal and external forces aligned against the Syrian uprising was formidable: it was not matched by organized challenge from a labour movement on the other side. To a greater degree even than in Egypt, any scope for independent rank and file action had been crushed by the time of the uprising. There was no equivalent of Gafsa or Mahalla: strikes or uprisings preceding a broader revolt. Following Bashar's neoliberal reforms, the Syrian trade unions lost even the limited access to the state they had held under Hafez.[99] Left parties were occasionally tolerated where they represented little threat, could be used as a counterweight to Islamists, or (very successfully) incorporated into the "anti-imperialist" regime. In the absence of independent political or economic organization (crushed by the weight with which the regime fell on all elements of civil society), it is unsurprising that little open working class struggle took place in Syria prior to the uprising. The corporatist state unions were used to mobilize shows of support for Bashar al-Assad.[100] Local strikes occurred but nothing on the scale of Tunisia or Egypt.

The class nature of the Syrian revolution was evident in a geographical split. The centres of opposition were mainly provincial centres and small towns (largely Sunni) that suffered the neglect and drought of the 2000s: the revolution encroached on the cities from the countryside, and on the centre of the cities from their destitute peripheries. Where the Syrian state fractured, its collapse was much deeper than in any of the other Arab revolutions but the areas involved were geographically limited. The heart of this self-organization was the Local Co-ordination Committees composed of activists directing demonstrations, in some cases merged with local committees formed to take over state functions, which then constituted higher levels of governance.[101] Parts of Syria saw the first free elections for decades and a degree of popular autonomy perhaps greater than in any other of the Arab revolutions. These bodies sometimes proclaimed social reforms reversing the policies of the Bashar years.[102]

However, this geographic limitation proved a fatal weakness. With no nationwide organization such as the UGTT, the external opposition was fractured into competing groups[103] and the revolution internally was locked into an unavoidable military struggle with the regime,[104] allowing the limited pockets of revolutionary Syria to be crushed from two sources.[105] On the one hand the regime, with the advantage of time and resources from its Iranian and Russian backers, was able to grind out a siege of the liberated areas until morale inevitably collapsed. On the other hand, sectarian forces such as *Da'esh* – opposed by the revolutionaries and ambiguous in its relationship to the regime – took advantage of the power vacuum in the liberated areas to replace Ba'thist authoritarianism with their own even grislier version.

Conclusion

Where does the comparative study of the balance of class forces and class alliances, histories of state autonomy and geopolitical conjunctures lead in the study of state tangents in the wake of the Arab uprisings? Representing as they do extreme and mid-points along a continuum of outcomes of the revolutionary uprisings, examination of these three cases using the approach of *Capitalist Development and Democracy* yields instructive conclusions.

To recapitulate these: "bourgeois" democracy most often accompanies proletarian organizational strength. Tunisia's constitutional settlement does not solely derive from the presence of the UGTT but, as demonstrated above, the organization did play a crucial role. In Syria, by contrast, there was no independent labour organization (despite an impressive previous history) to spread the popular uprising across the territory of the state. Of course, the uprising did spread, especially in the form of sympathy demonstrations for besieged cities: however, these never penetrated central Damascus in particular. Egypt formed a middle case, with an independent union movement playing a strong role in the revolution, but its leadership eventually siding with the *ancien régime* in its struggle with the Muslim Brotherhood.

These differences interacted with degrees of state autonomy and geopolitical interest. The Tunisian state, although not autonomous of capital, certainly had a degree of distance from the ruling clan and a unidirectional relationship with an external power. The Egyptian state, and its core in the armed forces, had an even greater stake in the economy but precisely for that reason a greater need to dispense with the Mubarak clique when they became a liability to the operation of these interests. Syria suffered an unhappy confluence of factors: a greater unity of state, ruling clique and business interests on the one hand and a particularly sharp geopolitical competition over the fate of the country on the other.

Democratic transition theory has sought explanations for the "failure" of the Arab revolutions in the nature of the "transition" negotiations and secular-Islamist but while these may have their part to play, as this article has sought to demonstrate, even the most minimal democratic guarantees are only likely when classes with the least to lose are weak, and those with the most to gain are strong.

Disclosure statement

No potential conflict of interest was reported by the author.

Notes

1. Brownlee et al., "Why the Modest Harvest?" 29.
2. See Schlumberger, "Opening Old Bottles in Search of New Wine"; Salame, *Democracy Without Democrats*; Valbjorn, "Upgrading Post-democratization Studies"; Cavatorta, "The Convergence of Governance"; Cavatorta and Pace, "The Arab Uprisings in Theoretical Perspective."
3. Stepan and Linz, "Democratization Theory," 15, 20–1.
4. O'Donnell and Schmitter, *Transitions from Authoritarian Rule*, 16.
5. Rueschemeyer et al., *Capitalist Development and Democracy*.
6. Teti, "Beyond Lies the Wub," 15.
7. Such as O'Donnell, *Bureaucratic Authoritarianism: Argentina*.
8. Brownlee et al., "Why the Modest Harvest?" 29–31.
9. Rueschemeyer et al., *Capitalist Development and Democracy*, 5–7.
10. Linz and Stepan, *Problems of Democratic Transition*, 2–7; Przeworski, *Democracy and the Market*, 9–12.
11. Przeworski, *Democracy and the Market*, 167–70.
12. Brown, "Egypt's Failed Transition," 52.
13. O'Donnell and Schmitter, *Transitions from Authoritarian Rule*, 16–7.
14. Landolt and Kubicek, "Opportunities and Constraints," 8.
15. Brown, "Egypt's Failed Transition," 51.
16. Stepan and Linz, "Democratization Theory and the Arab Spring," 28.
17. Ibid., 21.
18. Carrothers, "The End of the Transition Paradigm," 5–7.
19. Ibid., 10–12.
20. Ibid., 16.
21. See especially Brown, "Egypt's Failed Transition," 45–56; Landolt and Kubicek, "Opportunities and Constraints," 12–6; Stepan and Linz, "Democratization Theory," 23–7.
22. Stepan, "Tunisia's Transition and the Twin Tolerations," passim.
23. O'Donnell, *Bureaucratic Authoritarianism: Argentina*.
24. See also Therborn, "The Rule of Capital."
25. Rueschemeyer et al., *Capitalist Development and Democracy*, 10.
26. Ibid.
27. Ibid., 7–8.
28. Ibid., 6–8, 75–6.
29. Ibid., 58–9.
30. Ibid.
31. Ibid., 8.
32. Ibid.
33. Ibid., 72.
34. Ibid., 65–6.

35. Ibid., 7.
36. Ibid., 76–7.
37. Ibid., 59.
38. Ibid., 53.
39. Omri, "The Tunisian Constitution."
40. Ibid.
41. Hinnebusch, *Syria: Revolution from Above*, 2–9.
42. Hanieh, *Lineages of Revolt*, 77.
43. Ibid.
44. Ayubi, *Overstating the Arab State*, 355.
45. Achcar, *The People Want*, 92–3.
46. Hanieh, *Lineages of Revolt*, 5–6.
47. Achcar, *The People Want*, 83.
48. Hanieh, *Lineages of Revolt*, 40–1.
49. Ibid., 95.
50. Stepan and Linz, "Democratization Theory," 26; Achcar, *The People Want*, 76–7.
51. Hanieh, *Lineages of Revolt*, 65.
52. Achcar, *The People Want*, 179.
53. Ibid., 75.
54. Hanieh, *Lineages of Revolt*, 40–2.
55. Achcar, *The People Want*, 231.
56. For example Landolt and Kubicek, "Opportunities and Constraints," 8.
57. Ayubi, *Overstating the Arab State*, 211.
58. Ibid., 212–3.
59. Achcar, *The People Want*, 178.
60. Ibid., 180.
61. Torelli, "Tunisia."
62. Hanieh, *Lineages of Revolt*, 87–9.
63. Roccu, "David Harvey in Tahrir Square," 433–4.
64. Roccu, "Gramsci in Cairo," 110.
65. Marshall and Stacher, "Egypt's Generals and Transnational Capital."
66. Springborg, *Mubarak's Egypt*, 213–4.
67. Achcar, *The People Want*, 284–5.
68. Ibid.
69. International Crisis Group, *Lost in Transition*, 16–20.
70. Achcar, *The People Want*, 186–7.
71. Ibid., 228–9.
72. Teti et al., "Sisiphus."
73. Springborg and Henry, *Globalization and the Politics of Development*, 189.
74. Beinin, *The Rise of Egypt's Workers*, 4–5.
75. Beinin, *Workers' Rights in Egypt*, 49.
76. Beinin, "Egyptian Workers After June 30th."
77. Ibid.
78. Roccu, "David Harvey in Tahrir Square," 13–4.
79. El-Shazli, "Where Were the Egyptian Workers?"
80. Neumann, "Suspects into Collaborators."
81. Hinnebusch, *Syria: Revolution from Above*, 31–4.
82. Haddad, *Business Networks in Syria,* chapter 3.
83. Achcar, *The People Want*, 60.
84. Haddad, *Business Networks in Syria*, chapter 3.
85. Ibid.
86. Achcar, *The People Want*, 214.

87. Ibid.
88. Haddad, *Business Networks in Syria*, chapter 3.
89. Ibid.
90. Ibid.
91. Hinnebusch, *Syria: Revolution from Above*, 43.
92. Haddad, *Business Networks in Syria*, chapter 3.
93. Achcar, *The People Want*, 209–10.
94. Owen, *The Rise and Fall of Arab Presidents*, 45.
95. Achcar, *The People Want*, 219–20.
96. Heydemann, "Syria and the Future," 67–70.
97. Holliday, *The Assad Regime*, 10; Heydemann, "Syria and the Future," 69–70.
98. O'Bagy, *Jihad in Syria*, 22.
99. Hinnebusch, *Syria: Revolution from Above*, 112.
100. Naisse, "Al-Burjuwaziya al-Suriya," 93.
101. Gopal, "Welcome to Free Syria."
102. Ibid.
103. O'Bagy, *Syria's Political Opposition*, 13–9.
104. Achcar, *The People Want*, 175.
105. Ibid., 175.

Bibliography

Anderson, Lisa. "Searching Where the Light Shines." *Annual Review of Political Science* 9 (2006): 189–214.

Achcar, Gilbert. *The People Want: A Radical Exploration of the Arab Uprisings*. London: Verso, 2013.

Ayubi, Nazih. *Overstating the Arab State: Politics and Society in the Middle East*. New York: St Martin's Press, 1995.

Beinin, Joel. *Workers' Rights in Egypt*. Washington, DC: AFL-CIO Solidarity Center, 2009.

Beinin, Joel. *The Rise of Egypt's Workers*. Middle East: Carnegie Endowment for International Peace, 2012.

Beinin, Joel. "Egyptian Workers After June 30th." *Middle East Report Online*, August 23, 2013. http://www.merip.org/mero/mero082313

Bilgin, Klara. "Book Review of 'On the State of Egypt: What Made the Revolution Inevitable' by Alaa Al Aswany." *Democratization* 19, no. 1 (2012): 149–152.

Brown, Nathan J. "Egypt's Failed Transition." *Journal of Democracy* 24, no. 4 (2013): 45–58.

Brownlee, Jason, Tarek Masoud, and Andrew Reynolds. "Why the Modest Harvest?" *Journal of Democracy* 24, no. 4 (2013): 29–44.

Brynen, Rex, Peter W. Moore, Bassel F. Salloukh, and Marie-Joelle Zahar. *Beyond the Arab Spring: Authoritarianism and Democratization in the Arab World*. Boulder: Lynne Reiner, 2012.

Carrothers, Thomas. "The End of the Transition Paradigm." *Journal of Democracy* 13, no. 1 (2002): 5–21.

Cavatorta, Francesco. "The Convergence of Governance: Upgrading Authoritarianism in the Arab World and Downgrading Democracy Elsewhere?" *Middle East Critique* 19, no. 3 (2010): 217–232.

Cavatorta, Francesco, and Michelle Pace. "The Arab Uprisings in Theoretical Perspective – An Introduction." *Mediterranean Politics* 17, no. 2 (2012): 125–138.

Eley, Geoff. *Forging Democracy: The History of the Left in Europe 1850–2000*. Oxford: Oxford University Press, 2002.

El-Shazli, Heba. "Where Were the Egyptian Workers in the June 2013 People's Coup Revolution?" *Jadaliyya*, June 2013 http://www.jadaliyya.com/pages/index/13125/where-were-the-egyptian-workers-in-the-june-2013-p

Fradkin, Hillel. "Arab Democracy or Islamist Revolution." *Journal of Democracy* 24, no. 1 (2013): 6–13.

Gopal, Anand. "Welcome to Free Syria." *Harpers Magazine*, August 2012. http://harpers.org/archive/2012/08/welcome-to-free-syria/

Haddad, Bassam. *Business Networks in Syria: The Political Economy of Authoritarian Resilience*. Kindle Electronic ed. Stanford: Stanford University Press, 2012.

Hanieh, Adam. *Lineages of Revolt: Issues of Contemporary Capitalism in the Middle East*. Chicago: Haymarket, 2013.

Heydemann, Steven. "Syria and the Future of Authoritarianism." *Journal of Democracy* 24, no. 4 (2013): 59–73.

Hinnebusch, Raymond. *Syria: Revolution from Above*. London: Routledge, 2001.

Holliday, Joseph. *The Assad Regime*. Washington, DC: Institute for the Study of War, 2013.

International Crisis Group. *Lost in Transition: The World According to Egypt's SCAF*. Middle East/North Africa Report, 24 April, 2012, http://www.crisisgroup.org/en/regions/middle-east-north-africa/egypt-syria-lebanon/egypt/121-lost-in-transition-the-world-according-to-egypts-scaf.aspx

Landolt, Laura K., and Paul Kubicek. "Opportunities and Constraints: Comparing Tunisia and Egypt to the Coloured Revolutions." *Democratization* 21, no. 6 (2014): 984–1006.

Linz, Juan, and Alfred Stepan. *Problems of Democratic Transition and Consolidation: Southern Europe, South America, and Post-Communist Europe*. Baltimore: Johns Hopkins University Press, 1996.

Marshall, Shana, and Joshua Stacher. "Egypt's Generals and Transnational Capital." *Middle East Report*, 262, 2012. http://www.merip.org/mer/mer262/egypts-generals-transnational-capital

Naisse, Ghayath. "Al-Burjuwaziya al-Suriya Wa-l-thawra Al-sha"abiya [The Syrian Bourgeoisie and the Popular Revolution." *Al-Thawra Al-Da'ima [Permanent Revolution]* 4, 2013.

Neumann, Peter. "Suspects into Collaborators." *London Review of Books*, 3rd of April 2014 http://www.lrb.co.uk/v36/n07/peter-neumann/suspects-into-collaborators

O'Bagy, Elizabeth. *Jihad in Syria*. Washington, DC: Institute for the Study of War, 2012.

O'Bagy, Elizabeth. *Syria's Political Opposition*. Washington, DC: Institute for the Study of War, 2012.

O'Donnell, Guillermo. *Bureaucratic Authoritarianism: Argentina 1966–1973 in Comparative Perspective*. Berkeley: University of California Press, 1988.

O'Donnell, Guillermo, and Philippe C. Schmitter. *Transitions from Authoritarian Rule: Tentative Conclusions About Uncertain Democracies*. 2nd ed., 4 vols. Baltimore: Johns Hopkins University Press, 2013.

Omri, Mohamed-Salah. "The Tunisian Constitution: The Process and the Outcome." *Jadaliyya*, 2014 http://www.jadaliyya.com/pages/index/16416/the-tunisian-constitution_the-process-and-the-outc.

Owen, Roger. *The Rise and Fall of Arab Presidents for Life*. London: Harvard University Press, 2012.

Przeworski, Adam. *Democracy and the Market: Political and Economic Reforms in Eastern Europe and Latin America.* Cambridge: Cambridge University Press, 1991.

Roccu, Roberto. "Gramsci in Cairo: Neoliberal Authoritarianism, Passive Revolution and Failed Hegemony in Egypt Under Mubarak, 1991–2010." PhD London School of Economics, 2011.

Roccu, Roberto. "David Harvey in Tahrir Square: The Dispossessed, the Discontented, and the Egyptian Revolution." *Third World Quarterly* 34, no. 3 (2013): 423–440.

Roy, Olivier. "The Transformation of the Arab World." *Journal of Democracy* 23, no. 3 (2012): 5–18.

Rueschemeyer, Dietrich, Evelyne Huber Stephens, and John D. Stephens. *Capitalist Development and Democracy.* Cambridge: Polity Press, 1992.

Salame, Ghassan. *Democracy Without Democrats: The Renewal of Politics in the Arab World.* London: IB Tauris, 1994.

Schlumberger, Oliver. "Opening Old Bottles in Search of New Wine: On Nondemocratic Legitimacy In the Middle East." *Middle East Critique* 19, no. 23 (2010): 233–250.

Springborg, Robert. *Mubarak's Egypt: The Fragmentation of Political Order.* Boulder: Westview Press, 1989.

Springborg, Robert, and Clement Moore Henry. *Globalization and the Politics of Development in the Middle East.* 2nd ed. Cambridge: Cambridge University Press, 2010.

Stepan, Alfred. "Tunisia's Transition and the Twin Tolerations." *Journal of Democracy* 23, no. 2 (2012): 89–103.

Stepan, Alfred, and Juan J. Linz. "Democratization Theory and the Arab Spring." *Journal of Democracy* 24, no. 2 (2013): 15–30.

Teti, Andrea. "Beyond Lies the Wub: The Challenges of (Post)Democratization." *Middle East Critique* 21, no. 1 (2012): 5–24.

Teti, Andrea, Vivienne Matthies-Boon, and Gennaro Gervasio. "Sisiphus." *Middle East Report Online* 10th of June 2014, http://www.merip.org/mero/mero061014

Therborn, Goran. "The Rule of Capital and the Rise of Democracy." *New Left Review* I, no. 103 (1980). http://newleftreview.org/I/103/goran-therborn-the-rule-of-capital-and-the-rise-of-democracy

Torelli, Stefano Maria. "Tunisia: A New Prime Minister for Old Politics?" *Jadaliya* 25th of December 2013. http://www.jadaliyya.com/pages/index/15720/tunisia_a-new-prime-minister-for-old-politics

Valbjorn, Morten. "Upgrading Post-democratization Studies: Examining a Re-politicized Arab World in a Transition to Somewhere." *Middle East Critique* 21, no. 1 (2012): 25–35.

Valbjorn, Morten, and Andre Bank. "Examining the 'Post' in Post-Democratization: The Future of Middle Eastern Political Rule Through Lenses of the Past." *Middle East Critique* 19, no. 3 (2010): 183–200.

Way, Lucan. "The Lessons of 1989." *Journal of Democracy* 22, no. 4 (2013): 17–27.

Back to the future: the Arab uprisings and state (re)formation in the Arab world

Adham Saouli

School of International Relations, University of St Andrews, St Andrews, Scotland, UK

> This article contributes to debates that aim to go beyond the "democratization" and "post-democratization" paradigms to understand change and continuity in Arab politics. In tune with calls to focus on the actualities of political dynamics, the article shows that the literatures on State Formation and Contentious Politics provide useful theoretical tools to understand change/continuity in Arab politics. It does so by examining the impact of the latest Arab uprisings on state formation trajectories in Iraq and Syria. The uprisings have aggravated a process of regime erosion – which originated in post-colonial state-building attempts – by mobilizing sectarian and ethnic identities and exposing the counties to geo-political rivalries and intervention, giving rise to trans-border movements, such as ISIS. The resulting state fragmentation has obstructed democratic transition in Syria and constrained its consolidation in Iraq.

This study examines the impact of the Arab uprisings on state formation in the Arab world, with emphasis on Iraq and Syria. I argue that the uprisings have exacerbated a process of state fragmentation, which has roots in long-term state-building processes in the postcolonial era. In this process, the ability of regimes to monopolize power domestically was eroding and the states' immunity against external penetration was waning. In Syria and Iraq, the uprisings had two direct impacts. First, they accelerated sectarian and ethnic mobilization, which was latent under the ideological hegemony of Arab nationalism, but had gradually became salient, especially after the fall of Saddam Hussein in 2003 and the uprising in Syria in 2011. This not only sharply increased long-standing challenges to the monopoly of power by ruling regimes, but also has contributed to state disintegration and blocked attempts to reform their political systems. Secondly, they accentuated Iraq and Syria's vulnerability to external penetration by rival regional powers, making state reformation even more difficult.

The article is divided into two main sections. Theoretically, I argue that an understanding of political change and continuity in the Arab world requires moving beyond the "democratization" and "post-democratization" frameworks. Following calls to refocus scholarly attention on the actualities of political dynamics, in the first section, I argue that an examination of state formation and the contentious politics that punctuate this process provide useful avenues to understand political change and continuity in the Arab world. Bringing in the state formation literature provides historical depth to current political upheavals in the Middle East, such as the Arab uprisings. By focusing on trajectories of state formation in varying contexts, we examine how state-building attempts engender anti-regime political mobilization, creating contentious politics. Contentious politics activate latent identities, mobilize passive populations, and give rise to new ideologies and actors, creating opportunities for political change, of which democratization is only one possibility. Whilst I argue that an understanding of the socio-political conditions that could facilitate or obstruct democratization is socially important, we should not allow this to determine or distort our analysis of politics in the region.

In the second section I present an empirical analysis on the impact of the Arab uprisings on Iraqi and Syrian state formation. First, I analyse how the post-colonial state-building processes in Iraq and Syria contributed to regime erosion. This will set the historical context to then examine the impact of the current uprisings on each of the two cases. I conclude the study by assessing the conditions that could facilitate or hinder democratization in Iraq and Syria.

Political change, continuity and development in the Arab world

Before and beyond democratization and authoritarian resilience

Attempts to understand political change and continuity in the Middle East have centred on two intersecting questions: First, how do we explain the absence of democracy in the Arab world? Second, how do we explain regime resilience in the region? Whilst the answer to the latter question should provide insights to the former, the two waves of literatures that contributed frameworks to answer these questions remained analytically divorced. The first, which emerged in the 1990s, focused on Arab states' resistance to the "third wave" democratizations, continuing a legacy initiated by modernization theories of the 1950s and 1960s.[1] The absences of a civil society, a strong bourgeoisie, democratic political culture or democratic interlocutors were all advanced as explanations for the absence of democracy in the region[2]. However, disenchanted by the faltering hope of political change in the region scholars moved to a "post-democratization" paradigm that examined "*how* political rule in the Arab countries is effectuated, organized, and executed" to generate stability and regime survival.[3]

AFTER THE ARAB UPRISINGS

Then came the Arab uprisings in 2010/11. Two ostensibly entrenched authoritarian leaders (Bin Ali of Tunisia and Mubarak of Egypt) were toppled in a matter of few weeks, triggering a wave of uprisings in other Arab countries. Academic responses to the uprisings reflected the two dominating paradigms. Some regional experts argued that a focus on the "myth of authoritarian stability" had missed the underlying factors that caused the winds of change.[4] However, with the return of the military to power in Egyptian politics, emergence of civil wars in Syria, Libya, Iraq and Yemen, constrained transition in Tunisia, and regime survival in Morocco, Jordan and the Gulf, others observed continuities in Arab politics.[5]

Nevertheless, despite the greater pace, intensity, and innovations in political protest, the latest uprisings do not represent a total break with previous forms of political contention in the Arab world. For example in 2005, Beirut was engulfed by Midan al-Tahrir-like protests, framed as a "Cedar Revolution" after the assassination of Lebanon's Prime Minister Rafic Hariri. The ousting of Muammar al-Qaddafi in 2011 – a combination of accumulated domestic opposition and external military intervention – is, to a degree, similar to the ousting of Saddam Hussein in 2003. In Egypt, the toppling of Mubarak in 2011, which paved the way for the election of the Muslim Brotherhood, which in turn led to a deep political polarization in Egypt providing the opportunity for the military to return to the political arena, is comparable to the elections of the Islamists in Algeria; there the refusal of the army to surrender to the ballot boxes triggered a civil war of the 1990s. A comparison between the current civil war in Syria and the Baathist-Muslim Brotherhood bloody struggle of 1978–1982 reveals similar processes, albeit with different outcomes. In each case the main political contention was between entrenched and ostensibly secular regimes and an Islamist opposition.

Hence, it should not come as a surprise that scholarly responses to the uprisings have fluctuated between explanations of change and continuity. However, the analytical link between political change and continuity in Arab politics remains to be established. One reason for the absence of such an analytical link is the democracy factor. This factor has framed and in some cases determined how we think about political change in the Arab world. In searching for the "absence of democracy", scholarly attention has been diverted away from developing methods, concepts and theories to understand how politics actually works.[6] The call for a "post-democratization" paradigm may have contributed to bring politics back in to the analysis; however, its focus on regime resilience comes at the expense of missing interesting forms of resistance against domination, and hence an understandings of potential originators of change.[7] An examination of the "genealogy of resistance",[8] for example the politicization, rise and development of Shi'a political Islam in opposition to Baathist domination in Iraq, could be very useful to understand and explain strategies of regime adaptation, state reformation or political change in contemporary Iraq.

Moving beyond democratization and post-democratization requires the settling of two issues. First, there is a need to move one step back to analyse politics as a domain of domination and resistance that, especially in the Arab world, takes place in processes of state making and unmaking in varying political contexts.[9] This involves a "return to the classic question about what politics is and what are the relevant political fields and actors".[10]

Second, it is important to free political analysis from normative frames, while recognizing that normative concerns continue to shape societies' interests in the political world. Political analysis cannot be indifferent to many Arabs' resistance to the violence, injustice and corruption of authoritarianism,[11] and understanding its causes and the conditions for democratic transition are socially important – not only for a Western audience of American political science, donors or policy-makers.[12] However, answers to this normative goal would first require an understanding of the political world.

Bringing politics back in: state formation and contentious politics

In this section, I will argue that a focus on state formation/deformation processes and the contentious politics they generate offers two main advantages in understanding political change in the Arab world. First, it contributes to the identification of the underlying struggles that gives politics its shape and direction. Despite the *varying* paths to state formation, the *direction* of the process is universally similar: a drive to centralize (especially coercive) power as a pre-requisite to institutionalize order and to facilitate socio-economic development. Second, this drive almost always generates resistance by dissatisfied challengers, spawning contentious politics. I start by sketching the state formation process.

The collapse of the Ottoman Empire led to the emergence of political boundaries (initially envisioned as European spheres of influence). Unlike European state formation processes, boundaries in the Arab world came *before* states and constituted the social environments within which states could form, deform or develop. State formation pits regimes against their challengers in struggles aiming to dominate three analytically separate but interrelated domains of social life: the *coercive*, the *ideological*, and the *socio-economic*.[13]

By monopolizing coercion (control over the tools of violence such as the police, security, army, courts) an actor prevents its rivals from similar tools of violence that would otherwise threaten it. Starting in the 1950s in republics such as Egypt, Iraq, Syria, Yemen or Libya, we observe a varying but steady process of increasing domination by the army over political life, usually at the expense of other social and political forces.[14] In monarchical regimes, such as Jordan or Saudi Arabia, royal families directly monopolized coercion. Secondly, depending on the cultural composition of a society, regimes articulated relevant ideologies to legitimize their rule and dominate the ideological sphere. In Saudi Arabia, King Abdel Aziz used a Wahhabi interpretation of Islam to help overcome tribal and regional divisions in the nascent kingdom; it then became the state ideology. Populist regimes (Egypt, Iraq, Syria, Yemen) of the 1950s and 1960s championed ideas of Arab Nationalism, socialism, anti-colonialism and national independence, delegitimizing the rule of their predecessors and repressing competing frameworks, such as Islamism. The Arab uprisings have shown that the ideological sphere continues to be an area of contention among Islamists, nationalists and, increasingly, sub-state sectarian communities. Finally, controlling the economic sphere was essential to state formation. Whilst tax-collection in European state formation was crucial for kings to wage war and suppress internal rivals,[15] in the Middle East rent from natural resources or external patrons has been essential to augment the co-optative power of regimes in oil-rich monarchies or strategically located states, such as Jordan. In populist republics of the 1950s and 1960s, redistribution from state-led development (agrarian reform, industrialization, import-substitution) became comparable vehicles for co-optation needed for regime survival.

Successful domination over the coercive, economic and ideological spheres gave rise to political regimes[16] of varying types. But these were far from consolidated "states", understood here as institutions (set of norms, rules and practices) that regulate but stand above political struggles and actors. In early state formation, a regime is *one* dominant group ruling over others in a particular jurisdiction. As Max Weber argues: "Like the political institutions historically preceding it the state is a relation of men dominating men, a relation supported by means of legitimate (i.e. considered to be legitimate) violence".[17] While a certain co-optation of social forces in rentier monarchies and populist republics was necessary for regime survival,[18] this was far from being fully *politically* inclusive, as facilitated by competitive elections allowing participation by all social forces. The limits of inclusion made the Arab state vulnerable, not only to political shocks (such as the Arab uprisings) but also to external infiltration.[19] The drive for regime survival engenders resistance against such attempted domination. Resistance forces seek to *de-monopolise* a regime's grip over the above-mentioned three spheres by offering competing ideologies, economic strategies and, in certain cases, armed resistance; thus, oppositional forces create the basis for *alternative* regimes.

Whilst state formation provides a generic framework that highlights a regime's drive for domination and an opposition's resistance, this struggle is punctuated by periods of what students of social movements call Contentious Politics (CP):

> episodic, public, collective interaction among makers of claims and their objects when (a) at least one government is a claimant, an object of claims, or a party to the claims and (b) the claims would, if realized, affect the interests of a least one of the claimants.[20]

The CP research agenda raises key questions and provides interesting conceptual tools to understand political change, continuity and democratization in the Arab world: When and under what conditions do passive populations collectively *mobilize* for change? How and why does an *opportunity* become visible for regime contenders? What kind of *frames* do the contenders *construct* as they struggle for power? What effects would this contention have on identity?

Departing from state formation and CP, the latest Arab uprisings appear an episode of collective interaction that pitted previously passive populations against regimes under varying socio-political conditions. By presenting alternative socio-political visions (democracy, Islamism, freedom, pluralism), contenders challenged the incumbent regimes' monopoly over the ideological sphere, whilst attempting to engage and mobilize the latent public.[21] For example, the Midan al-Tahrir Square collective action was a site of political protest that challenged Mubarak's monopoly over the national narrative, whilst seeking to mobilize the public for change; it did so by imagining and promising an alternative society.[22]

The uprisings opened an opportunity for change, but whether the opportunity would be realized or not is a different question. What contenders perceive as an opportunity, which is "an activating mechanism responsible in part for the mobilization of previously inert populations",[23] regimes and their supporters perceive as a threat. To delegitimize antagonists, regimes engage in framing processes, accusing the latter of being "terrorists", "agents of foreign states" or "instigators of instability". In heterogeneous societies, such as Iraq or Syria, interactive framings can activate or aggravate identity divides; this occurs when "political entrepreneurs draw together credible stories from available cultural materials, similarly create we–they boundaries, activate both stories and boundaries as a function of current political circumstances, and manoeuvre to suppress competing models".[24]

Contentious politics also involves collective violent campaigns that defy a regime's capacity to monopolize coercion. When this occurs, it provides the space for contenders to establish new forms of authority: establish order (monopolizing coercion in "liberated areas"), institutionalize courts, capture sites of economic significance, raise new flags and protect the "boundaries" of the areas they occupy. Regime's and "counter-regimes" engage in rival projects of state formation.[25] Contentious politics, however, need not always be about state (re)formation; I analytically connect state formation to CP because most Arab states remain prone to reconstruction, and contentious politics are integral to this process. The Arab uprisings are an episode of intense struggle between regimes and their contenders; but the quantitative *change* in intensity of the struggle, its visibility, and the emergence of new actors, claims and forms of political mobilization should not conceal the qualitative *continuity* of the struggle from the pre-uprising period.

But what does the examination of state formation and contentious politics imply for the democratization debate? Contentious politics, which in the Arab world is directly linked to state formation/reformation, is a necessary but not sufficient condition for democratization. Necessary because contentious politics reflect periods of intense struggles between regimes and their rivals, juxtaposing opposing socio-political claims and generating conditions for political change, including democratization. However, as the cases of Syria and Iraq will illustrate, there are several variables that can intervene between contentious politics and democratization. Such variables include, but need not be limited to, sectarian and ethnic fragmentation, the internalization of external geopolitical rivalry, and collective violence, which not only constrain democratization but also threaten to fragment the state as a territorial entity.

Back to the future: the Arab uprisings and state (re)formation in Iraq and Syria

State-building and regime erosion in Iraq (1968–2003) and Syria (1963–2011)

The state formation process in Iraq and Syria – the attempt by Arab nationalist regimes to attain political independence, socio-economic development and nation-building – since the 1960s fomented the seeds of *regime erosion*, returning these states to square one of state formation half a century later.[26] Regime erosion can be attributed to three interrelated trajectories that had varying effects on the two cases: (1) intra-regime and regime-opposition struggles for domination led to the monopolization of power in the hands of a few and to mass political exclusion; (2) to reproduce their domination at the state level, regimes resorted to kinship ties, contributing – intentionally or unintentionally – to the activation and reproduction of identity divides within their societies, divides which political contenders utilized for political mobilization; and (3) because of political exclusion and the activation of identity divides, regimes and the territorial states in which they dominate became more vulnerable to unanticipated shocks (such as the Arab uprisings) and external penetration, which aggravated regime erosion and state disintegration.

First, colonial divisions of the region and later colonial domination in Iraq and Syria gave rise to various political ideologies (Arab Nationalist, Baathist, Communist, Nationalist, Islamist), seeking liberation, economic development and, for Arab Nationalists, Arab political union. These views reflected the socio-political grievances of the time, and contradicted the interests of the ruling elites. But the absence of democratic means that could channel these socio-political grievances transformed the military, which began to be infiltrated by these ideologies into a vehicle of political change. Whilst the military began to infiltrate the political realm as early as 1936 in Iraq and 1949 in Syria, two military coups in 1958 (Iraq) and 1963 (Syria) would trigger state formation processes and have lasting effects on both countries. The coups, which brought coalitions of revolutionary forces to power, initiated an intra-coalition elimination contest: first between Baathists and their Arab Nationalist, Communist and nationalist foes; and second among the Baathists when they reached power in Iraq (1968) and Syria (1963). The elimination contests among Baathists culminated in the emergence of the narrowly based regimes of Saddam Hussein in Iraq (indirectly since 1968 and directly since 1979) and Hafez Assad in Syria (1970). In these processes, political foes were purged, detained and killed, laying the foundations of authoritarian regimes where the monopoly over the use of violence determined the patterns of other social, economic and judicial spheres.[27]

To maintain a monopoly over coercion, Assad and Hussein designed in-built protection against military coups by diversifying military, security and intelligence agencies and creating paramilitaries. The monopoly over coercion facilitated the domination of the ideological level. Baathist ideology, as interpreted by the wielders of coercive power, became the state ideology: first through the "Baathification" of the military and then of society through education, party socialization and the media. Alternative ideologies were excluded or suppressed. At socio-economic levels, both regimes attempted, either through agrarian reforms (Syria) or through oil rent (Iraq), to include previously marginal social forces in state-driven developments. Departing from his predecessor's socialist and minoritarian regime, Assad also integrated members of Sunni bourgeoisie from Damascus and Aleppo, giving them important political posts in the party and government; he, however, maintained a monopoly over security, military and foreign policy decisions.[28]

In both cases, political exclusion had adverse effects on state-building; the political system did not offer opportunities for accountability, especially of regime figures whose presence was crucial for regime survival.[29] As such, political exclusion eroded the regimes' socio-political ties with society. Whilst both regimes did not lose total support, political exclusion and repression and elite corruption eroded their legitimacy, and formed the basis for political mobilization when opportunities emerged (such as the 1978–1982 Islamic rebellion in Syria or the 1991 uprising in Iraq).

Second, ideological and personal rivalries within the Baath party, coupled with the struggle to monopolize coercive power, gave rise to the issue of political trust. In both cases, Baathist ideology and the political party ceased to form the political cement required to tie regimes together. Ideological erosion was countered by a reactivation of tribal and sectarian ties. Each regime attempted to install kin in key positions of party and state – in particular its coercive agencies. Under Saddam Hussein, the process starts with the "Tikitization" of the Baath in the early 1970s and culminates in direct family rule by the late 1990s.[30] In Syria, the intra-regime struggles among Baathists began to take a sectarian dimension when Salah Jadid purged first several Sunni officers and then Ismaili and Druze comrades. In the last round, Assad and Jadid remained as the last Alawi Baathist leaders, before Assad's "Corrective Revolution" overthrew Jadid. Under Assad, key security, intelligence and military posts were primarily allocated to trusted Alawi officers.[31]

This process eroded regimes' alienation from and legitimacy in society. In Iraq, the Baathification and Tikritization of the state not only alienated contenders within the Sunni community, but also gradually contributed to the demarcation of sectarian – Sunni-Shi'a – cleavages and exacerbated ethnic – Arab-Kurdish – boundaries. Fearing a Shi'a rebellion in the 1970s, Saddam Hussein initiated a repressive campaign against all expressions of Shi'a religious and political contention, reinforcing Shi'a perception of marginalization. But the activation of sectarian boundaries is not a one-way road, generated only by regime actions; in Iraq it was also stimulated by the increasing political consciousness of Iraqi Shi'as. The emergence of the Islamist Dawa Party in 1958, which initially came as a response to the Communist ideological challenge, formed an early expression of this consciousness. By the late 1970s, the Dawa's ability to mobilize the Shi'as community against the Baath formed a significant threat to Saddam Hussein.[32] The identity divides separating the Iraqi Arabs from the Kurds started earlier and was aggravated by the failure of successive Iraqi regimes to accept Kurdish cultural and regional autonomy.[33] In the 1990s, Iraqi Kurds began to enjoy de facto autonomy before, as we shall see below, this became constitutional in 2005.

In Syria, Assad faced an Islamic rebellion culminating in civil war in 1978–1982.[34] This civil war and the regime's attack on the Sunni bastion of Hama, which killed thousands, in 1982 reinforced sectarian divisions and perceptions within Syria, undermined the regime's secular ideology and gave regime contenders the opportunity to frame it as sectarian and Alawite. To be sure, the presence of heterogeneous society, made up of various sectarian and ethnic communities, as that of Iraq and Syria, does not in itself *cause* sectarian divisions, nor does it imply that the conflict is purely cultural; but a heterogeneous society provides the cultural material for political contenders to frame the conflict in cultural terms in order to mobilize support. The Islamists targeting of Alawite officers, as in the Aleppo's artillery school 1979, and the discourse employed, which framed the regime in sectarian terms, activated identity divides in this contentious episode.[35] In this case – unlike after 2011 – the sectarian cleavage was muted by the fact that the largely Sunni peasantry remained in the regime coalition, co-opted by Baathist agrarian reforms[36].

Thirdly, the combination of domestic political exclusion and identity divides exposed Iraq and Syria to external infiltration. The strategic location of both states, in the Arab-Israeli conflict region (Syria) and the heart of the Middle East (Iraq), has meant that domestic rivalries become integral to the regional (and international) balance of power. In the state formation process, the fear of external subversion exacerbated the drive to monopolize power domestically.[37] Regimes and their contenders perceived regional developments as opportunities or threats to alter and maintain the domestic power balance. For example, the Syrian civil war in 1978–1982 cannot be divorced from Egypt's pressure on Assad after ties between the two states soured in the wake of the Camp David agreements. The Islamists perceived this as an opportunity to topple Assad; but it also increased the regime drive to maintain power.[38]

Similarly, the 1991 uprising in the southern provinces of Iraq came with the perception of (and promise made by the US to) the Shi'as of Iraq that Hussein's regime would be toppled. However, during that uprising, Hussein capitalized on the regional and international decision to keep him in power to crush the uprising. Saddam Hussein framed the uprisings as an Iranian conspiracy aiming to transform Iraq into an Islamic state. The repression of the uprising, however, ingrained sectarian and ethnic boundaries in the country.[39]

The Arab uprisings and state formation in Iraq and Syria, 2011–2014

It is in the context of the state formation trajectories examined above that we can understand the impact of the uprisings on Iraq and Syria. In the eyes of the Syrian and Iraqi opposition groups, the "Arab Spring" presented an opportunity to readdress the Iraqi balance of power, which emerged in 2003, and to reform or overthrow the Syrian regime. The effects of the uprisings on Iraq and Syria, however, vary.

When the uprisings erupted in 2010/11, Iraq had already established regime change and inaugurated a proto-democratic experiment. Contrary to the 1991 uprisings which failed to materialize in regime change, in 2003 the interests of the Iraqi opposition, especially Kurdish and Shi'a organizations, converged with the US's strategy to topple Saddam Hussein. The removal of Hussein from power paved the way for the Iraqi opposition to initiate a new political regime centred on the two main Kurdish movements, the Kurdish Democratic Party and Popular Union of Kurdistan, and Shi'a movements, al-Dawa, the Sadr Movement, the Supreme Islamic Council in Iraq and, to a lesser extent, the Sunni Iraqi Islamic Party. A new constitution was ratified, satisfying the aspirations of the Kurdish movement, guaranteeing cultural and administrative autonomy and federal democracy in Iraq; the new order also brought the Shi'a to the heart of the political system, making them the dominant actor in the new state-building process. A series of largely fair national elections in January and December 2005 and 2010 consolidated the new political arrangement and demarcated the sectarian and ethnic political map of the country.[40] What emerged, though not formally presented as such, was a form of consociational democracy, which, theoretically at least, accepted the presence of political, religious and ethnic communities. As in Lebanon, the apportionment of posts in the state aimed to represent and incorporate the main communities of the country: the Shi'as took the executive prime minister post, the presidency was given to the Kurds, and house speaker to the Sunnis.

But this state-building process was fraught with domestic and external problems. Domestically, not all Sunni factions accepted the new political order. In opposition to the US occupation, to increasing Iranian influence, and to Shi'a and Kurdish political dominance, many Sunnis, with some exceptions, refused to legitimize the new regime.[41] Shi'a forces filled the main offices of the state and used state resources to augment their social bases and to blackmail and repress their political opponents. This increased Sunnis' perception of marginalization. The US decision to dismantle the army and the "De-Baathification" programme left hundreds of thousands, of whom many were Sunnis, jobless. This further weakened regime legitimacy in Sunni governorates, especially Anbar and Salaheddine.[42]

Resistance to the new form of domination and the US-led occupation began to turn both political and violent as early as 2004. Violent resistance targeted the rebuilding of security and military institutions, with concentrated attacks on recruitment centres and the occupying forces. Sunni resistance provided the opportunity for former Baathists and Saddamists, Sunni tribal forces and Islamists, especially Al Qaeda related organizations, to capitalize on Sunni marginalization to advance their political goals.[43] This resistance, in turn, reinforced the Shi'a drive to monopolize power. The Shi'as fear of a reversal of the state-building process and Sunni perception of marginalization entrenched the Shi'a-Sunni divide.

The post-2003 Iraqi state-building process intersected with regional geopolitical rivalries. Syria, which aimed to destabilize and deter US control in Iraq, hosted former Baathists and facilitated the transfer of Islamist jihadists to Iraq.[44] For Al Qaeda's Iraqi version, the Islamic State of Iraq (ISI)-the original version of the Islamic State of Iraq and Syria (ISIS)-Iraqi state failure provided opportunities to fight the US, the Shi'as, which were targeted by suicide bombers, and Iran, and to establish a "caliphate". Faced with the threat of regime change, Iraqi military and security forces in collaboration with Shi'a militias in turn sought to repress Sunni Islamist militants and cleanse Sunnis of certain areas of Baghdad, thereby further marginalizing the community. By 2007, Iraq was facing a sectarian civil war. For Sunnis, the new regime intended to repress them, impose a Shi'a-dominated system, and provide Iran with greater influence; thus challenging Iraq's Arab identity. For Shi'as, many Sunnis are intent on reversing the nascent democratic system, paving the way for the return of the Baath and legitimizing Al Qaeda attacks on Shi'as. These mutual interpretations not only weakened the democratic experience in Iraq, but also eroded the capacity and legitimacy of the new regime in Sunni areas of Iraq.

It is against this background that the Arab uprisings began to impact Iraq in 2011. In 2011, the US withdrew most of its troops from Iraq. US occupation had, in varying degrees, constrained the behaviour of Iraqi political forces. However, American withdrawal juxtaposed Iraqi communities, with their varying visions of the country, against one another. In a drive to monopolize coercive power in the state, Prime Minister Nuri al-Maliki of the Dawa Party clashed with both Shi'a and Sunni militias; in his drive to centralize power he installed his own supporters in the state, including family members, overriding official institutions.[45] Maliki's confrontation with Sunni politicians, such as Tarek Hashemi, Rafi al-Issawi and Saleh al-Mutlak, who accepted the political process but aimed to curb Maliki's power and sought greater Sunni incorporation, diminished the remaining Iraqi government channels to the Sunni community.

The first impact of the Arab uprisings, and the geopolitical rivalries they engendered, was to exacerbate Iraq's sectarian and ethnic divisions. In March 2011, the tide of the Arab uprisings reached Syria and assumed a sectarian dimension by 2012. The rise of sectarian discourse in the region and the emergence of ostensibly sectarian camps, with Iran, the Syrian regime, and Hizbullah on the one hand, and Turkey, Qatar and Saudi Arabia on the other hand came to directly affect Iraq, which became an arena for regional rivalries. Saudi Arabia and Turkey capitalized on Sunni disenchantment within Iraq to weaken the Shi'a-dominated regime and to curb Iran's influence in the region. This aggravated Shi'a worries and led al-Maliki's government to transform its previous enmity against Assad into support for his survival; Shi'as feared that the coming of a "Sunni" regime in Syria would empower Iraqi Sunnis and weaken, if not topple, the newly established Shi'a-dominated regime in Iraq. The Iraqi government's support of Assad heightened the domestic Sunni-Shi'a divisions. Many Iraqi Sunnis supported the Syrian rebellion against Assad, connecting their own grievances to that of their Syrian coreligionists.[46] By 2012, Iraqi Sunnis of Anbar and other Sunni regions began protests calling for an end to "Sunni marginalization", release of detainees and for Maliki to step down. Dismissing the uprisings as an "external conspiracy", Maliki failed to accommodate the demands of the protestors who began to garner support from Sunni MPs and politicians.[47]

Exploiting the Sunni uprising and regime erosion in Sunni areas, ISIS and former Baathists began to occupy areas of western and northern Iraq. In early June 2014, Mosul fell to ISIS and, by the end of the month, the Al Qaeda breakaway declared its "Islamic State" on a wide swath of territories ranging from the east of Aleppo in Syria to the Sunni-majority regions, including Anbar, Ninenevah and Mosul in Iraq.[48] The quick collapse of the Iraqi army in these Sunni areas exposed its weak legitimacy.[49] Indicative of the sectarian framing encouraged by rival regional powers, when Mosul fell to ISIS, Saudi Arabia considered it to be a "revolution" by Sunnis who were frustrated by Maliki's rule.[50]

The occupation of most of the Sunni areas by the Islamic State led Mazuud Barazani to exploit the Iraqi army's weakness to occupy the oil-rich and contested territory of Kirkuk. Barazani then announced that the Iraqi political process had failed and conditions for Kurdish statehood had emerged.[51] By August 2014, the state-building process in Iraq and the impact of the Arab uprisings did not only besiege democratic consolidation, as will be argued in the conclusion, but also threatened the disintegration of Iraq as a state.

Compared to Iraq, the Arab uprisings had a more damaging effect on Syria. The coming of Bashar Assad to power in 2000 reflected a continuation of the regime his father had established in Syria. Despite the favourable external opportunities (after the 2006 Lebanon war, which increased regime legitimacy; the Saudi opening to Syria in 2008; improved relations with Turkey and France), Bashar al-Assad failed to create a more politically inclusive regime. This failure made his regime, and in consequence Syria's territorial integrity, vulnerable to the Arab uprisings, which reached Syria in March 2011. Within a few weeks, the realm of politics, which was concentrated in a few hands, and which contained and repressed any attempts to promote alternative political visions, opened widely for numerous political actors that rose to challenge Assad's rule. In this contentious episode, we observe both a continuation of and innovation in regime-society contention.

Initially, Syrian protestors consciously avoided any sectarian or ethnic slogans that might alienate Syria's minorities and that the regime could use to delegitimize the opposition. The peaceful protesters called for "reform" and advanced a democratic and pluralistic vision, thus challenging Assad's monopoly over the national narrative.[52] But the regime's strategy to prevent any Midan al-Tahrir-like contentious performance led it to overreact violently. Beyond the use of violence, Assad, relying on the support of state employees, some segments of the urban middle classes, his own Alawi base and the Syrian crony capitalists that had benefited from privatization schemes,[53] staged counter political rallies in most of Syria's cities; he called for a national dialogue and drafted and then held a referendum on a new constitution, ending the Baath's "legal" monopoly over the political system.[54] Whilst these regime adaptations could have contributed to political reform, they, however, failed to attract support from the Syrian opposition, the Syrian National Council (SNC), most of which was in exile and expected a swift fall of the regime.[55]

Assad's survival, however, and the absence of a political agreement on transition gave rise to an armed struggle, transforming Syria into a collapsed state marred by a civil war. In a span of two years (2011–2013), Syria turned from an influential regional actor into a battlefield for geopolitical rivalries. In the eyes of the opposition, political protest, on its own, had revealed its limits.[56] However, despite many defections, the army and the Republican Guard remained largely intact. Due to fear of regime's violence or because of the absence of a clear alternative, Syria's main cities (Damascus and Aleppo) did not instantly rise against the regime. Whilst the Arab uprisings had had a demonstration effect, sectarianism in Iraq since 2003 and the bloody fall of Qaddafi in Libya, formed counter demonstration effects that restrained revolt in Syria's big cities. Despite the varying origins of the rebellion – from the rise of Salafism in Dera, to opposition against religious restrictions in Banyas, to a revolt against the Alawi *shabbiha* in Latakia – it was concentrated in the periphery, where state services and control has weakened, before moving to Sunni hotbeds in Hama and Deir el-Zur.[57] Assad's military strategy aimed to concentrate efforts on the main cities in order to preserve the strategic link between Damascus-Homs-Latakia, but this came at the expense of leaving peripheral areas to the control of rebel groups.

With state weakening and regime loss of territory to the opposition, initially to the Free Syrian Army (FSA) of military defectors, Islamist jihadist groups began to see an opportunity to establish a foothold in Syria.[58] The rise of jihadist groups, such as Jabhat al-Nusra and ISIS, aggravated the sectarian divide which the civil war had activated. The regime's Alawite core, memories of the Hama massacre in 1982 and regime's alliance with Shi'a Iran and Lebanon's Hizbullah fostered sectarian framings and mobilization. The erosion of secular Arab nationalist ideology in the state-building process, and Bashar Assad's failure to articulate a new ideology since 2000,[59] left a vacuum that was filled by sectarian and tribal identities. But despite this, in its discourse and through its media outlets, the regime continued to promote a national narrative, aiming to demobilize sectarian divisions and framing the conflict as one between the "state", which represents plurality, stability and sovereignty, and the "terrorists", who are agents of external powers wanting the disintegration of the Syrian state.[60] The failure of the opposition to unite ranks made radical Islamism, manifested in the jihadist ISIS and Jabhat al-Nusra, the main political alternative to Assad. Fearing for their survival should the Islamists win, most of Syria's minorities and many of urban Sunnis backed the regime.

What exacerbated the Syrian conflict and shaped its development were regional geopolitical rivalries. The opportunity that the uprisings offered to unseat Assad led many of his regional foes, Saudi Arabia, Turkey and Qatar, to capitalize on domestic opposition to achieve their strategic goals. For Saudi Arabia, toppling Assad and installing a friendly regime would curtail Iranian expansion, weaken the "Resistance Axis" and potentially isolate Iran and Hizbullah. For Turkey and Qatar, the rise of a potentially Islamist (Muslim Brotherhood) regime in Syria would not only contain Iran and isolate Saudi Arabia, but would also likely facilitate Turkey's bid to establish economic and political hegemony in the Arab region in alliance with moderate Islamist movements. This strategy aimed to fill the vacuum left by the diminishing US Middle East role under the Obama administration.[61] For Iran, Hizbullah and, as mentioned above, the Iraqi regime, a fall of Assad would be a strategic loss and a threat to Shi'a influence in the region. Lebanon's Hizbullah feared that Assad's fall would diminish the movement's strategic depth in its conflict with Israel.[62]

The rivalries of these geopolitical camps began to directly affect the civil war in Syria. Each camp began to channel money, arms and men to its domestic allies in Syria. On the one hand, these external infiltrations contributed to the further erosion of the Syrian state; but on the other hand, Hizbullah's direct military intervention and support from Iran and Russia kept the regime intact. Geopolitical rivalry pitting Saudi Arabia against Qatar and Turkey weakened and further divided the Syrian opposition, contributing to Assad's survival and to the rise of the more robust Jihadist groups. The control of the rebel areas by Jihadists provided them with the opportunity to apply their political vision. The execution of rivals, the violent application of Islam and the sectarian attitude of these groups augmented the feeling of fear among Syria's minorities and gave credence to the regime's proposition that the most viable alternative to its rule would be the jihadists.

By the end of 2013, the Syrian war had caused more than 100,000 deaths, two million refugees,[63] and the disintegration of the country. In June 2014, more than half a century after the Baath Party found roots in Syria and Iraq, a new ideological movement represented in ISIS announced its "Caliphate", straddling the Sykes-Picot political boundaries and dominated over most of eastern Syrian and western Iraq.[64]

Conclusion: prospects and obstacles to democratization in Iraq and Syria

The Arab uprisings was an episode of contentious politics that challenged the existing political order in Iraq and Syria and formed an opportunity to renegotiate the basis of political rule in each of the two cases. However, due to the coercive state-building process in Iraq and Syria, their heterogeneous social composition and geo-political locations, the Arab uprisings led to state disintegration in both countries. Whilst the challenge to the state boundaries represented by ISIS may not endure, largely due to the socio-political resistance this movement faces in Arab societies and to the resistance of the international and regional systems to a revision of state boundaries, both countries face long term challenges to consolidate (Iraq) or reconstruct (Syria) political systems.

Whilst the politicization of sectarian and ethnic identities in Iraq and Syria appears to cause state disintegration and civil wars, this politicization, under the right conditions, might contribute to democratization. Iraq has already made an important transition towards political pluralism, accepting the presence of various sectarian and ethnic grievances, visions and interests. In ratifying a constitution, holding elections, allowing for a pluralist press and designing state institutions, Iraq had begun to translate political pluralism into political institutions. However, the US occupation until 2011, Sunni dissatisfaction, and sectarian and geopolitical rivalries, especially under the rule of al-Maliki, stalled the attempt to build a consociational democracy. As a divided state with a fragile democracy, Iraq's political development and stability, like that of Lebanon, largely depends on its regional setting. A favourable and less polarized regional setting might contribute to stabilizing Iraq and furthering its democratic experiment – and vice versa. To find a solution to the crisis, the US called for a "national unity" government, indicating the need to reincorporate the Sunnis. When Iran and the Iraqi Shi'a supreme leader Ayatollah Sistani made similar calls, the room for al-Maliki to seek a third term diminished, paving the ground for the appointment of Haidar al-Abadi. Regional fears of ISIS expansion, especially into Irbil or Baghdad, led regional rivals to converge in calling for national unity in Iraq. Saudi Arabia was among the first to recognize the newly-appointed Shi'a Prime Minister.[65]

Whilst the incorporation of various communities in a consociational system is a prerequisite for its success, this system, as the experience of Lebanon suggests, generates its own problems. The participation of different actors in "national unity" governments, which usually includes the main representatives of each community, leaves little room for an effective political opposition and, hence, accountability. The apportionment of state positions – in the judiciary, security and intelligence forces, central banks – among the ruling multi-communal coalition weakens these institutions since most of the main appointments are political patronage meant to serve the political power position of rival politicians within the state apparatus. These appointments increase the vulnerability of political institutions to political rivalries and hinder their capacity to become effective regulators of the political system.

Unlike Iraq, Syria still has to make the transition to political pluralism. The inability of the opposition to topple Assad and of Assad to reproduce his former domination is lengthening the war. Geopolitical rivalries over Syria are directly contributing the continuation of the struggle. Syria takes a central place in the strategies of the vying camps in the region since developments there are key to regional shifts in the balance of power. Whilst prospects for democratization in Syria are remote, an external agreement that would preserve the minimum interests of regional (Saudi Arabia and Iran) and international (USA and Russia) actors could still trigger a political process that would facilitate internal political change. Such a framework, similar to the Taif Accord, which brought the Lebanese civil war to an end, would widen the political scope to include various political forces. In their discourses, both the regime and the opposition have avoided explicitly proposing a consociational (sectarian) arrangement, preferring to present a "national" platform. However, any political opening and dialogue is very likely to juxtapose heterogeneous Syrian communities against on another; beyond the Syrian national identity that binds all groups, and in the absence of ideological divides (with the possible exception of Islamism-non-Islamism) among different Syrian groups, sectarianism and – in the case of Syria's Kurds – ethnicity are very likely to form the new boundaries of a future political system. Minority groups, including the one represented by the regime, would require assurances that a future political system would guarantee them influence at the centre of decision-making, in coercive agencies of the state, and in parliament.

Whilst state formation and crystallization long preceded democratization in Europe, in countries like Iraq and Syria, and for that matter Lebanon, Libya and Yemen, these two processes are *converging*. Iraq and Syria are finding that to reconstruct (and avoid the dissolution of) their states they will need to open the political arena to various communal and political actors, triggering a process of democratization. Successful state formation will mean democratization. But this process is, and will be, burdened by major challenges, not least the geopolitical rivalries; by political Islam, especially extremist versions, such as ISIS, that challenge democracy as a political system; by transnational sectarianism that is inflaming divided societies; and by the sectarian/ethnic apportionment that enervate institutions, decrease accountability, and facilitate corruption in consociational versions of democracy.

Acknowledgement

I would like to thank Francesco Cavatorta, Raymond Hinnebusch, and an anonymous reviewer for their very useful comments and suggestions on previous versions. I am responsible for any remaining flaws.

Disclosure statement

No potential conflict of interest was reported by the author.

Notes

1. For a critical overview, see Hinnebusch, "Authoritarian Persistence," 373–95.
2. For examples see Salame, "Introduction"; Waterbury, "Democracy Without Democrats?"; Brynen et al., *Political Liberalization and Democratization*.
3. Schlumberger, "Arab Authoritarianism," 6 (emphasis in original); Bellin, "The Robustness of Authoritarianism," 148.
4. Gause III, "Why Middle East Studies Missed the Arab Spring," 81–90.

5. Valbjorn, "Upgrading Post-democratization Studies," 29; Brynen et al., *Beyond the Arab Spring*, 1.
6. Anderson, "Searching Where the Light Shines," 209.
7. Schlumberger, "Arab Authoritarianism," 7–8.
8. Tripp, *The Power and the People*, 4.
9. Saouli, *The Arab State*.
10. Valbjorn, "Upgrading Post-democratization Studies," 31; see also Anderson, "Searching Where the Light Shines," 210; Cavatorta and Durac, *Civil Society and Democratization*, 9; Hinnebusch, "Toward a Historical Sociology," 214; Saouli, *The Arab State*, 3.
11. See also, Teti, "Beyond Lies the Wub," 18–20; Valbjorn, "Upgrading Post-democratization Studies".
12. Anderson, "Searching Where the Light Shines," 199.
13. Compare with Raymond Hinnebusch, "Toward a Historical Sociology," 201–16.
14. As Hinnebusch, *Syria: Revolution from Above*, 60, observes of Syria "when the legitimacy of party institutions and the holders of coercive power were confronted in the starkest fashion, the latter triumphed".
15. Tilly, *Coercion, Capital, and European States*.
16. A regime is "an alliance of dominant ideological, economical, and military power actors coordinated by the rulers of the state"; Mann, *The Sources of Social Power*, 18.
17. Weber, *Politics as a Vocation*, 78.
18. Hinnebusch, "Toward a Historical Sociology".
19. Saouli, *The Arab State*.
20. McAdam et al., *Dynamics of Contention*, 5.
21. Snow and Benford quoted in Snow, "Framing Processes, Ideology, and Discursive Fields," 384.
22. Saouli, "Performing the Egyptian Revolution".
23. McAdam et al., *Dynamics of Contention*, 43.
24. Tilly, *Identities, Boundaries, and Social Ties*, 216.
25. For an illustration of this point, see the documentary produced by Vice News on ISIS's state-making processes in territories occupied in Iraq and Syria https://www.youtube.com/watch?v=AUjHb4C7b94 Accessed 3 October 2014.
26. For an alternative argument on the emergence of consolidated states in Syria and Iraq with "strong state institutions" that "aimed at securing and enhancing national sovereignty", see Mufti, *Sovereign Creations*, 9.
27. For Syria, see Van Dam, *The Struggle for Power in Syria*, 34–75. For Iraq, see Saouli, *The Arab State*, 109–24.
28. Hinnebusch, *Syria: Revolution from Above*, 115–38.
29. Van Dam, *The Struggle for Power in Syria*, 91.
30. For a detailed analysis of this process, see Saouli, *The Arab State*, 118–20.
31. Van Dam, *The Struggle for Power in Syria*, 48–74.
32. For the rise of Shi'a political consciousness, emergence of Shi'a political organizations and regime-Shi'a contention, see Jabr, *The Shi'ite Movement in Iraq*.
33. On the 1991 Shi'a uprising, see Jabr, *The Shi'ite Movement in Iraq*, 269–71. On regime-Kurdish relations, see Gunter, *The Kurds of Iraq*.
34. Van Dam, *The Struggle for Power in Syria*, 105–17.
35. Ibid., 91.
36. Hinnebusch, "Syria: From 'Authoritarian Upgrading' to Revolution?".
37. For a theoretical and empirical base for this argument, see Saouli, *The Arab State*, 49–65.
38. During the crisis, Sadat highlighted Assad's regime as "firstly Alawi, secondly Ba'thist, and thirdly Syrian", hoping to contribute to the weakening of his regime. Sadat quoted in Van Dam, *The Struggle for Power in Syria*, 73.

39. For the uprising and the activation of sectarian boundaries in Iraq, see Haddad, *Sectarianism in Iraq*, 65–86.
40. Saouli, *The Arab State*, 128–33.
41. On Sunni perception of the new Iraq, see Haddad, *Sectarianism in Iraq*, 143–78.
42. Saouli, *The Arab State*, 130–2.
43. On the rise of Sunni resistance, see Dodge, *Iraq*, 44, 57, 89–90.
44. Ibid., 193–4.
45. Ibid., 147–80.
46. For Iraqi responses to the Syrian uprisings, see Saouli, "The Foreign Policy of Iraq and Lebanon".
47. *Guardian*, 26 December 2012 http://www.theguardian.com/world/2012/dec/26/iraq-protests-tension-sunni-shia
48. *Guardian*, 10 June 2014 http://www.theguardian.com/world/2014/jun/10/iraq-sunni-insurgents-islamic-militants-seize-control-mosul
49. BBC, 30 June 2014 http://www.bbc.co.uk/news/world-middle-east-28082962
50. Reuters, 16 June 2014 http://www.reuters.com/article/2014/06/16/us-iraq-security-qatar-idUSKBN0ER1JF20140616
51. *New York Times*, 13 June 2014 http://www.nytimes.com/2014/06/13/world/middleeast/iraq.html?_r=0
52. Ismail, *The Syrian Uprising*, 538–49; see also, Tripp, *The Power and the People*, 55–8.
53. Hinnebusch, "Syria: From 'Authoritarian Upgrading' to Revolution?" 98–100.
54. BBC, 29 March 2011 http://www.bbc.co.uk/news/world-middle-east-12892870; *Guardian*, 26 February 2012 http://www.theguardian.com/world/2012/feb/26/syria-referendum-constitution-homs-shelling
55. Hokayem, *Syria's Uprising*, 71–2.
56. International Crisis Group, *Syria's Metastasising Conflicts*, 143.
57. Hinnebusch, "Syria: From 'Authoritarian Upgrading' to Revolution?" 107.
58. On the Islamist factions of the opposition, see, Hokayem, *Syria's Uprising*, 93–102.
59. Hinnebusch, "Syria: From 'Authoritarian Upgrading' to Revolution?" 99.
60. For example, the Syrian regime continues to pay the salaries of state employees in territories occupied by the opposition "maintaining an image of the state", see Firas Khalife, "Life continues in Damascus ... with an eye on the 'Coalition' war [Dimashq tamdee bi hayatiha ... wa iynaha ala harb 'al-tahaluf'] *as-Safir* http://assafir.com/Article/5/374920.
61. Hokayem, *Syria's Uprising*, 105–48.
62. For Hizbullah's perception of the uprising in Syria, see Saouli, "Hizbullah, Hamas, and the Arab Uprisings," 37–44.
63. *Guardian*, "Humanitarian Crisis: Syria's Nightmare", 4 September 2013 http://www.theguardian.com/commentisfree/2013/sep/04/humanitarian-crisis-syria-nightmare-editorial Accessed 19 October 2013.
64. BBC, 30 June 2014 http://www.bbc.co.uk/news/world-middle-east-28082962
65. *Guardian*, 14 August 2014 http://www.theguardian.com/world/2014/aug/14/iraqi-prime-minister-maliki-step-aside-abadi

Bibliography

Anderson, Lisa. "Searching Where the Light Shines: Studying Democratization in the Middle East." *Annual Review of Political Science* 9, no. 1 (2006): 189–214.

Bellin, Eva. "The Robustness of Authoritarianism in the Middle East: Exceptionalism in Comparative Perspective." *Comparative Politics* 36, no. 2 (2004): 139–157.

Brynen, Rex, Bahgat Korany, and Paul Noble, eds. *Political Liberalization and Democratization in the Arab World: Theoretical Perspectives*. Boulder, Colorado: Lynne Rienner Publishers, 1995.

Brynen, Rex, Pete W. Moore, Bassel F. Salloukh, and Marie-Joelle Zahar, eds. *Beyond the Arab Spring: Authoritarianism & Democratization in the Arab World*. Boulder: Lynne Rienner, 2013.

Cavatorta, Francesco, and Vincent Durac. *Civil Society and Democratization in the Arab World: The dynamics of Activism*. London: Routledge, 2010.

Dodge, Toby. *Iraq: From War to a New Authoritarianism*. Abdington: Routledge, 2012.

Gause III, Gregory F. "Why Middle East Studies Missed the Arab Spring." *Foreign Affairs* 90, no. 4 (2011): 81–90.

Gunter, Michael M. *The Kurds of Iraq: Tragedy and Hope*. New York: St. Martin's Press, 1992.

Haddad, Fanar. *Sectarianism in Iraq: Antagonistic Visions of Unity*. London: Hurst and Company, 2011.

Hinnebusch, Raymond. *Syria: Revolution from Above*. London: Routledge, 2001.

Hinnebusch, Raymond. "Authoritarian Persistence, Democratization Theory and the Middle East." *Democratization* 13, no. 3 (2006): 373–395.

Hinnebusch, Raymond. "Toward a Historical Sociology of State Formation in the Middle East." *Middle East Critique* 19, no. 3 (2010): 201–216.

Hinnebusch, Raymond. "Syria: From 'Authoritarian Upgrading' to Revolution?." *International Affairs* 88, no. 1 (2012): 95–113.

Hokayem, Emile. *Syria's Uprising and the Fracturing of the Levant*. Abingdon: Routledge, 2013.

International Crisis Group. *Syria's Metastasising Conflicts*, no. 143. Brussels: International Crisis Group, 2013.

Ismail, Salwa. "The Syrian Uprising: Imagining and Performing the Nation." *Studies in Ethnicity and Nationalism* 11, no. 3 (2011): 538–549.

Jabr, Faleh A. *The Shi'ite Movement in Iraq*. London: Saqi, 2003.

Mann, Michael. *The Sources of Social Power*. Cambridge: Cambridge University Press, 1993.

McAdam, Dough, Sidney Tarrow, and Charles Tilly. *Dynamics of Contention*. Cambridge: Cambridge University Press, 2001.

Mufti, Malik. *Sovereign Creations: Pan-Arabism and Political Order in Syria and Iraq*. New York and London: Cornell University Press, 1996.

Salame, Ghassan. "Introduction: Where are the Democrats?." In *Democracy without Democrats?: The Renewal of Politics in the Muslim World*, edited by Ghassan Salame, 1–22. New York: I.B. Tauris, 1994.

Saouli, Adham. "Performing the Egyptian Revolution: Origins of collective restraint action in the Midan." *Political Studies* 54 (2014): 37–44, doi:10.1111/1467-9248.12135

Saouli, Adham. "Hizbullah, Hamas, and the Arab Uprisings: Structures, Threats, and Opportunities." *Orient* 54, no. 2 (2013): 37–44.

Saouli, Adham. *The Arab State: Dilemmas of Late Formation*. London: Routledge, 2014.

Saouli, Adham. "The Foreign Policy of Iraq and Lebanon." In *The Foreign Policies of Middle East States*, edited by Raymond Hinnebusch and Anoushiravan Ehteshami, 105–132. Lynne Rienner: Boulder, 2014.

Schlumberger, Oliver. "Arab Authoritarianism: Debating the Dynamics and Durability of Nondemocratic Regimes." In *Debating Arab Authoritarianism: Dynamics and Durability in Nondemocratic Regimes*, edited by Oliver Schlumberger, 1–20. Stanford, CA: Stanford University Press, 2007.

Snow, David A. "Framing Processes, Ideology, and Discursive Fields." In *Blackwell Companion to Social Movements*, edited by David A. Snow, Sarah A. Soule, and Haspeter Kriesi, 380–412. Victoria, Australia: Blackwell Publishing, 2004.

Teti, Andrea. "Beyond Lies the Wub: The Challenges of (Post) Democratization." *Middle East Critique* 21, no. 1 (2012): 5–24.

Tilly, Charles. *Identities, Boundaries, and Social Ties*. Boulder, Colorado: Paradigm, 2005.

Tilly, Charles. *Coercion, Capital, and European States*, AD 990-1990. Oxford: Basil Blackwell.

Tripp, Charles. *The Power and the People: Paths of Resistance in the Middle East*. Cambridge: University of Cambridge Press, 2013.

Valbjorn, Morten. "Upgrading Post-democratization Studies." *Middle East Critique* 21, no. 1 (2012): 25–35.

Van Dam, Nicholas. *The Struggle for Power in Syria: Politics and Society Under Asad and the Ba'th Party*. London: I.B. Tauris, 2011.

Waterbury, John. "Democracy Without Democrats?: The Potential for Political Liberalization in the Middle East." In *Democracy without Democrats?: The Renewal of Politics in the Muslim World*, edited by Ghassan Salame, 23–47. New York: I.B. Tauris, 1994.

Weber, Max. "Politics as a Vocation." In *From Max Weber: Essays in Sociology*, edited by Hans Heinrich Gerth and Charles Writght Mills, 77–128. London: Routledge, 2001.

Globalization, democratization, and the Arab uprising: the international factor in MENA's failed democratization

Raymond Hinnebusch

School of International Relations, University of St Andrews, St Andrews, UK

> What explains the almost wholly negative impact of international factors on post-uprising democratization prospects? This article compares the utility of rival "diffusionist" and neo-Gramscian political economy frames to explain this. Multiple international factors deter democratization. The failure of Western democracy promotion is rooted in the contradiction between the dominance of global finance capital and the norm of democratic equality; in the periphery, neo-liberalism is most compatible with hybrid regimes and, at best, "low intensity democracy". In MENA, neo-liberalism generated crony capitalism incompatible with democratization; while this also sparked the uprisings, these have failed to address class inequalities. Moreover at the normative level, MENA hosts the most credible counter-hegemonic ideologies; the brief peaking of democratic ideology in the region during the early uprisings soon declined amidst regional discourse wars. Non-democrats – coercive regime remnants and radical charismatic movements – were empowered by the competitive interference of rival powers in uprising states. The collapse of many uprising states amidst a struggle for power over the region left an environment uncongenial to democratization.

Do international level variables advance or retard democratization in MENA? The Arab uprising, when local agents finally embraced democratic discourse, seemed a sign that the globalization of democracy had finally overcome "Middle East exceptionalism". Despite this, the impact of the international level on the uprising has been almost uniformly negative. It has helped destabilize the region, but has done little to enable democratic transition, much less consolidation.

The conventional democratization approach to the international variable might be called the *diffusionist* model by which democracy is exported from the Western core via a combination of emulation, leverage and linkage, with regional lags increasingly overcome by globalization-driven homogenization. Although utilizing evidence by those working in this tradition, this article adopts an alternative *neo-Gramscian framework,*[1] that sees the export of a "democratic" capitalist order to MENA as highly contingent. In this view, the stability of a global or regional order depends on congruence between the system of production and ideological hegemony promoted by global institutions and by a hegemonic state. While MENA has been incorporated into circuits of Western finance capital and brought under US military hegemony, the hegemony of Western norms remains highly contested, the regions' alternative state formation pathways highly resilient, and ongoing power struggles over the region productive of norm fragmentation little congenial to democratization.

The article first examines the literature on the international export of democratic capitalism in the age of globalization; then looks at its impact on MENA prior to the uprising; and finally examines the impact of post-2011 international and regional power struggles in shaping the outcome of the uprisings.

Democratization within the frame of globalization

Democratization, in the neo-Gramscian view, must be understood within the framework of *economic globalization*, a process constituted by the internationalization of production and the dominance of Western finance capital and a Westcentric transnational corporate class. The globalization of capitalism requires the sustained agency of the global hegemon of the age, now the US, empowered by the dominance of its finance capital[2] and working through international financial institutions, to promote "disciplinary neo-liberalism"[3] manifest in international contractual arrangements such as the World Trade Organization. Especially in the world periphery, the hegemon plays a key role in forcing open markets to Western penetration, using economic crises and debt relief to enforce neo-liberal measures such as Anglo-American legal practices, tariff removal, privatization and structural adjustment.[4] The hegemon seeks thereby to transform states into transmission belts of global neo-liberalism.[5] With the demise of Soviet countervailing power, this US project acquired enhanced leverage; for example, war could again be used to force open the most recalcitrant and lucrative periphery markets, notably oil-rich Iraq.[6]

At the levels of institutions and ideology, sociological institutionalists (world polity theory) see a parallel process in which a world culture of capitalist democracy is diffused outward from core to periphery.[7] Buzan and Little noted that the expansion of European international society through imperialism globalized a formally Westphalian states system and stimulated an internalization of Western norms of sovereignty and nationalism, that made denial of the independence of the periphery too costly.[8] In a geopolitical dynamic recognizable to realists whereby the international system shapes the states, via socialization and emulation, a convergence in governance took place: since the capitalist national state is best able to mobilize power in international competition, all states emulated this model through defensive modernization.[9] In the era of de-colonization, these twin dynamics propelled a real diffusion of power to the periphery; however, Clark showed that, to compensate, the core engineered the globalization of neo-liberal practices, creating an international society of only *semi*-sovereign states in the periphery.[10]

What is the link between neo-liberal globalization and democratization? While globalization created a capitalist global political economy that ostensibly facilitated democratization, Western states also actively manipulated it to export democracy. As theorized notably by Levitsky and Way,[11] globalization gave Western states leverage over weaker less developed countries (LDCs) via sanctions, diplomatic pressures, conditionality and intervention. However, their pressures were most effective where paralleled by linkage: socio-economic penetration and interdependencies resulting from economic integration. Linkage, via diasporas, media penetration and the internet could tilt the internal power balance toward democratization, by creating and empowering constituencies pressing for it: Western-financed transnational non-governmental organization (NGO) networks built up civil society, and emergent regional elites were socialized through educational exchanges. Solingen[12] saw responsiveness to Western democracy promotion as advanced by the rise inside non-democratic regimes of business-dominated "internationalist coalitions" at the expense of statist-nationalist ones, a function of the move from bi-polarity, when authoritarian national security states had been fostered by super-power patrons, to a US-centric neo-liberal world empowering Western-linked bankers, finance ministers, and trading bourgeoisies. Finnemore and Sikkink[13] showed that states were socialized into standards of "civilized" international society notably by international organizations and NGOs that linked external and internal liberal norm entrepreneurs, such as democratization activists, to spread norms domestically. Huntington[14] identified a "snowballing" effect in which the de-legitimation of authoritarian governance made democracy appear to be the only legitimate form of rule and Rosenau[15] stressed how transnational linkages encouraged anti-authoritarian movements to spill across borders, as was famously the case in the Arab spring. The dominant ideology was that economic success required democratization, which alone had the legitimacy, predictability and informational advantages needed to encourage investors and innovation – while authoritarian regimes fostered economically counterproductive rent seeking.

In parallel, as reflected in "World Society"[16] approaches, there was a normative shift from an international society based on sovereign equal states to one wherein sovereignty was made conditional on "good governance" and states' fulfilment of their "responsibility to protect", with human rights violations justifying intervention – all as judged and implemented by the great powers, above all the US hegemon. The export of the non-violent resistance paradigm, popularized by Gene Sharp and theorized by Stephan and Chenoweth[17] publicized the techniques by which activists could use non-violent protest to provoke the collapse of authoritarian regimes; this is said to have played some role in inspiring the techniques of the Arab uprising. Less often observed was, as Ayoob and Lustick[18] suggested, how human rights and democratization campaigns aimed to deprive late developing states, for better or worse, of the tools of violence earlier used in the consolidation of core states, hence perpetuating state weakness in the periphery that sustained core dominance over it.

These one-way diffusionist models capture important tendencies, but greatly oversimplify reality, in neglecting three important counter-realities. Firstly, there is arguably a *contradiction* within the norm package exported by globalization that works against smooth norm diffusion. Thus, paradoxically, even as globalization appears to be an engine in the horizontal spread of democratization, it paradoxically also *dilutes* it: in locking states into trade pacts that remove much economic policy, particularly economic rights, from political contestation, democracy is hollowed out as the economic policies of all political parties converge on the neo-liberal consensus, big money and big corporate media manipulate elections and electorates are de-politicized or set against each other over race and immigration issues. The function of states changes from the provision of social needs to disciplining their societies as needed to attract global finance capital via a "race to the bottom"; the state becomes more accountable to transnational capital and less to its citizenry. In the periphery, the consequences have been particularly damaging. While in the core, Sorensen observed,[19] democratic consolidation was normally accompanied by periods of growing affluence and equality, globalization produces inequality on a world scale[20] and, as Boix[21] found, this high inequality undermined democratization in the periphery. What the West exported to the periphery was democratic procedure without the *substance* of political equalization or, in Robinson's words, "low intensity democracy".[22] For Huntington, unless economic development consolidated new democracies, a reverse authoritarian wave was likely;[23] and, as Petras and Veltmeyer[24] argued, globalization often generated some hybrid form of "electoral" or "neo-authoritarianism". In short, while the global hegemony of Westcentric international financial capital has reconstituted massive economic inequality on a global scale, the core simultaneously exports the formal procedures of democracy (elections, independent judiciaries) but emptied of its substance – political equality.

Second, the diffusionist narrative obscures the fact that democratization is a *power struggle*, and hence depends on the power of the global hegemon, backed by a Westcentric "collective hegemon", that promotes it. The legitimacy of the US hegemon is, however, strongest in the core and weakest in the periphery and the less legitimacy it enjoys, the more it must rely on more costly hard power to enforce democratic capitalism. As Hegemonic Stability Theory acknowledges, such "liberal imperialism" makes the hegemon very vulnerable to imperial overreach which damages its economy and encourages rising alternative powers to contest its hegemony;[25] while the US was, in the 1990–2002 period, largely unconstrained by such countervailing power, beginning with the highly contested Iraq war, other powers began to soft-balance against Washington and after the failure of the Iraq intervention and the global financial crisis, the US retreated to "offshore balancing" in the Middle East. After Iraq, authoritarian regimes were able to undermine the legitimacy of democracy-promotion by depicting it as American interventionism. Also, as Levitsy and Way[26] acknowledged, Western leverage was diluted when applied to larger states that the West could not afford to destabilize (Saudi Arabia) or ones with alternative global patrons (Iran); indeed, Brazil, Russia, India and China (the BRICS) had coalesced to soft balance against the US. They aimed to promote a global power balance supportive of a renewed plurality of global norms and a return to the primacy of state sovereignty in international society. Democracy promotion had provoked a backlash by the second half of the 2000, with a growing number of governments expelling Western NGOs and prohibiting local groups from taking foreign funds.[27] In these new conditions, when democratic revolts took place, rather than provoking a global consensus against authoritarian regimes, they were more likely to become a matter of international power contestation, with pro-democracy intervention countered by non-democratic or neighbouring states fearful of the demonstration effect or the threat to the regional power balance.[28] Contesting sides inside states undergoing revolt sought to draw in outside powers on their side, further destabilizing rather than democratizing them.

Thirdly, intervening between the global core and the periphery states is, as Buzan and Wæver[29] argue, the level of *regions*, which have their own structures – norms, power balances, patterns of amity-enmity – and are at least partly constituted "bottom upward", hence reflective of "thicker" regionally specific variations in inter-human society that are buffers against global influence. March and Olsen showed that path dependencies from historically specific regional experiences prevent quick adaptation to what are promoted as superior global models, with a typical outcome *hybridity*; thus, for Sharabi, Western penetration of MENA's patriarchal societies created a reinforced neo-patriarchal order.[30] In regions outside the Western core, liberalism, far from a triumphant, has to compete with (or accommodate itself to) nationalism and religion. In MENA it encounters a "grass roots counter-hegemony"[31] in the form of Islam, which has superseded socialism as the ideology of protest for the deprived. Islamists created patriarchal versions of civil society activism that could provide the social basis of semi-democratic regimes in which popular sovereignty would be checked by the "sovereignty of God" (the ulama interpreting the sharia). The socializing effect of "linkage" would also be much diluted where substantial cultural differences overlapped with political economy factors: thus, the reinforcement of tribal culture by oil rent-funded clientelism in the Gulf short-circuits the linkage posited by modernization and democratization theory between increased education and increased participatory demands. Where, as in the Middle East, no (legitimized) hegemonic order has been established, rival norms will be promoted by rival agents in their power struggles, with the likely outcome *hybridity*.[32] Political change may still mean movement away from authoritarianism but toward various hybrids ranging from low intensity consociational democracy as in Lebanon to competitive authoritarianism such as Iran's theo-democratic power sharing between ulama and elected politicians.

MENA under neo-liberal globalization

The political economy of MENA: between authoritarianism and democratization

The main longer-term structural factor shaping regime formation in MENA is its distinctive political economy – to which correspond state institutions and agents with ideologies, initially shaped in a first wave of globalization in which the Western world expanded into MENA. The Marxist theory of uneven and combined development tells us that late developers' defensive modernization leads to hybrid institutions mixing capitalist and pre-capitalist features.[33] In the MENA case where the modern states system was literally imposed from without by Western imperialism in what David Fromkin[34] called a "peace to end all peace", and in violation of the dominant identities of the region's peoples, artificial states had to compete with powerful pre-existing sub- and supra-state forces for the loyalties of their populations, and hence suffered built-in legitimacy deficits. In these circumstances, formally liberal, actually oligarchic, institutions that Western imperialism had put in place quickly collapsed and Arab state builders gravitated toward *neo-patrimonial* practices that combined time-honoured indigenous state-building formulas (Ibn Khaldun's[35] *assabiya* or elite solidarity built on primordial ties) with imported modern bureaucratic machinery and surveillance technology. In parallel, at the level of political economy, the penetration of the capitalist mode of production into MENA, articulating with pre-capitalist modes, produced, according to Ayubi,[36] a fluid social structure lacking a hegemonic class wherein a dominant state filled the vacuum. Populist authoritarian (PA) regimes originating in the military coups of petit bourgeois officers, often bound by a particular communal solidarity (*assabiya*), seized the command posts of the army and bureaucracy. These state elites balanced between communally and territorially fragmented classes while forging populist alliances against the old oligarchy joining national capital and workers/peasants, incorporated thru corporatist syndicates, rather than pluralist civil society. In the PA Arab republics that emerged in the 1950s–1960s, "Bonapartist" states (prefigured in Marx's analysis of Napoleon III) launched "passive" revolutions "from above". While demolishing the class power of the old oligarchy through nationalizations and land reform, they generated their own state bourgeoisies via statist import substitution industrialization; and balanced in international politics between communism and capitalism, getting aid from both sides. This formula was empowered, perhaps beyond its shelf life, by the exceptional availability of hydrocarbon and geopolitical rent in the region after the mid-1970s, which enabled the lubrication of clientele networks, the clientelization of "pre-democratic" regime-supportive tribes and communal minorities, and also a populist "social contract" with the masses. Rents gave the state considerable autonomy of society and allowed it to co-opt segments of the business class, a context hostile to democratization which requires a class balance between the state and bourgeoisie. At the ideological level both governing elites and masses were illiberal, depriving the small secular liberal middle class of leverage while authoritarianism was successfully legitimized in the name of nationalist resistance to imperialism.[37]

The exhaustion of state capitalism and economic and fiscal crisis into which PA regimes fell from the 1980s onward made them extremely vulnerable to Western international financial institutions (IFIs), such as the World Bank and International Monetary Fund (IMF), which used debt relief to force them into "structural adjustment". In parallel, within regimes, as Higgott and Dodge[38] argued, neo-liberalism started winning as power shifted from public sector managers to finance and economy ministries staffed by Western educated technocrats with direct connections to international financial institutions and reflecting neo-liberal ideological hegemony at the global level. But as Guazzoni and Poppi[39] showed, economic liberalization did not lead to diminishing state control or a more independent civil society or bourgeoisie; rather, Presidential families exploited IFI's demands for privatization of the public sector to seize its choicest elements as their private property and to generate supportive crony capitalists who were heavily invested in relations with the West. IFIs commended Tunisia and Egypt, where the cronies of Gamal Mubarak and the Ben Ali family took advantage of their pressures for privatization to turn public sector assets into private monopolies, as models of good economic governance.[40]

Globalization in MENA was not, therefore, associated with democratization. Rather, authoritarian power persisted but was now used, not to attack inequalities, as in the populist period, but to reconstruct and protect the new inequalities unleashed by the region's opening (infitah) to the global economy. Under this new "post-populist" authoritarianism, regimes restructured their social bases. Thus, privatization provided regime elites with new patronage resources to foster and co-opt a supportive crony capitalist class.[41] This new class base was, contrary to globalization discourse, incompatible with democratization: crony capitalists would be threatened by democratic transparency but also even productive capitalists wanted rule of law for themselves but not rights for workers. Rather than a hegemonic bourgeoisie capturing the state and instituting limited democracy for itself, much of the bourgeoisie became dependent on the state for contracts, business opportunities, rent and the disciplining of labour, allowing rulers to play off rival business cliques. While capitalism is said to empower bourgeoisies and working classes who combine to force democratization, in MENA economic liberalization and privatization obstructed such a democratic coalition and was used to build anti-democratic coalitions – "networks of privilege"[42] – re-empowering authoritarianism.

At the same time, reviving capitalism meant investors had to be favoured over the mass public through reduction of labour rights and wages while IMF structural adjustments contracted populist welfare, producing "food riots" across the region (while leaving intact military purchases from Western arms dealers). Enforcing this required the old popular constituencies be demobilized; hence democratization, which could empower them to resist neo-liberalism, could not be promoted. Moreover, rollbacks of the populist social contract on which regimes had initially built their legitimacy and abdication of their developmental and welfare roles to the private sector and religious charity networks made regimes vulnerable to the rise of Islamic opposition, that powerfully attracted the marginalized strata victimized by neo-liberal policies and were well poised to win elections, should regimes democratize. Rulers, on the other hand, could hardly expect to win a democratic election when they were forcing austerity unequally on the majority and violating people's sense of moral economy, excluding, not including them, as the populist regimes had initially done. Contrary to mainstream globalization discourse, neo-liberalism, *reinforcing* rather than diluting regional neo-patrimonialism, posed a major obstacle to democratization.

As such, globalization was paralleled by a move toward hybrid regimes via "lopsided political liberalization", in which greater access was accorded the beneficiaries of post-populism: the interest groups of the bourgeoisie were given greater corporatist and parliamentary access to power and more rule of law. Elections were manipulated to empower bourgeois parties supportive of neo-liberalism and marginalize populist ones, with safety valve opposition parties for the middle class tolerated only within strict limits; and corporatist arrangements, which in the populist era had allowed mass organizations access to decision-makers, becoming instruments for disciplining and demobilizing mass strata.[43] It was against this "post-populist authoritarianism" that the Arab intifada of 2011 mobilized.

Authoritarian persistence was reinforced by the role of the region in the world system. Democracy develops when governments need their citizenry to pay taxes or to fight in wars but in the Middle East many states depended on the outside: on rents (oil revenues or foreign aid) in lieu of taxes and on foreign bases and security treaties instead of citizen armies. Democracy achieves hegemony when associated with nationalism, as in the French and American revolutions; but MENA regimes forfeited nationalist legitimacy through their alignment with the US, which was, with Israel, the most unpopular state in Middle East public opinion.[44] Thus, where democratization even partly proceeded in MENA, it unleashed anti-Western or anti-Israeli sentiments that challenged regimes' Western-aligned foreign policies and which Islamic movements exploited, prompting a halt or reversal of these experiments. The case of Jordan shows most dramatically how a regime's responsiveness to Western demands – for peace with an Israel unwilling to concede Palestinian rights – was necessarily paralleled by a contraction of domestic democratization. Conversely, the "war on terror" cemented new political alliances between the US, Britain and France and MENA authoritarian regimes against the common threat from radical Islam. In some cases (Syria), authoritarian upgrading took advantage of a certain authoritarian solidarity (Russian or Chinese support) and in some cases also the use of anti-Western nationalism to discredit democracy discourses. Both threats from the West and from Islamists were used to securitize politics.

AFTER THE ARAB UPRISINGS

Western democracy promotion in MENA

During the first decade of Western democracy promotion, MENA was largely exempted, with security and stability of allied regimes given priority over democratization. In the 1990 Gulf war the US punished Jordan and Yemen for following public opinion and rewarded Mubarak for ignoring it. Washington's post-war presence in the Gulf depended on absolute monarchies and it even expressed alarm that Yemen's democratization would infect Saudi Arabia. The war on terror aligned Washington with authoritarian regimes against Islamic opinion: the US backed the Algerian military's overturning of an Islamist electoral victory and its violent suppression of Islamists while US NGOs praised Algeria's 1997 elections that excluded Islamists. The biggest US aid recipients, Egypt and Jordan, did not hold free elections.[45] Ray Takeyh attributes this to the fear Islamists would benefit from democratization and from the need for partner regimes willing to deal with Israel, help in the "war on terror" and deliver oil.[46] In parallel, Amaney Jamal sees the Arab bourgeoisie embracing authoritarianism and alliance with the US as a bulwark against Islamists and popular power.[47]

Much more proactive in MENA was the European Union (EU) which, through the Mediterranean Partnership, acted collectively vis-a-vis the fragmented MENA states in a systematic drive to pry open regional markets for European businesses. The partnership, in ending protection for industries in the southern Mediterranean while only marginally expanding access to European markets for MENA agricultural products, reversed the advantages given LDCs under Cold War preferential trading arrangements.[48] Hyde-Price[49] argues that the EU promoted market opening while neglecting democratization and human rights. EU defenders claimed the economic development that the partnership supposedly promoted would lead to democratization over the long run and that EU officials encouraged incremental political progress through dialogue and economic incentives rather than antagonizing regimes with predictably ineffective political demands. This strategy would, however only be effective if neo-liberalism *did* lead to economic development; however, as Joffe[50] observed, no economy has ever developed under the economic openness the EMP mandated; rather authoritarian regimes were needed to implement free trade agreements that pauperized MENA populations.[51]

The Bush administration announced an end to tolerance of authoritarianism after 9/11 on the grounds that it was the root cause of terrorism, hence that Western security required democratization. Washington launched new democracy promotion campaigns without consulting pro-US regimes, as if, declared Egypt's Mubarak, MENA states had no sovereignty.[52] Coming in parallel with the war on Iraq and a sharp US tilt toward Israel, the initiative triggered a strong negative reaction by Arab commentators and journalists, congruent with public opinion, among whom it was seen as serving Israel's interests by debilitating Iraq and a means of pressuring regimes to be more cooperative on Palestine and Iraq's occupation. The US calls for human rights while ignoring Palestinian rights had no credibility; also the Gulf oil regimes were always exempted. Many intellectuals and civil society groups were pulled between their nationalist rejection of Western interference and fear that democracy would not come without some outside pressure; in Egypt, Western pressures opened limited space that allowed the strongly anti-Mubarak Kefiya movement to emerge. The technical approach of the West, notably the stress on elections and on fostering civil society was widely criticized; and, despite the emphasis on elections, when Hamas won a free election in Palestine, the West refused to recognize or deal with it and the fear of Islamist victories eased the pressure on regimes for elections.[53] Lynch[54] argued that US support for Israel and antagonism to Iran so alienated regional publics that US regional influence depended on marginalization of publics by authoritarian regimes; it was no surprise that Bush soon abandoned democracy promotion.

The Western export of democracy to the region was widely seen to fail, indeed, to deter democratization in spite of considerable leverage and a reasonable level of linkage. It was seen as an instrument of US hegemony; as Teti [55] argued, it put the West in a privileged position to judge governance in MENA states and the West's insistence on secular liberal versions of democracy combined with neo-liberal economics, while marginalizing Islamic versions of democracy and discouraging redistributive measures, had limited appeal in MENA. The democratization promoted by the West was of the "thin" variety compatible with neo-liberal globalization. While as an ideology democracy made gains in the region, it faced too much competition from counter ideologies to be hegemonic, and the balance of social forces produced by the articulation of global neo-liberalism with MENA crony capitalism was most compatible with hybrid regimes and at best with "low intensity" democracy (Tunisia, Lebanon).

The uprising: democratization between structure and agency
Global level precipitants
Global level pressures played a key role in destabilizing the fragile post-populist authoritarian regimes in MENA. While the globalization of neo-liberalism reduced their ability to satisfy the welfare of mass publics, the parallel promotion of democratization and the spread of Internet technology encouraged anti-regime political mobilization by middle class youth "overproduced" by population growth and educational expansion. Activists trained by US government funded democracy promotion campaigns and West European NGOs played a certain role in spreading the uprising.[56] The "responsibility to protect" doctrine conveyed the misapprehension to dissident activists that the West would intervene should repression exceed certain limits. The US invasion of Iraq had also empowered sectarian discourses that spread outward across the region, reinforced by Saudi-Iranian rivalry; the nominally consociational democracy left behind by the US in Iraq, with its built-in Shia majority, was actually a failed state that would provide fertile ground for the anti-democratic ISIS movement.

AFTER THE ARAB UPRISINGS

The uprisings provided a new context for competitive interference by global powers that blocked any straightforward export of democracy. The US was ambivalent about the uprisings, which constituted a threat to key allies, notably Egypt, where Mubarak was deposed and Saudi Arabia, which was threatened by insurgents in Yemen and protests in Bahrain. But the West also saw opportunities to reincorporate Libya and Syria into the Westcentric democratic capitalist order and to roll back the growing regional influence of Russia and China, which had growing stakes in arms deals, energy partnerships, and trade with authoritarian regimes. What was remarkable was that while Western democracy promotion was, for once, in sync with social movements in the region, the outcome was no straightforward expansion of the democratic-capitalist world. The West's abuse of the United Nations resolution authorizing humanitarian intervention in Libya to effect regime change activated Russia and China's strong interest in defending the norm of sovereignty against Western expansion in MENA at the expense of the multi-polar world order they sought,[57] which was also congruent with the interests of anti-Western MENA regimes and movements. Also, with regional turmoil not lending itself to management by military means and chastened by its adventure in Iraq and lingering austerity from the world financial crisis, Washington retreated to its traditional "off shore balancing" in MENA, content to contain and exploit regional cleavages, notably the Sunni-Shia conflict most manifest in Syria and Iraq where anti-Western Shia and Sunni movements were fighting each other.

The regional trans-state level: the construction and de-construction of democratic ideological hegemony

The first regional manifestation of the uprising was the unleashing of a trans-state ideological struggle. The uprisings were accompanied by a powerful mobilization of pro-democracy sentiment in the region, parallel to the weakening and collapse of several authoritarian states. What was remarkable was that while Bush's forced democratization, unleashing civil war in Iraq and Lebanon, had seemingly discrediting the notion in the 2000s, the demands of the 2011 youth movements and rebellions were chiefly for democracy and freedom in their *own states*, rather than the traditional Pan-Arab, anti-imperialist, concerns that had dominated the 2000–2010 "New Arab Cold War".[58] Even more remarkable was that significant segments of regional opinion put aside their traditional suspicion of Western interference to call for intervention under the banner of responsibility to protect against the heavy repression deployed by regimes in Libya and Syria in particular.

In parallel to democratization discourses, the uprisings also empowered Islamic identity. The main initial beneficiary was the Muslim Brotherhood whose electoral prowess, backed by Turkey and Qatari money and media, propelled its simultaneous rise toward the levers of power in several states, seemingly on the brink of realizing its moderate Islamic version of democracy; had it prevailed, the third wave might finally have penetrated the Arab world. With variants from the *Ikhwan* tradition ruling in the pivotal capitals of Ankara and Cairo, and kindred movements empowered or in government in Tunisia, Morocco, Yemen, Palestinian Gaza and Libya, a new Islamic version of democracy that eschewed anti-democratic and sectarian exclusionary Wahhabi Islam, seemed on the cusp of achieving hegemony. Other Islamists, such as the formerly anti-democratic Salafis, joined the democratic political game while Al-Qaeda was marginalized by the peaceful overthrows of dictators, especially when its new leader Ayman Al-Zawahiri, denounced the principle of majority rule, defying the yearning of Muslim populations for democracy.

However, in parallel, Saudi Arabia fostered conservative Salafis in Egypt and Syria against both secular democratic youth and the Brotherhood and also used Sunni Salafism against Iran as part of their geo-political struggle; combined with the parallel use of non-Sunni sectarian solidarity by the Syrian and Bahraini regimes against their uprisings, sectarian conflicts soon spread insecurity and defensive sectarian solidarity in Lebanon, Syria, Bahrain, Yemen and Iraq, which would make democratization impossible. In parallel, the ailing fortunes of Al-Qaeda and its various avatars was reversed, thriving on sectarian polarization and new opportunities in the failing states of Libya, Yemen, Syria and Iraq. Moreover, by the third year of the uprisings, state national security establishments were recovering some of their lost capacity in a fightback, notably in Egypt and Syria, against both democratization and Islamization. A watershed was the overthrow of President Morsi in Egypt by an alliance between secularist liberals and the army and deep state. It was encouraged by a tacit alliance of Israel, which covered the Egyptian military's flank in Washington, with Saudi Arabia, which provided copious financial support and brought Egypt's Salafis into the new military dominated ruling coalition. This marked a triumph of counter-revolutionary and anti-democratic forces regionally. On the one hand, liberals began to abandon a democracy that would empower Islamists; on the other hand, the trend toward democratization of Islamic movements was reversed by the demonstration in Egypt that Islamic movements that won elections would not be allowed to rule. The absolute monarchies, Saudi and UAE especially, which had encouraged the military, along with their polarizing sectarian Sunni discourse, were empowered and the democratic Islamic threat to them diluted. Far from the democratic mobilization leading to the hegemony of democratic norms, it had unleashed normative fragmentation.

Competitive interference amidst the regional struggle for power

At the regional level the uprising intensified the pre-existing regional power struggle between the Iran-led "resistance axis" and the Sunni-dominated pro-Western axis led by Saudi Arabia. Three regional powers, Saudi Arabia, Iran and Turkey, had enough material and soft power and sufficient invulnerability to the uprising to try to use it to bid for regional hegemony in the name of quite different models of governance, with only Turkey ostensibly promoting democratization. This precipitated the inter-state power balancing which realism expects will block bids for hegemony: as a result, the region was fragmented as no power managed to use the uprising to shape a new regional order under its hegemony.

Saudi Arabia (and the Gulf Cooperation Council): A new "Holy Alliance"

The uprising initially appeared to be a major threat to the monarchies. The fall of Mubarak in Egypt; state failure in Yemen, where they and Iran backed opposing sides in the Houthi rebellion in the north, and Al-Qaeda was also finding space to operate; and the possibly-contagious Shia uprising in Bahrain were perceived as opportunities for Iran. But the monarchies dampened the potential spread of revolt to their own populations via a combination of repression, most obvious in Bahrain; political concession, most obvious in Morocco, and economic blandishments to citizens, most obvious in Saudi Arabia where US$5000/citizen worth of jobs and benefits were promised.[59] The Gulf Cooperation Council (GCC) was ungraded into a counter-revolutionary "Holy Alliance", *de facto* incorporating Morocco and Jordan, with the rich GCC states transferring billions of dollars to the poorer monarchies to enable them to similarly appease discontent, crowned by anti-revolutionary intervention in Bahrain. Their financial liquidity glut allowed them to fund trans-state Islamists against secularists and buy influence on a massive scale in uprising states, particularly Egypt.[60] The GCC also went on the offensive, taking advantage of its media dominance and its bloc vote in the Arab League to legitimize the Western intervention against old foes Qaddafi and Asad. Al-Jazeera was overtly political, exaggerating and widely disseminating regime violence in Syria while ignoring repression in Bahrain and instances of violence by the Syrian opposition. However, splits between Riyadh and Doha over their sponsorship of rival (Muslim Brotherhood, Salafi) Islamists put the GCC at cross-purposes: the two backed rival Islamists in Egypt and in also in Syria where Gulf-funded Islamists fought both the regime and each other, helping to produce a failed state. In inflaming Islamist militancy and anti-Shia sentiment, the GCC helped empower Al-Qaeda avatars such as ISIS. Saudi Arabia's backing for the military in Egypt against Turkish and Qatari promotion of the Muslim Brotherhood helped precipitate an internal conflict that ended in a hybrid regime in Cairo.

Turkey: failed liberal hegemon

The rise of the Adalet ve Kalkınma Partisi (AKP) government to power in 2000 initiated a transformation in Turkey's Middle East policy. Its policy of "zero problems" with its neighbours aimed to ameliorate the interminable regional conflicts left behind by the fall of the Ottoman empire by exporting the liberal practices of the zone of peace. An active diplomacy sought to resolve disputes, project Turkey as a model of an economically successful Islamic democracy, and appeal to an Islamic civilization shared by Turks and Arabs. Economic integration aimed to construct new cross-border "liberal" interdependencies that would also permit the export of Turkish business in need of regional markets.[61]

The Arab uprising initially upset Turkey's strategy, which had prioritized economic integration with its Arab neighbourhood regardless of their authoritarian governance. Turkey initially opposed North Atlantic Treaty Organization intervention in Libya where it had close business ties with the regime. But the then prime minister, now president, Recep Tayyip Erdoğan switched his discourse to the championing of democratization as the region-wide rise of kindred business/Islamist coalitions similar to the AKP in the apparently-emerging Sunni democracies in Tunisia and Egypt provided new openings to Turkish soft power. The congruity of its political system – a democracy that incorporates Islamic forces – with regional popular aspirations, was demonstrated by the hero's welcome given Erdoğan in his 2011 tour of these countries.[62]

It was in Syria that Turkish policy ran aground. Syria had been the showcase of its zero-problems strategy where trans-state issues of conflict, such as the disputed Turkish annexation of Iskanderun, Euphrates water, and Kurdish separatism, had been resolved amidst the opening of borders to free passage and free trade agreements, which were meant to be extended into the Levant and Gulf areas. However, when the Syrian uprising started and Asad dismissed Turkey's calls to contain it through political reforms and instead continued repressing protestors, the AKP now professed to see repressive dictatorships as the most serious threat to its ambition for a pacific neighbourhood and democracy as the solution. It sacrificed its ties with Asad's regime, helped organize the Syrian opposition and gave it safe haven to operate an insurgency from Turkish territory. If, as Turkey expected, the minority Alawi regime had quickly collapsed and been replaced by the Muslim Brotherhood opposition, the AKP could have expected to enjoy special influence in Damascus. However, Erdoğan had grossly underestimated the tenacity of the Asad regime, bolstered by its allies in the resistance axis, Iran and Hizbollah. Turkey appeared impotent even to manage the spillover of the crisis – refugee flows, Kurdish empowerment – on its borders. Its attempt to export democracy to its neighbour had the same outcome as the earlier US attempt in Iraq: collapse into a failed state. In calling on the West to intervene in Syria, Ankara jettisoned its earlier notion of a Middle East zone of peace as an alternative to misguided American interventions. In deploying Sunni Islamic identity against the secular/Alawi regime in Damascus, Ankara contributed to the sectarianization that was destabilizing the region. Turkey was soon on bad terms with other Middle East states, too. Over Syria it sacrificed its good relations with Iran. Iraq's Shia-led government objected to Ankara's manipulation of its ties to Iraqi Sunnis and Kurds against Baghdad. When Turkey objected to the overthrow of President Morsi and Egyptian moves to isolate Hamas in Gaza, ties with Cairo turned sour.

The new struggle for Syria: the perils of exporting the non-violent resistance paradigm

In Syria, the uprising began as a mobilization of protestors demanding democratization against a repressive authoritarian regime, arguably a test of the non-violent resistance model which anticipates the use of violence against mass non-violent protest will precipitate either defections in the security forces or external sanctions and intervention. Indeed, the possibility of external military intervention shaped both opposition and regime strategies. Western funded Syrian expatriates, young cosmopolitans that were instrumental in initiating and internationalizing the uprising, understood that they could not succeed without external intervention to restrain the regime's repressive options. External activists told those on the ground, pointing to the Libya no-fly zone, that "the international community won't sit and watch you be killed". They claimed that another Hama was not possible because "Everything is being filmed on YouTube, and there's a lot of international attention on the Middle East".[63] This encouraged Syrian activists to risk their lives and to eschew the compromise with the regime needed for a pacted transition. The Libyan intervention gave decisive momentum to the uprising.[64]

The regime, for its part, having survived several decades of Western isolation, had always seen itself as besieged by foreign enemies; the role played by external exiles and internet activists abroad in provoking or escalating the uprising was congruent with its perceptions of conspiracy and tarnished the indigenous opposition with the suspicion of treasonous dealings with foreign enemies, justifying the resort to repressive violence. The regime tried to calibrate its violence within limits that would not trigger an international bandwagon toward intervention, although over time this bar was steadily raised. Later yet, it felt the need to quickly smash resistance so as not to lose control of territory that could be used to stage intervention as had happened in Libya, thus precipitating a transition from the "security solution" to the "military solution". This did not precipitate Western intervention for, in contrast to Libya, the consensus behind humanitarian intervention had been destroyed by Western-led regime change in Libya.

Repression did precipitate some defections from the Syrian military, not enough to precipitate regime collapse but enough that the regime lost control of wide swathes of the northeast of the country to armed insurgents. The struggle for Syria became a regional and international proxy war; regionally, with Turkish, Saudi and Qatari support for the opposition being offset by Iranian, Hizbollah and Iraqi support for the regime; and internationally, through American and European support for the uprising offset by Russian and Chinese support for the regime. Iran proved a tenacious power balancer: on the defensive, Tehran sought to create a protective land belt from Iraq (where post-US occupation, the move of the Maliki regime against Sunni rivals made it more dependent on Iran) to Syria, and Hizbollah. These external involvements, each blocking the other, contributed to the stalemating of the Syrian conflict, especially as the insurgents began to fight among themselves, pitting more moderate Syrian rebels against transnational Al-Qaeda avatars, Jabhat al-Nursa and the Islamic State of Iraq and Syria (ISIS). With rising levels of jihadist involvement, the West became more concerned with the "international war on terror" than with the "Responsibility to Protect".

Egypt and Tunisia: neo-liberalism Redux

Democratic uprisings do not guarantee democratic consolidation: the two regional states with the least fragmented societies and most developed institutions, hence the best prospects for democratization, faced a political economy stacked against consolidation. The revolutions in Egypt and Tunisia were a reaction against the acute social inequalities resulting from neo-liberalism, but the revolutions remained purely political, with no attempts to attack unjust economic inequalities. This was because enduring dependencies on the Western-centred international financial system locked them into neo-liberal practices. Indeed, because the uprisings has actually worsened economic growth, hence prospects for addressing unemployment, by deterring investors and tourism, they were more dependent on Western IFIs. Particularly in Egypt IFIs tried to exploit the post-uprisings economic crises by making loans conditional on further opening to international finance capital, notably privatizations that would allow Western and Gulf investors to buy up prime parts of Egypt's infrastructure and public services.[65]

In this context, the least bad outcome was the "low intensity democracy" that appeared possible in Tunisia where long-term Western cultural penetration may indeed have assisted democratic consolidation – ironically, even when the West supports the authoritarian leader, as was the case with Ben Ali. If democracy is consolidated in Tunisia, it will be because moderates were able to reach a pact to marginalize the radicals on both sides, despite the French supporting anti-clericalists and the Gulf supporting Salafists. But even in Tunisia, nostalgia set in for the stability and relative prosperity of the Ben Ali period; all that had changed for the unemployed was increased political freedom to express their frustrations. In Egypt, where political competition was diverted from economic injustice to identity issues framed in destabilizing zero-sum terms and backed by competitive interference from the US, Saudi Arabia and Qatar, the result was a hybrid regime: mixing limited political pluralism with doses of authoritarian power needed to manage identity conflicts and turn back demands for social justice that could not be accommodated in a global neo-liberal economic order.

Conclusion

The diffusionist approach, with its image of both benign and inevitable global diffusion of democratic capitalism (each believed to reinforce the other) from the core provides little explanation for the failure of democratization in post-uprising MENA, except the notion of time lags, perhaps attributable to cultural exceptionalism, a mechanical view that neglects agency. Neo-Gramscianism offers a far more robust explanation; for it, the exportability of a stable democratic-capitalist world order to the periphery depends on congruence between forces of production and hegemonic norms. However the contradictions within the Western core's version of world order debilitated its exportable power.

AFTER THE ARAB UPRISINGS

The West has certainly left a profound impact on MENA but it has not been benign and has therefore inevitably generated resistance. In a first wave of globalization the West imposed an arbitrary and flawed states system made up of fragile regimes wherein early liberal experiments rapidly failed and more indigenous hybrids of neo-patrimonialism and populism became the main state building formulas. The second wave of globalization at the end of the Cold War exposed these regimes to the powerful homogenizing material forces (finance capital, markets), triumphant liberal ideology (via transnational linkages and the new globalized communications technology) and the dominance of a liberal global hegemon, the US, which increasingly penetrated the region. However, rather than these reinforcing each other, the incongruence in the Western project prevented achievement of hegemony over the region.

The core's export of democracy suffered, first of all, from a built-in contradiction between the global inequality generated by neo-liberalism and the democratic norm of equality. The US hegemon cannot bridge this contradiction because it lacks both the hard and soft power to control the region and provokes anti-hegemonic balancing by global and regional powers. The incoherence of global liberalism inevitably generates regional backlashes, with counter-ideologies, nationalist populism and Islamism, retaining remarkable power in MENA; the latter remains the only credible counter-hegemonic ideology opposing triumphant world liberalism.

Moreover, pre-Arab uprising regimes proved extremely resilient in the face of globalization, and indeed adept in using global resources – investment, arms, technology – to adapt. In the oil-poor republics, regimes, such as the Tunisian and Egyptian ones, selectively exploited global neo-liberal pressures to reconstitute statist authoritarian regimes in inegalitarian crony capitalist forms quite resistant to democratization. In parallel, the Arab regimes *most* incorporated into West-centric global financial networks, the Arab Gulf state were the *least* democratic, not only internally, but also in their use of finance capital to promote anti-democratic forces.

To be sure, the vulnerabilities of the authoritarian republics were exposed in the Arab uprising, when communications globalization, enabling the export of democratization discourses – pushing for the empowerment of populations even as regional incarnations of neo-liberalism generated grievances among them – precipitated the Arab revolt, profoundly destabilizing the region. The Arab uprisings were both a symptom of globalization and a backlash against it, a continuation and intensification of struggle between those seeking to make regional states transmission belts of neo-liberalism and those wanting to protect the indigenous moral economy.

In spite of the opportunity presented by the uprisings to tilt internal power balances, Western and regional intervention in the Arab uprisings states promoted not democratization but intensified destabilization. Neither leverage or linkage gave the West the influence to peacefully promote democratization while militarized intervention proved disastrous in Libya, as it had earlier been in Iraq, with the state demolished, empowering militias and trans-state jihadists rather than democrats; even when intervention was expected but not delivered, as in Syria, it encouraged rebellion and with similar results.

Further diluting any democratizing normative impetus was the global norm fragmentation deepened by the Arab uprising, pitting the West's "liberal imperialist" "humanitarian" interventionism against Russian and Chinese defence of sovereignty in which each checkmated the other rather than cooperating to facilitate a stable regional transition. Similarly, at the regional level, uprising states became targets of competitive interference by rival powers backing opposing forces and also largely checkmating each other. Even the presence of an aspirant liberal-Islamic hegemon, Turkey, was unable make democracy normatively hegemonic. Rather, external intervention (sanctions, arms supplies) in internal power struggles (Syria, Libya) magnified and prolonged a deepening destabilization of states that was profoundly inhospitable to democratization.

As regional states fractured under the effect of internal revolt, contrary norms were wielded in domestic power struggles between middle class liberal activists, "deep" state establishments and rival versions of Islamism that either rejected or selectively embraced aspects of Western defined democratic norms. Democrats proved inferior to statist authoritarians and Islamist radicals who had either more guns, money or ideological motivation – and much of it came from external sources. Indicative of the negative impact of external – global and regional – interference in the Arab uprising states was the inverse relation between the likelihood of democratization and the intensity of external competitive interference: where it was most intense, the result was failed states (Libya, Syria); where it was significant, Bonapartist restoration (Egypt); and only where it was most muted did "low intensity democracy" result (Tunisia).

Disclosure statement

No potential conflict of interest was reported by the author.

Notes

1. Cox, "Social Forces, State and World Orders."
2. Arrighi and Silver, "Capitalism and World (dis) Order."
3. Gill, *Power and Resistance.*
4. Gowan, *The Global Gamble*; Harvey, *The New Imperialism.*
5. Cox, "Social Forces, State and World Orders."
6. Barkawi and Laffey, "The Imperial Peace," 403; Hartnett and Stengrim, *Globalization and Empire.*
7. Finnamore, "Norms, Culture and World Politics."
8. Buzan and Little, "The Historical Expansion."
9. Waltz, *The Theory of International Politics*; Finnamore, "Norms, Culture and World Politics."
10. Clark, "Another Double Movement."
11. Levitsky and Way, "International Linkage and Democratization."
12. Solingen, *Regional Orders at Century's Dawn.*

13. Finnamore and Sikkink, "International Norm Dynamics."
14. Huntington, "Democracy's Third Wave."
15. Rosecrance, *Linkage Politics.*
16. Buzan, *From International to World Society.*
17. Stephan and Chenoweth, "Why Civil Resistance Works."
18. Ayoob, *The Third World Security Predicament;* Lustick, "The Absence of Middle Eastern Great Powers."
19. Sorensen, *Democracy & Democratization,* 125–6.
20. Hartnett and Stengrim, *Globalization and Empire,* 140.
21. Boix, *Democracy and Distribution.*
22. Robinson, *Promoting Polyarchy.*
23. Huntington, "Democracy's Third Wave."
24. Petras and Veltmeyer, *Globalization Unmasked,* 70.
25. Gilpin, *War and Change in World Politics,* 153–6, 217–9.
26. Levitksy and Way, "International Linkage and Democratization."
27. Carothers, "The Backlash Against Democracy Promotion."
28. Halliday, *Revolution and World Politics,* 207–33.
29. Buzan and Weaver, *Regions and Powers,* 6–26.
30. Sharabi, *Neo-Patriarchy.*
31. Adamson, "Global Liberalism vs. Political Islam"; Murden, *Islam, the Middle East and the New Global Hegemony,* chapter 4.
32. Bacik, *Hybrid Sovereignty.*
33. Callinicos and Rosenberg, "Uneven and Combined Development."
34. Fromkin, *A Peace To End All Peace.*
35. Salame, "'Strong' and 'Weak' States."
36. Ayubi, *Overstating the Arab State,* 26–30.
37. Pratt, *Democracy and Authoritarianism.*
38. Dodge and Higgott, *Globalization and the Middle East.*
39. Guazzone and Pioppi, *The Arab State.*
40. Saif, "Arab Leaders and Western Countries"; Zurayk, "Feeding the Arab Uprisings."
41. King, *The New Authoritarianism.*
42. Heydemann, *Networks of Privilege.*
43. Hinnebusch, "Authoritarian Persistence"; Glasser, *Economic Development and Political Reform.*
44. Furia and Lucas, "Determinants of Arab Public Opinion."
45. Gambill, "Explaining the Arab Democracy"; Lynch, *The Arab Uprising,* 223–5.
46. Takeyh, "Close but no Democracy."
47. Jamal, *Of Empires and Citizens.*
48. Hinnebusch, "Europe and the Middle East."
49. Hyde-Price, "Normative Power Europe."
50. Joffe, "Relations between the Middle East and the West," 66–8.
51. Durac and Cavatorta, "Strengthening Authoritarian Rule thorough Democracy Promotion."
52. Ehteshmai, *Globalization and Geopolitics*; Ottoway and Carothers, "The Greater Middle East Initiative."
53. Delacoura, "US Democracy Promotion."
54. Lynch, *The Arab Uprising,* 217.
55. Teti, "The Globalization of Democracy."
56. Nixon, "US Groups."
57. Blank, "Russia's Anxieties."
58. Tamlali, "The 'Arab Spring'."
59. Shehadeh, "Economic Costs, the Arab Spring and the GCC."

60. Heydarian, *How Capitalism Failed the Arab World,* 128–50.
61. Hinnebusch and Tur, *Turkey-Syria Relations.*
62. Barkey, "Turkey and the Arab Spring."
63. Seelye, "Syria Unrest."
64. Lynch, *The Arab Uprising,* 165.
65. Hanieh, "International Aid."

Bibliography

Adamson, Fiona. "Global Liberalism vs. Political Islam, Competing Ideological Frameworks in International Politics." *International Studies Review* 7, no. 4 (2005): 547–569.

Arrighi, Giovanni, and Beverly Silver. "Capitalism and World (dis) Order." In *Empires, Systems and States: Great Transformations in International Politics,* edited by Michael Cox, Tim Dunne, and Ken Booth, 257–279. Cambridge: Cambridge University Press, 2001.

Ayoob, Mohammed. *The Third World Security Predicament, State Making, Regional Conflict and the International System.* Boulder, CO: Lynne Rienner Publishers, 1995.

Ayubi, Nazih. *Overstating the Arab State: Politics and Society in the Middle East.* London: I.B Tauris, 1995.

Bacik, Gokhan. *Hybrid Sovereignty in the Arab Middle East: the Cases of Kuwait, Jordan and Iraq.* New York: Palgrave-Macmillan, 2008.

Barkawi, Tarik, and Mark Laffey. "The Imperial Peace: Democracy, Force and Globalization." *European Journal of International Relations* 5, no. 4 (1999): 403–434.

Barkey, H. J. "Turkey and the Arab Spring." http://carnegieendowment.org/2011/04/26/turkey-and-arab-spring/2s3#comments

Blank, Stephan. "Russia's Anxieties About The Arab Revolution." *E-Notes,* Foreign Policy Research Institute. July 2012. www.fpri.org

Boix, Carles. *Democracy and Distribution.* Cambridge: Cambridge University Press, 2003.

Buzan, Barry. *From International to World Society: English School Theory and the Social Structure of Globalization.* Cambridge: Cambridge University Press, 2004.

Buzan, Barry, and Richard Little. "The Historical Expansion of International Society." In *The International Studies Encyclopedia,* edited by Robert Allen Denemark, 59–75. Chichester, UK: Wiley-Blackwell, August 2008.

Buzan, Barry, and Ole Weaver. *Regions and Powers: The Structure of International Security.* Cambridge: Cambridge University Press, 2003.

Callinicos, Alex, and Justin Rosenberg. "Uneven and Combined Development: The Social Relational Substratum of the International?" *Cambridge Review of International Affairs* 21, no. 1 (2008): 77–112.

Carothers, Thomas. "The Backlash Against Democracy Promotion." *Foreign Affairs*, March/April, 2006.
Clark, Ian. "Another Double Movement: the Great Transformation after the Cold War." In *Empires, Systems and States: Great transformations in International Politics*, edited by Cox et al., 237–255. Cambridge: Cambridge University Press, 2001.
Cox, Richard. "Social Forces, State and World Orders." In *Approaches to World Order*, edited by Richard Cox and Timothy Sinclair, 85–123. Cambridge: Cambridge University Press, 1996.
Delacoura, Katerina. "US Democracy Promotion in the Arab Middle East after 11 September 2001: A Critique." *International Affairs* 81, no. 5 (2005): 963–979.
Dodge, Toby, and Richard Higgott, eds. *Globalization and the Middle East: Islam, Economy, Society and Politics*. London: Royal Institute of International Affairs, 2002.
Durac, Vincent, and Francesco Cavatorta. "Strengthening Authoritarian Rule thorough Democracy Promotion: Examining the Paradox of EU and US Security Strategies." *British Journal of Middle Eastern Studies* 36, no. 1 (2009): 3–19.
Ehteshmai, Anoushirivan. *Globalization and Geopolitics of the Middle East*. London: Routledge, 2007.
Finnamore, Martha. "Norms, Culture and World Politics: Insights from Sociology's Institutionalism." *International Organization* 50, no. 2 (1996): 325–347.
Finnamore, Martha, and Kathryn Sikkink. "International Norm Dynamics and Political Change." *International Organization* 52, no. 4 (1998): 887–917.
Fromkin, David. *A Peace To End All Peace: Creating the Modern Middle East 1914–1922*. New York: Henry Holt & Company, 1989.
Furia, Peter A., and Russell E. Lucas. "Determinants of Arab Public Opinion on Foreign Relations." *International Studies Quarterly* 50 (2006): 585–605.
Gambill, Gary C. "Explaining the Arab Democracy Deficit, Part II: American Policy." *Middle East Intelligence Bulletin* 5, nos. 8–9 (August-September 2003).
Gill, Stephen. *Power and Resistance in the New World Order*. Basingstoke: Palgrave/Macmillan, 2003.
Gilpin, Robert. *War and Change in World Politics*. Cambridge: Cambridge University Press.
Glasser, Bradley Louis. *Economic Development and Political Reform: The Impact of External Capital on the Middle East*. Cheltenham, UK: Edward Elgar, 2001.
Gowan, Peter. *The Global Gamble: Washington's Faustian Bid for World Dominance*. London: Verso, 1999.
Guazzone, Laura, and Daniela Pioppi. *The Arab State and Neo-Liberal Globalization: The Restructuring of the State in the Middle East*. Reading: Ithaca Press, 2009.
Halliday, Fred. *Revolution and World Politics*. Basingstoke: Macmillan, 1999.
Hanieh, Adam. "International Aid and Egypt's Orderly Transition." *Jadaliyya*, May 29, http://www.jadaliyya.com/pages/index/1711/egypts-'orderly-transition'-international-aid.
Hartnett, Stephen, and Laura Stengrim. *Globalization and Empire: The US Invasion of Iraq, Free Markets and the Twilight of Democracy*. Tuscaloosa, AL: University of Alabama Press, 2006.
Harvey, David. *The New Imperialism*. London: Oxford University Press, 2005.
Heydarian, Richard Javad. *How Capitalism Failed the Arab World: the Economic Roots and Precarious Future of the Middle East Uprisings*. London: Zed, 2014.
Heydemann, Steven. *Networks of Privilege in the Middle East: the Politics of Economic Reform Revisited*. Palgrave: Macmillan, 2004.
Hinnebusch, Raymond. "Authoritarian Persistence, Democratization Theory and The Middle East: An Overview and Critique." *Democratization* 13, no. 3 (June 2006): 373–395.
Hinnebusch, Raymond. "Europe and the Middle East: From Imperialism to Liberal Peace?" *Review of European Studies* 4, no. 3 (July 2012): 18–31.

Hinnebusch, Raymond, and Ozlem Tur. *Turkey-Syria Relations: Between Enmity and Amity.* Farnham: Ashgate, 2013.
Huntington, Samuel P. "Democracy's Third Wave." *Journal of Democracy* 2, no. 2 (Spring 1991): 12–34.
Hyde-Price, A. "Normative Power Europe: A Realist Critique." *Journal of European Public Policy* 13 (2006): 217–234.
Jamal, Amaney. *Of Empires and Citizens – Pro-American Democracy or No Democracy at All?* Princeton: Princeton University Press, 2012.
Joffe, George. "Relations between the Middle East and the West: A View from the South." In *The Middle East and Europe: The Power Deficit*, edited by B. A. Roberson, 45–73. London: Routledge, 1994.
King, Stephan. *The New Authoritarianism in the Middle East and North Africa.* Bloomington: Indiana University Press, 2009.
Levitsky, Steven, and Lucian A. Way. "International Linkage and Democratization." *Journal of Democracy* 16, no. 3 (July 2005): 20–34.
Lustick, Ian. "The Absence of Middle Eastern Great Powers: Political Backwardness in Historical Perspective." *International Organization* 51, no. 4 (1997): 653–683.
Lynch, Marc. *The Arab Uprising: The Unfinished Revolutions of the New Middle East.* New York, NY: Public Affairs, 2012.
Murden, Simon. *Islam, the Middle East and the New Global Hegemony.* Boulder, CO: Lynne Rienner Publishers, 2002.
Nixon, R. "US Groups helped nurture Arab Uprising." *New York Times* 2011.
Ottoway, Marina, and Thomas Carothers. "The Greater Middle East Initiative: Off to a False Start." *Carnegie Endowment Policy Brief*, March, 2004.
Petras, James, and Henry Veltmeyer. *Globalization Unmasked: Imperialism in the 21st century.* London: Zed, 2002.
Pratt, Nicola. *Democracy and Authoritarianism in the Arab World.* Boulder, CO: Lynne Rienner Publishers, 2007.
Robinson, William I. *Promoting Polyarchy: Globalization, US Intervention, and Hegemony.* New York: Cambridge University Press, 1996.
Rosecrance, Richard. *Linkage Politics.* New York: Free Press, 1969.
Saif, Ibrahim. "Arab Leaders and Western Countries Swapping Democracy for Business Interests." *Perspectives Middle East #2: People's Power – The Arab World in Revolt*, Beirut: Heinrich Boll Foundation, 2011, 106–11, http://www.boell.de/en/2011/05/06/perspectives-middle-east-2-peoples-power-arab-world-revolt
Salame, Ghassan. "'Strong' and 'Weak' States: A Qualified Return to the Muqaddimah." In *Foundations of the Arab State*, edited by G. Salame, 29–64. London: Croom Helm, 1987.
Seelye, Kate. "Syria Unrest 'Cannot Be Contained.'" *The Daily Beast*, March 28, 2011. http://www.thedailybeast.com/articles/2011/03/28/syria-unrest-cannot-be-contained-dissidents-say.html
Sharabi, Hisham. *Neo-Patriarchy: A Theory of Distorted Change in Arab Society.* Oxford: Oxford University Press, 1996.
Shehadeh, Nael. "Economic Costs, the Arab Spring and the GCC." *Gulf Research Bulletin* (November 24, 2011).
Solingen, Etel. *Regional Orders at Century's Dawn: Global and Domestic Influence on Grand Strategy.* Princeton: Princeton University Press, 1998.
Sorensen, Georg. *Democracy & Democratization.* Boulder, CO: Westview Press, 1998.
Stephan, Maria J., and Erica Chenoweth. "Why Civil Resistance Works: The Strategic Logic of Nonviolent Conflict." *International Security* 33, no. 1 (2008): 7–44.
Takeyh, Ray. "Close But No Democracy." *National Interest*, no. 78 (Winter 2004/5): 57–64.

Tamlali, Yassin. "The 'Arab Spring': Rebirth or Final Throes of Pan-Arabism?" In *Perspectives Middle East #2: People's Power – The Arab World in Revolt*, 46–49. Beirut: Heirich Boll Foundation, 2011.

Teti, Andrea. "The Globalization of Democracy and the Location of the Middle East in the Contemporary World Order." In *The Middle East and Globalization*, edited by Stephan Stetter, 77–97. New York: Palgrave Macmillan, 2012.

Waltz, Kenneth. *The Theory of International Politics*. New York: McGraw-Hill, 1979.

Zurayk, Rami. "Feeding the Arab Uprisings." In *Perspectives Middle East #2: People's Power – The Arab World in Revolt*, 119–125. Beirut: Heirich Boll Foundation, 2011.

Conclusion: agency, context and emergent post-uprising regimes

Raymond Hinnebusch

School of International Relations, University of St. Andrews, St. Andrews, UK

This conclusion summarizes the evidence explaining the divergent trajectories taken by post Arab uprising states in terms of multiple variables, each illustrated by an iconic case, namely: State Failure and Competitive governance (Syria), Regime Restoration and Hybrid Governance (Egypt) and Polyarchic Governance (Tunisia). Factors include the starting point: levels of opposition mobilization and regimes' resilience – a function of their patrimonial-bureaucratic balance; whether or not a transition coalition forms is crucial for democratization prospects. Context also matters for democratization, particularly political economic factors, such as a balance of class power and a productive economy; political culture (level of societal identity cleavages) and a minimum of international intervention. Finally, the balance of agency between democracy movements, Islamists, the military and workers shapes democratization prospects.

The introduction to this issue surveyed how starting points – regimes and uprisings against them – made some subsequent trajectories more likely than others. Thus, violent uprisings and state failure sharply narrowed democratization prospects, while relatively peaceful transitions widened them. However, as the subsequent chapters showed, agency – the struggle of rival social forces in the period after uprisings began – also contributed to outcomes. Such agency was itself affected by the political economy, cultural and international contexts. Together, starting points, subsequent agency and context shaped divergent trajectories of post-uprising regime re-formation.

Agency

Anti-regime democracy movements

Secular middle class youth with their internet proficiency were instrumental in overcoming atomization and enabling anti-regime mobilization. In particular, the unemployed educated, seeking themselves as the victims of discriminatory crony capitalism, embraced democracy as the answer. The peaceful protest their discourse promoted was compatible with a democratic transition. They were the vanguard of movements that forced the departure of authoritarian leaders and/or won potentially democratic constitutional changes. However, the youth movements proved unable to capitalize on the fall or weakening of old regimes.

Vincent Durac pointed to the leaderless, highly heterogeneous nature of the anti-regime movements that shared only the desire for the fall of the regime, and that, once this happened, quickly divided into contentious factions. Their lack of ideology and organization meant they did not constitute a counter government that could replace incumbent regimes, nor mobilize empowering mass votes. Moreover, splits between secularists and Islamists broke the anti-regime front, enabling the deep state to recover. In Egypt and Morocco, secular liberals' inability to compete with the Islamists in elections quickly compromised their commitment to democracy and revived the ability of the "deep state" – the military or the monarchy – to use them against the Islamists. Only in Tunisia did secular forces remain united enough to both balance and compromise with Islamists. In cases such as Syria and Libya, the heterogeneity and fragmentation of the movements meant they could not reach any kind of pacted transition with incumbent rulers and, as a result, soon became armed factions, propelling state failure and much reducing the prospects of a democratic outcome.

Islamists

Islamist movements were key actors in post-uprising political contestation. Variations in their relations with ruling regimes and other political forces were central to outcomes. Islamists' critics widely predicted that democratic elections could bring anti-democratic Islamists to power who would end democracy. Others argued that inclusion in the political process incentivized Islamists to moderate their ideologies in order to enable anti-authoritarian coalitions with secular opposition groups, maximize their voter appeal, and negotiate constraints from secular institutions such as the military and judiciary.[1]

Initially, Islamists appeared to be the main beneficiaries – with their organized committed activist followings, electoral experience, charity networks, schools and television stations, welfare services and ability to speak for the deprived, funding from the Gulf, competitive advantage from use of mosques and madrassas for recruitment – and the greater debilitation of the secular political opposition under authoritarian rule. Post-uprising, while liberals and secularists focused on street protests, the Islamists concentrated on organizing for elections and, in Tunisia and Egypt, Islamists got pluralities in the first democratic elections, but not solid majorities needed to marginalize opposition and govern effectively.[2]

However Islamists were themselves variegated, all were not equally empowered and inter-Islamist splits soon cost them their opportunity to achieve hegemony. In their contribution to this special issue, Frédéric Volpi and Ewan Stein assessed the fortunes of three brands of Islam after the uprising. Initially the Muslim Brotherhood's state-oriented "electoral Islam" appeared to be empowered by the removal of authoritarian presidents, as well by the support and inspiration of Turkey's Adalet ve Kalkınma Partisi (AKP), a model of apparently successful pragmatic Islamic governance. Salafists, already on the rise before the uprising, were energized and propelled into the political arena by the uprising and by funding from Saudi Arabia, which saw them as an instrument against both the Muslim Brotherhood and secular revolutionaries. The behaviour of the Brothers in Egypt where, outflanked and pushed right by the Salafists, they broke several promises not to push their agenda too far, alarmed secularists, with similar tensions observable in Tunisia.[3] Trans-state jihadist movements inspired by Al Qaeda initially appeared discredited by the prospect of democratization via peaceful protest. However, the new opportunities in failed states resulting from civil war in the Levant and North Africa, combined with the military's repression of the Muslim Brothers in Egypt, reversed the relative power balance within the Islamist camp. This empowering of non-democratic and violent jihadists (Syria/Iraq); the military's political exclusion of a significant sector of Islamic civil society (Egypt); and the renewed ability of revived regimes to play off rival brands of Islamists and secularists halted moves toward democratization. Without inclusion of Islamist movements willing to play by democratic rules, such as the Brothers, with their mass constituencies, greatest capacity among social forces to balance the power of the state, and unique ability to confer legitimacy on market capitalism, no democratic transition is likely.[4]

The military and security forces

Eva Bellin[5] argued that a main ingredient of authoritarian resilience had for many decades been the reliability of large effective security forces and that, similarly, militaries' responses to the uprisings were crucial to outcomes. These responses varied depending on factors such as the institutional autonomy, repressive capabilities, and interests (political, economic, communal, professional) of military establishments.[6] Initially, seeing the rapid departure of presidents in Tunisia, Egypt and Yemen, many judged that political mobilization had exceeded the repressive containment powers of the old regimes; however, the military and security forces have regrouped, restoring some of the old state-society (im)balance. In his contribution to this special issue, Joshua Stacher, observes that while *states* may have been weakened by the uprising, *regimes*, and particularly their coercive cores, have not only survived but also dramatically expanded the use of violence to rescue old orders.

Variations in the military's role were pivotal for outcomes. In Egypt, where the military retained institutional autonomy of the top political leadership and also had conflicts of interest with the presidential family as well as a large stake in the preservation of the establishment, including considerable command of large sectors of the economy, it sacrificed the president to preserve itself and the institutions and territorial integrity of the state. Its dependence on Western support also made it unwilling to risk its funding via mass repression on behalf of the president. Once Mubarak departed, Egypt's large politicized army attempted to retain command of the transition process and steer it in such as way as to preserve its interests. When it faced resistance, it did not hesitate to repress protestors when they targeted its own interests and particularly in its attacks on the Muslim Brothers after al-Sisi's coup it showed that an institutionalized US funded military was no less willing than patrimonial leaders to use massive violence to defend its vital interests. Moreover, it possessed the repressive capacity to reassert control over Egyptian society and territory (even if contested in Sinai). This was pivotal in enabling *restoration* of a *hybrid regime*. By contrast in Tunisia the limited repressive capacities and de-politicization of the military was decisive for enabling democratic transition.

In Syria, sectarian penetration and Baathist politicization of the military reduced its autonomy, keeping the bulk of it loyal to the regime. Identity differences between the military and protestors much reduced the chances of defections from the security forces when they were ordered to fire on civilians, hence the chances of a transition pact. The Syrian military retained enough institutional cohesion to defend the regime from collapse; yet incremental defections on identity grounds, acquired enough critical mass to staff a rival "Free Syrian Army", leading to militarized *civil war and stalemate*.

In Libya and Yemen militaries were least institutionalized and most communally riven, thus most vulnerable to fairly rapid and major splits along tribal and family lines. Where they split, with part remaining loyal to the leader and part opposed, the outcome was *stalemate* (Yemen). Where, as in Libya, the military disintegrated, a function of Qaddafi's weakening it as an institution, the result was *state failure*.

Workers

In his contributory article, Jamie Allinson examines the variable impact of the working classes on post-uprising trajectories. Where workers movements were, as a result of greater industrialization, larger and better organized, as in Egypt and Tunisia, even though their top leadership had long been co-opted by regimes, they played key roles in anti-authoritarian mobilization. Workers' unions were pivotal in the mobilization against the president in Tunisia where the formal union structure recovered its autonomy and helped organize the uprising. In Egypt, Tripp[7] argues that nationwide strike action made it clear to the Egyptian military that opposition to Mubarak was too deep and widespread to be rolled back.

In alliance with the middle class, workers, as Rueschemeyer, Stephens and Stephens show,[8] are crucial elements of a democratic coalition that is necessary to drive democratization. Aschar observes that workers constituted the real alternative to the other two post-uprising contending forces, the military/state establishment and Islamist movements, both of which stood for variations of the neoliberalism against which the uprisings initially mobilized.[9] Yet, the outcome has not been uniform, with the official unions co-opted by the military in Egypt and playing the key brokerage role in democratic consolidation in Tunisia. The marginalization of organized workers during the uprisings in Syria, Libya and Yemen was associated with both state failure and democratic failure.

Generally, it can be hypothesized that the *balance of agency* between these four actors will bias trajectories in certain ways. Where pro-democracy social movements and organized workers are strong, the military weak or non-political, and Islamists moderate, chances for polyarchy are best (Tunisia); where the military is strong and politicized, Islamists moderate, and democracy and workers movements fairly strong, a hybrid formula results (Egypt); a strong military, radicalization of Islamists, and weakened democracy movements and worker unions biases the outcome toward state failure and civil war (Syria).

The political economy context

Outcomes are, however, not merely the result of agency, which must operate within a pre-existing political economy structure. Historical sociologists such as Barrington Moore[10] showed that variations in modernizing coalitions shape democracy possibilities: where the state joined with the landed oligarchy to repress and exploit the peasantry to serve an agricultural export strategy, the result was conservative authoritarianism, while if the peasants were included in a radical coalition against the landed class, authoritarianism of the left resulted – as in the Arab populist republics. Moore and later Rueschemeyer, Stephens and Stephens showed that inclusive democratization requires a balance of class power, including some state autonomy of the dominant classes and a bourgeois alliance with the organized working class to extract power sharing from the state.

In MENA, however, political economy is unfavourable to democratization. First, rentier states produce state-dependent bourgeoisies and clientalized citizens (combined, in many cases, with readily expelled expatriate labour); indeed, states with copious rent have proved most resistant to the uprising. Second, the pathway of the earlier populist regimes, under which a more inclusive ruling coalition corresponded to social reform and import substitute industrialization, was cut short by some combination of capital accumulation failures, lost wars and international financial institution (IFI) pressures for "structural adjustment." The neo-liberal "solution" to the populist crisis – re-empowering investors and export strategies that required the repression of labour costs – shaped new state-crony capitalist coalitions to exclude labour as well as deepening dependencies on global finance capital. Neo-liberalism drives a wedge between bourgeoisie and workers at the expense of the democratic coalition between them needed to check the power of the deep state.

While the uprisings were rooted in protest at the neo-liberal "solution," Aschar[11] observes that they remained purely political, with no attempts to attack economic injustice or dysfunction; rather, they actually worsened economic growth, hence prospects for addressing unemployment, by deterring investors, particularly in manufacturing. Moreover, a root cause of under-investment, the exceptional export of MENA capital to the West by family dynasties in oil rich mini-states, at the expense of regional investment, can hardly be addressed by revolutions in the republics. In parallel, the enduring dependence on the Western-centred international financial system locked Egypt and Tunisia, the two states with the best prospects for democratization, into neo-liberal practices that removed the big issues of politics – distribution of wealth – from domestic political agendas.

With socio-economic alternatives off the political agenda, political competition in the post-uprising states was diverted into *cultural wars* over identity issues framed in destabilizing zero-sum terms (Islamist vs. secularist, Sunni vs. Shia). Under such conditions, political pluralism, where it survives, is likely to be mixed with doses of authoritarian power in order to manage identity conflicts and turn back demands for social justice that cannot be accommodated in a global neo-liberal economic order. The least bad outcome under neo-liberalism has tended to be "low intensity democracy" in which elections serve as an institutionalized mechanism for elite circulation that may constrain the state but only marginally empowers the masses;[12] this may well lead to their disillusionment and support for alternatives such as Salafism or even for restorations of elements of the old regime. Indeed, in Tunisia where democratic transition was most advanced, disillusionment with democracy set in, political contestation was diverted into cultural wars and the October 2014 elections led to a certain restoration of old elites. This does not mean indigenous agency and resistance is unimportant: Tripp suggests that within the global neo-liberal order, resistance can alleviate the worse effects of the system or carve out a space for autonomous action. For Aschar, outcomes depend on freedom for organized workers' movements and on the "unblockage" of investment propensities among an industrial bourgeoisie in order to restart growth.[13] One could therefore hypothesize, that a degree of economic "unblockage" and some balance between classes (bourgeoisie and workers) and between classes and the state (as in Tunisia) facilitates democratic transition; their absence underlies either autocracy *or* state failure if radical movements fill the vacuum; while a middle scenario of *some* balance enables hybrid regimes.

Between structure and agency: the political cultural variable

Political culture is a residue of historical structures that constrain agency as well as being reproduced and altered by it. Given that culture changes only over long periods while the Arab world has experienced both authoritarian quiescence and attempted democratic revolution in a period of mere decades, culture, per se, would appear to carry limited explanatory power.[14] It might be argued that the historic cycles of popular submission when the state is strong and revolt when it is weak reflects a durable political culture inhospitable to democracy.[15] Yet polling evidence that Arabs, including pious Muslims, value democracy[16] and the demand for it expressed by millions of Arabs in the uprising, seems incompatible with the exceptionalist image of an unchanging Middle East cultural propensity for authoritarian rule.

However, Stepan and Linz [17] suggest that disputes over the role of religion in politics have made it difficult for Arab societies to arrive at a consensus on democratic rules of the game. Symptomatically, all parties in Egypt wanted limits on majorities built into the constitution: secularists wanted the military to introduce guarantees against Islamist majorities while the Muslim Brotherhood wanted legislation vetted by a religious body like Iran's Council of Guardians. This suggests that support for democracy can be wide but shallow: middle class secularists may value personal liberty more than democracy and sacrifice the latter if it means Islamists can curtail the former; Islamists can value democracy but subordinate it to religious law.

Nevertheless, culture and identity are far from fixed. Dialogue can enable compromise across cultural differences and contentious politics tends to harden them. In this respect, a main locus of cultural interaction, the media, played a prominent but two-sided role. While the new media – satellite television and the internet – had, prior to the uprisings, apparently produced an Arab public sphere that promoted an informed and active citizenry tolerant of a pluralism of views, once they became instruments of political struggle during the uprising, democratic civility gave way to hyperbole and polarization. With the much renewed permeability of weakened states, the internet became a vehicle of misinformation, while satellite TV channels, owned by Gulf states, business tycoons, salafi preachers or sectarian groups, became instruments to fight proxy cultural wars that fragmented the new public.[18] Where, in the many multi-identity societies of the region, elements of shared civic identity were shattered by the instrumentalist use of sectarian cleavages, as in Bahrain and Syria, media-spread sectarian discourse diverted mass mobilization into sectarian conflict; even in homogeneous societies such as Egypt, cultural wars were constructed as the secularists and the military launched a sustained media campaign to demonize the Muslim Brotherhood. Such identity cleavages tend to produce exclusionary governance strategies and are a major obstacle to creating a consensus for prioritizing democratic rules of the game.

What made Tunisia somewhat different was that these cleavages were more muted, partly because of the country's long history of secularism, down to the agency of the founding father, Bourguiba. Tunisia's more civic political culture was reinforced, as Durac observed, because exiled secularist and Islamist elites had a history of dialogue before the revolution. The mainstream Islamist party was relatively liberal and the role of Gulf funded salafis relatively contained – although not entirely, since several assassinations of secular leaders almost precipitated a breakdown similar to Egypt's.

In summary, the more homogeneous the identity and the greater the propensity to compromise between Islamists and secularists, the more a civic culture supportive of democracy exists (Tunisia). Where identity is fragmented and compromise blocked, the uprising challenge to states resulted in failed states (Syria). A homogeneous culture plus failed religio-secular compromise is compatible with a hybrid regime (Egypt).

The international variable

The international variable contributed both to precipitating the uprising and to the failure of democratic transition. First, not only did the globalization of neo-liberal economics generate post-populist crony capitalism, but also the West's democracy campaigns, empowered by globalization of communications, delegitimized post populist regimes. Then, in the wake of uprisings, mounted in good part against neo-liberalism, Western IFIs sought use the weakening of economies in uprising states to deepen neo-liberalism in the region, threatening to hollow out democratization before it had even began.

The external factor was important too, in affecting the power balance between regimes and oppositions. The restraint of the army in Egypt was partly a function of foreign dependency. While its oil riches ought to have given the Qaddafi regime the resources to survive, its relative international isolation opened it to foreign intervention; conversely, the survival of the oil-poor Asad regime was contingent on significant external financial and military support and protection by its Russian and Iranian allies.

At the regional level, the *competitive interference* of rival powers (Iran, Saudi Arabia, Qatar, Turkey) in uprising states, where they backed warring sides and alternative governance models, contributing to democratic reversal or civil war. The Sunni Gulf Cooperation Council powers and Turkey (themselves split over support for rival kinds of Islamists) and Iran deployed sectarian polarization against each other. Moreover, both sides used rent transfers to bolster anti-democratic forces – the non-oil monarchies, the military in Egypt, the Asad regime, salafis. But with neither side able to sweep the board, the result was both the destabilization of states and the fragmenting of publics between secularists and varieties of rival Islamists. Democratic transition was blocked and reconstituted regimes emerging from such communal power struggles were likely to incorporate some identity communities in order to exclude others. The resulting norm fragmentation meant democracy had little chance of becoming "hegemonic" in the region.

It can therefore be hypothesized that the more a country becomes an arena of competitive interference, the less likely is democratic transition; thus, while Tunisia managed to avoid such intervention, Libya suffered its most extreme form, with the result being polar opposite outcomes – democratic transition and state failure; Egypt, a middle case, facilitated a hybrid state.

The partial reconstitution of governance: emergent regime types

There is a widespread belief that the popular mobilization unleashed by the uprising cannot be "put back in the box." The uprisings unleashed a new wave of instability similar to that experienced in the Arab post-independence years, albeit now with much larger, more mobilized and, in some places, highly armed, populations. But whether this means democratization is unavoidable or whether political participation will, instead, take new forms in failed or hybrid regimes remains in contention. As Morten Vallbjorn explained in his contribution to this special issue, the notion of re-politicization implies a struggle between a *re-politicized*, more mobilized citizenry less deterred by the fear barrier and rulers trying to bring them under control through old oligarchic practices, new authoritarian upgrading techniques and, as Stacher points out, unrestrained violence. Elites will have to work harder at appeasing, co-opting and dividing the citizenry; but they are likely to be so divided themselves that this will not prove easy. The result is likely to be *neither* stable authoritarian nor democratic states, but unstable and "failed" hybrids. Politics is likely to be a deepened version of Huntington's[19] "praetorianism" – mixtures of military repression, ballot box contestation, street protest and "terrorism" – in which, as he put it, "clubs are trumps." As Stacher points out in his article, quantitative studies indicate contested transitional periods suffer greater violence: "more murder in the middle." Nevertheless, a partial reconstruction of authority is also underway, even in failed states, with three major observable trajectories driven by different conjunctions of forces.

Outcome 1: State failure and competitive governance

A major unintended consequence of the uprising has been state failure. In his article, Adham Saouli traced the special vulnerability of the more identity-fragmented Arab states to the limited inclusion of identity groups by regimes constructed around sectarian cores and with artificial borders exposing them to the destabilizing effect of trans-state interference. In such states there is a high risk that *regime weakening or failure will lead to state failure*. In the most immediate sense, states' failure resulted from the incapacity of the military to defend their territorial integrity, either because it was kept weak (Libya), was decimated by foreign intervention (Iraq, Libya) or suffered significant defections (Syria). There are variations, of course, notably Libya wherein the regime and state disintegrated in parallel vs. Syria and Iraq where regimes regrouped around a sectarian and territorial core but the state's overall territorial integrity was debilitated.

The consequent breakdown of order, particularly in multi-communal societies, ushers in the *security dilemma*, as people fall back on primordial solidarity groups – tribes, sects – for survival while demonizing the "other," with the supposedly "defensive" actions of each group making all more insecure. Moreover, as government loses the capacity to deliver services and the normal economy fails, rival movements acquire a stake in a war economy through smuggling, looting, the arms trade, and exploitation of natural resources (oil), while ordinary persons, insecure and deprived of their livelihoods, gravitate to warlords and militias for survival or exit the country as refugees.

Yet, amidst civil war, "competitive state reconstruction"[20] takes place. Ibn Khaldun identified cycles of state collapse and reformation in MENA where historically a new dynasty (regime) was founded by a charismatic leader, possessing followers bound both by kinship *asabiyya* (social solidarity) and religious zeal. As Tilly[21] and others indicate, opposition movements prevail that combine an ideological message, ability to provide security through command of armed violence, and control of resources enabling provision of social goods. Charismatic leaders with armed followings seeking to construct alternative states are most evident in ISIS's trans-state operations, straddling eastern Syria and western Iraq, aiming to create a caliphate and overthrow "artificial" boundaries imposed by "Sykes-Picot," but similar phenomenon are also evident in North Africa as a result of Libyan state collapse and in Yemen. In parallel, the surviving cores of pre-existing regime became more dependent on ethno-sectarian *asabiyya* and therefore less institutionalized and inclusive. Whichever side prevails, this form of state formation is likely to result in the exclusion of the losers and eventual decline into neo-patrimonial rule. However, where neither side can defeat the other, a "hurting stalemate" could create conditions for a power-sharing settlement, provided the "commitment problem" – that neither side can trust the other to keep their agreements and not seek revenge – could be overcome, possibly through international guarantee of a settlement and international peace-keepers. The loss of control of formerly centralizing states over their territory, combined with the surge of sectarian identities at the expense of state identities, suggests that political reconstruction will require new forms of consociational ethno-sectarian power-sharing. This is, however, likely to result in a hybrid authority formula, with mixtures of authoritarian and pluralist, informal and formal, governance.

Outcome 2: Regime restoration and hybrid governance

Where the state remains intact and the regime survives the uprising, one possible outcome is "restoration." The exceptional mass activism of revolutionary outbursts cannot be sustained: Brinton's classic exploration of post-revolutionary "Thermidor" sees a yearning for order empowering a "man on horseback." Political sociologists such as Mosca and Michels[22] exposed the practices used to restore or sustain elite or class rule in spite of increased politicization, revolution and competitive elections: an Iron Law of Oligarchy is sustained through elites' disproportionate resources (information, wealth), command of the levers of bureaucracies and relative cohesion compared to the divided public. In the Marxist tradition democracy remains purely formal – "bourgeois," "for the few" – when the grossly unequal distribution of wealth robs formally equal citizenship of substance. The inequality accompanying the globalization of finance capital everywhere "hollows out" democracy. [23] When powerful bureaucracies, crony capitalists and co-opted worker unions survive an uprising, it only takes the onset of mass weariness of disorder to open the door to "restoration."

Yet, in the wake of the Arab uprising, elites need new forms of "authoritarian upgrading" to manage more mobilized masses. While the redistributive populism through which the early republics consolidated themselves is incompatible with economic globalization, the subsequent post-populist crony capitalism was an immediate cause of the uprising and cannot be wholly restored either. As such, some hybrid formula combining features of both seems likely, with forms of populist jingoism (sectarianism, "war on terror") mixed with electoral authoritarianism. States possessing rents can sustain patrimonial practices of co-optation and enable a modicum of welfare populism in order to deter cross-class mobilization. This is compatible with hybrid regimes, featuring middle levels of both elite contestation and mass inclusion (Egypt).

Outcome 3: Polyarchic governance

The final possible pathway from the uprising is where democratic transition ends in polyarchy. The democratization literature identifies several enabling conditions. The existence of a shared political community enabling peaceful electoral contestation[24] has been problematic in MENA owing to strong sub- and supra-state identities rivalling loyalty to the state; the Arab uprising unleashed further powerful cultural wars. However, the states are less vulnerable to these rival identities in relatively homogeneous societies where they have historical roots (Egypt, Tunisia) as compared to the "artificial" fragmented states of the Levant; democratization prospects are better in the former.

Second, democratic consolidation rests on a balance of class power and a "democratic coalition" able to extract democratization from the state. While rent is widely used by MENA regimes to deter such a coalition by clientalizing society and co-opting bourgeoisies, where rent is modest and where more advanced modernization and industrialization enables a democratic coalition between the educated middle class and the organized working class, a class balance might be approximated (Tunisia).

For Weberians such as Huntington,[25] polyarchy requires that power be both *concentrated* in institutions – an executive with centralized command of bureaucracies – and *diffused* through incorporation of mass participation via mass political parties. The prototype is Turkey where Ataturk first concentrated power and built institutions; at a later stage, when the requisites of democratization were thought sufficient, elites presided over democratization from above by transformation of the single ruling party into a two-party system with competitive elections. This scenario was vastly facilitated by Ataturk's successful nation-building project that endowed nationalist legitimacy on state institutions. However, in Arab countries, despite political liberalization and pluralization experiments starting in the 1990s, Turkish-style democratic institutionalization from above never acquired momentum, in good part because nationalist legitimacy was prematurely lost, and instead change was initiated by the Arab Spring's mobilization from below. Democratization requires a *transitional insider-outsider ruling coalition* – "clean" remnants of the old regime, notably the bureaucracy, and leaders of peaceful protests – with the authority to steer a democratization of the institutions of the old regime via multi-party elections.

AFTER THE ARAB UPRISINGS

Unfortunately, the conditions of democratic consolidation, a shared identity, a balance of class forces, institutions capable of incorporating mass participation, and an insider-outsider transition coalition were largely absent in the post-Arab uprising period, with the possible exception of Tunisia.

Diverging pathways: The determinants of three prototypical cases

Multiple variables shaped the different trajectories followed by uprising states. These are summarized in Table 1 and are here brought together to explain the three prototypical cases: Syria, where transition failed; Egypt, where it was reversed; and Tunisia, where it was relatively successful.

Syria: failed transition, failed state

Conditions for democratic transition were not favourable in Syria: identity fragmentation and the lack of a class balance weakened society, while a robust combination of *both* patrimonial authority and bureaucratic institutions gave the regime exceptional resilience. Owing to the cross cutting of class inequalities by urban-rural and sectarian cleavages, the narrow opportunity structure (weak civil society) and the willingness of the loyal military to use violence against protestors, mobilization was insufficient to overthrow the regime but enough to deprive it of control over wide parts of the country. The soft-liners were marginalized on both sides by the regime's use of violence, the maximalist demands of the opposition and the identity cleavages between regime security forces and the protestors. Defections from the military were sufficient, together with high levels of external intervention, to militarize the conflict, resulting in protracted civil war and a failed state. This diverted the country away from democratization and along other pathways. Anti-democratic agents – the military, jihadists – were empowered while democratic forces – the protesting youth, the trade unions – were marginalized. The uprising greatly sharpened identity cleavages along both sectarian and secular-Islamist lines. No cross-class democratic coalition was conceivable as the destruction to the political economy infrastructure debilitated capitalist production relations and generated a parasitic war economy that locked Syria into a much-deepened crisis for at least the immediate future.

Egypt: Reversed transition

In Egypt an anti-regime cross-class coalition and a favourable opportunity structure – manifest in considerable civil society experience and internet penetration – enabled a massive bandwagoning against the ruler; the relative autonomy of the military, which prioritized its own interests, enabled an insider-outsider coalition to engineer presidential departure. In spite of a relatively peaceful transition from Mubarak's rule, the post-uprising power struggle between secular revolutionaries, the military and Islamists was unconstrained by agreement on rules of

Table 1. Variables shaping divergent tangents.

Variables	Syria	Egypt	Tunisia
MASS MOBILIZATION			
Cleavages	Mobilization diluted by cross-cutting cleavages	Bandwagoning via cross-class coalitions	Bandwagoning via cross-class coalitions
Opportunity Structure	Diluted by Low civil society experience	Facilitated by high civil society experience	Facilitated by high civil society experience
REGIME CAPACITY (co-optative and coercive)	Patrimonial-bureaucratic balance	Patrimonialism bureaucratically constrained	Patrimonialism bureaucratically constrained
Military role	Low autonomy-loyal to leader	High autonomy	High autonomy
Bureaucratic territorial penetration	Medium	High	High
TRANSITION COALITION	No → presidential survival + protracted insurgency → state failure	Yes → presidential removal, transition starts → state establishment survival	Yes → presidential removal, transition starts → state establishment survival
POLITICAL ECONOMY			
class balance	Lack of class balance	Lack of class balance	Some class balance
economy	War economy	Rentier economy	Productive economy
POLITICAL CULTURE			
societal identity	Fragmented	Homogeneous	Homogeneous
secular-religious cleavage	High	High	Low
COMPETITIVE EXTERNAL INTERVENTION	High	Medium	Low
AGENCY			
Dominant forces and their relations	Military vs. radical Islamists	Military vs. moderate Islamists	Moderate Islamists + trade unionists +civil society
OUTCOME	**Failed State**	**Hybrid regime**	**Polyarchy**

the game. The lack of a strong organized pro-democracy movement and autonomous trade unions, compared to the over-sized politicized military, and the split between secularists and divided Islamists allowed a substantial "restoration" of the old regime. This reflected the lack of a balance of class power able to check a rent-funded state. Post-uprising authoritarian upgrading depended on sophisticated versions of divide and rule, as exemplified by military's cooptation of the Muslim Brotherhood to demobilize street protests followed by its co-optation of the "Tamarod" (grassroots protest) movement to destroy the Brotherhood's President

Morsi. No democracy that excludes one of the most important socio-political forces in Egypt can be consolidated and only a hybrid regime, retaining extra-constitutional powers for the security forces, can cope with the violent spillover of Islamist resistance. Saudi Arabia played a crucial role in encouraging and supporting the counter-revolution, both in funding the al-Sisi regime and in encouraging its Salafist clients to break with the Brotherhood and support the military. A populist-xenophobic intolerance of dissent more repressive than under Mubarak was combined with electoral authoritarianism manifested in Sisi's election and the rather dim prospects of free parliamentary elections amidst the exclusion of the Brotherhood.

Tunisia: Transition and institutionalization

As in Egypt, cross-class grievances and a favourable opportunity structure – civil society experience – enabled bandwagoning mobilization that, given the refusal of an autonomous military to protect the president, enabled an insider-outsider democratic coalition. Yet Tunisia's transition was not similarly stalled. Political culture inheritances – Tunisia's secular tradition, relative homogeneity and long history of statehood – consolidated the political community needed to underpin contestation over other issues. Its historically more moderate Islamist movement enabled compromise between Islamists and secularists. What made the big difference from Egypt was Tunisia's larger middle class, greater mass literacy and a small unpoliticized army. The Islamist en-Nahda party won a plurality in the first post uprising elections but, unlike the Egyptian Brotherhood, shared power with two secular parties, and a secularist politician became president alongside an Islamist prime minister. Moderate democratic Islamists were much stronger that Salafists and, contrary to the case in Egypt, entered a coalition with secularists rather than the Salafists. Nevertheless, before long the secularist-Islamist cleavage threatened to destabilize the country: militant salafists' attempts to restrict cultural expression they considered anti-Islamic seemed tolerated by the government and the murders of secular political leaders critical of the en-Nahda government plunged the country into a crisis in 2013 similar to what was, in parallel, happening in Egypt. However, by contrast to Egypt, there was no "man on horseback" in Tunisia's small politically unambitious military that rival political forces could call upon to "rescue" the country from the other; hence they had to compromise their differences through dialogue. The constituent assembly was more inclusive than in Egypt and was able to reach a compromise constitutional formula. Crucially, the balance of agency favoured democratic forces. The limited role of the military in public life and the exceptional role of the trade union movement in brokering a consensus had its origins in the fact that the independence movement had combined a powerful political party, the Destour, and an equally powerful union movement, pre-empting the role of national vanguard assumed elsewhere, including Egypt, by the army.

As a result, Tunisia experienced the most thorough democratization. Still, the revolution remained purely political: only the top political elite was renewed, with the ouster of the ruling family and some ruling party elites while the bourgeoisie and the military establishment survived. Indeed, Tunisia experienced a mild restoration as a result of the October 2014 elections in which a "Bourguibist" party dominated by old regime elites was voted into power at the expense of the post-Ben Ali currents, both the secular democratic movements and an-Nahda; the elections reflected both cultural cleavages and nostalgia for order and economic stability. Ultimately, the better prognosis for democratic transition in Tunisia than elsewhere was rooted in the success of the uprising in ameliorating (rather than aggravating) the pre-uprising crisis.

Conclusion

Immediate post-uprising outcomes varied significantly in line with differing combinations of the factors indicated in Table 1. While in Egypt and Tunisia bandwagoning mobilization against the regime and military autonomy combined to produce presidential removal and regime survival, initiating a relatively peaceful transition from authoritarian rule, in Syria the dilution of mobilization by cross cutting cleavages and presidential control of the military precluded such a peaceful transition.

Differing political economy and political cultural contexts drove further divergence among the cases. Homogeneous cultures in Tunisia and Egypt kept the state together compared to the state failure resulting from cultural fragmentation in Syria. However, the greater culture of compromise in Tunisia allowed agreement on rules of the game, while contests over the rules split Egypt. While Tunisia came closest to a class balance, given the relative strength of industrialization and organized labour, external rent in Egypt and a rent-fuelled war economy in Syria weakened or precluded such a balance. In Tunisia the balance of agency – a combination of a weak military, moderate Islamists and strong trade unions – facilitated democratic transition; in Egypt the domination of the political arena by the strong politicized military reversed this transition; while the combination of strong military and radical Islamists in Syria led to militarized conflict and the division of state territory. Finally, external intervention in Tunisia was too limited to disrupt democratization; medium intervention facilitated democratic reversal in Egypt; and intense competitive interference in Syria blocked any resolution of civil war.

Disclosure statement

No potential conflict of interest was reported by the author.

Notes

1. Brynen et al., *Beyond the Arab Spring*, 119–46.

2. Heyderian, *How Capitalism Failed*, 95–110; Lynch, *The Arab Uprising*, 146–59.
3. Lynch, *The Arab Uprising*, 210–3.
4. Brynen et al., *Beyond the Arab Spring*, 119–46.
5. Bellin, "Authoritarianism in the Middle East."
6. Gause III, "Why Middle East Studies Missed the Arab Spring."
7. Tripp, *The Power and the People*, 163.
8. Rueschemeyer et al., *Capitalist Development and Democracy.*
9. Aschar, *The People Want*, 152–99.
10. Moore, *The Social Origins of Dictatorship and Democracy.*
11. Aschar, *The People Want*, 13–8.
12. Robinson, *Promoting Polyarchy.*
13. Tripp, *The Power and the People,* 175; Aschar, *The People Want,* 290–3.
14. Brynen et al., *Beyond the Arab Spring*, 95–100.
15. Zubaida, "The 'Arab Spring' in Historical Perspective."
16. Brynen et al., *Beyond the Arab Spring,* 95–117.
17. Stepan and Linz, "Democratization Theory."
18. Brynen et al., *Beyond the Arab Spring*, 233–56; Heyderian, *How Capitalism Failed,* 151–71; Lynch, *The Arab Uprising.*
19. Huntington, *Political Order.*
20. Jones, "The Rise of Afghanistan's Insurgency," 17.
21. Tilly, *Coercion, Capital, and European States.*
22. Mosca, *The Ruling Class*; Michels, *Political Parties.*
23. Cavatorta, "The Convergence of Governance."
24. Rustow, "Transition to Democracy."
25. Huntington, *Political Order.*

References

Aschar, Gilbert. *The People Want: A Radical Exploration of the Arab Uprising.* London: Saqi Books, 2013.

Bellin, Eva. 2012. "Authoritarianism in the Middle East: Lessons from the Arab Spring." *Comparative Politics* 44, no. 2 (2012): 127–149.

Brinton, Crane. *The Anatomy of Revolution.* revised ed. New York: Vintage Books, 1965.

Brynen, Rex, Pete W. Moore, Bassel F. Salloukh, and Marie-Joëlle Zahar. *Beyond the Arab Spring: Authoritarianism and Democratization in the Arab World.* Boulder, CO: Lynne Rienner Publishers, 2012.

Cavatorta, Francesco. "The Convergence of Governance: Upgrading Authoritarianism in the Arab World and Downgrading Democracy Elsewhere?." *Middle East Critique* 19, no. 3 (2010): 217–232.

Gause, F. Gregory III. "Why Middle East Studies Missed the Arab Spring: The Myth of Authoritarian Stability." *Foreign Affairs* (July-August, 2011).

Heyderian, Richard Javad. *How Capitalism Failed the Arab World: The Economic Roots and Precarious Future of the Middle East Uprisings*. London: Zed Books, 2014.

Huntington, Samuel P. *Political Order in Changing Societies*. New Haven: Yale University Press, 1968.

Jones, Seth. "The Rise of Afghanistan's Insurgency: State Failure and Jihad." *International Security* 32, no. 4 (Spring 2008): 7–40.

Lynch, Marc. *The Arab Uprising: The Unfinished Revolutions of the New Middle East*. New York: Public Affairs, 2012.

Michels, Robert. *Political Parties: A Study of the Oligarchical Tendencies of Modern Democracy*. New York: Free Press, 1966.

Moore, Barrington. *The Social Origins of Dictatorship and Democracy*. Boston: Beacon Press, 1966.

Mosca, Gaetano. *The Ruling Class*. New York: McGraw-Hill, 1939.

Robinson, William I. *Promoting Polyarchy: Globalization, US Intervention, and Hegemony*. New York: Cambridge University Press, 1996.

Rueschemeyer, Dietrich, Evelyne Huber Stephens, and John D. Stephens. *Capitalist Development and Democracy*. Cambridge: Polity Press, 1992.

Rustow, Dankwart. "Transitions to Democracy: Toward a Dynamic Model." *Comparative Politics* 2 (April 1970): 337–363.

Stepan, A., and J. J. Linz. "Democratization Theory and the 'Arab Spring'." *Journal of Democracy* 24, no. 2 (2013): 15–30.

Tilly, Charles. *Coercion, Capital, and European States, AD 990–1990*. Cambridge, MA: Blackwell, 1990.

Tripp, Charles. *The Power and the People: Paths of Resistance in the Middle East*. Cambridge: Cambridge University Press, 2014.

Zubaida, Sami. The 'Arab Spring' in Historical Perspective, *Open Democracy*, 21 October, (2011). http://www.opendemocracy.net/sami-zubaida/arab-spring-in-historical-perspective

Index

Adalet ve Kalkınma Partisi (AKP) 143, 156
agency, context and emergent post-uprising regimes 154–70; agency 154–8; anti-democratic agents 165; anti-regime democracy movements 154–5; capital accumulation failures 158; "commitment problem" 163; competitive interference of rival powers 161; diverging pathways (determinants of prototypical cases) 165–8; economic "unblockage" 159; Egypt (reversed transition) 165–7; emergent regime types 161–2; institutionalized US funded military 157; international variable 161; Islamists 155–6; jihadist movements inspired by Al Qaeda 156; "low intensity democracy" 159; military and security forces 156–7; outcome (polyarchic governance) 164–5; outcome (regime restoration and hybrid governance) 163–4; outcome (state failure and competitive governance) 162–3; political competition 159; political cultural variable 159–61; political economy context 158–9; polyarchy 164; "praetorianism" 162; state failure 162; Syria (failed transition, failed state) 165; transitional insider-outsider ruling coalition 164; Tunisia (transition and institutionalization) 167–9; "unblockage" of investment propensities 159; variables shaping divergent tangents 166; workers 157–8
Al Qaeda: attacks 121; jihadist movements inspired by 156
Al Qaeda in the Arabic Peninsula (AQAP) 80

Al Qaeda in the Islamic Maghreb (AQIM) 80
Algeria, Armed Islamic Group 80
"anachronistic" regimes 74
Armed Islamic Group (GIA) 80
Asad, Hafez al- 61
Assad, Bashar al- 104, 122
"authoritarian-democratic hybrid" 22
authoritarianism, contradictory dynamics of 21; in Maghreb, 23; vulnerability 4–6
Aziz, King Abdel 114

Baathists, elimination contests among 117
Bahrain, mobilization in 6; state violence in 62
Banna, Hasan al- 77
Barazani, Mazuud 122
Ben Ali, Zine al-Abidine 18, 37, 55, 97
bourgeois democracy 96, 105
Brazil, Russia, India and China (the BRICS) 135

"caliphate" 121, 124
Camp David agreements 119
capitalist development 95
car bombs 60
"Cedar Revolution" 113
change and continuity in Arab politics 111–30; absence of civil society 112; Al Qaeda attacks 121; alternative regimes 115; "Baathification" of the military 118; before and beyond democratization and authoritarian resilience 112–14; "caliphate" 121, 124; Camp David agreements 119; "Cedar Revolution" 113; colonial domination 117; consociational democracy, attempt to build 125; Contentious Politics 115; "Corrective Revolution" 118;

INDEX

"counter-regimes" 116; Dawa Party 119, 121; "De-Baathification" programme 120; domestic political exclusion and identity 119; establishment of economic and political hegemony 124; Free Syrian Army 123; geopolitical rivalries 125; Midan al-Tahrir Square collective action 116; monopolizing coercion 114; "myth of authoritarian stability" 113; "national unity" government, US calling for 125; peaceful protesters 122; political change, continuity and development in the Arab world 112–17; political dynamics, actualities of 112; "post-democratization" paradigm 113; prospects and obstacles to democratization in Iraq and Syria 124–6; proto-democratic experiment 120; regime adaptations 123; regime erosion 111, 117; "Resistance Axis" 124; sectarian cleavage 119; socio-economic development 114; state-building process, problems of 120; state-building and regime erosion in Iraq (1968–2003) and Syria (1963–2011) 117–19; state formation and contentious politics 114–17; state formation in Iraq and Syria (2011–2014), Arab uprisings and 120–4; state (re)formation in Iraq and Syria, Arab uprisings and 117–24; Sunni Islamist militants 121; "third wave" democratizations 112; "Tikitization" of the Baath 118; US-led occupation 120; Wahhabi interpretation of Islam 114

China, regional influence of 141

Civil Coalition of Revolutionary Youth 44

civil-military relations 26

class forces, transition and the Arab uprisings 90–110; anti-democratic class 94; 'Arab Spring', harvest 90, 96; bourgeois democracy 96, 105; "breakthrough" phase of democratization 92; capitalist development 95; case study (Egypt) 99–102; case study (Syria) 102–5; case study (Tunisia) 96–9; crony capitalist faction 100; democratic transition theory, critique of 92–3; economic dependency 94; electoral campaigning 92; emergence of regime types 93; empowerment of working class 95; geopolitical dependency 94; historical sociology of democratization and role of the labour movement 93–6; *infitah* 99; levels of analysis 95; Local Coordination Committees 104; mobilizing factor for democracy 94; "national dialogue" 99; nationalist corporatism 101; "passing-over" of workers' struggles 101; "passive revolution" 96; patrimonialism 97; prevailing perception 90; privatization 97; redistributed land 97; rhetorical commitment to anti-imperialism 104; "secular liberals" 92; "secular Westernised middle class" 95; social cleavages 93; "stages" of transition 93; *status quo ante* 99; "Sultanism" 97; Sunni elements, Gulf funding to 104; "transnational power relations" 94; "troika" 98; urban working class 94, 95; web of state, class and familial interest 97; Western democracy 92; Western influence 98; working class, role of 91

Cold War, second wave of globalization following, 147

comparison of Tunisia, Egypt and Syria *see* class forces, transition and the Arab uprisings

competitive state making 2

"compromised democracy" 58

consequences of Arab uprisings 1–13; alternative post-uprising trajectories 2–4; anti-regime mobilization 2, 6; authoritarian resilience 2, 9–10; communal cleavages 7; dynasticism 9; food riots 5; grievances 5; information technology penetration 7; insider-outsider coalitions 8, 10; neopatrimonialism 9; opportunity structure 7; path dependency 4–10; Qatar support of 100; regime type 2, 3; roots of crisis, authoritarian vulnerability 4–6; starting point 2; state consolidation 2; "Sultanism" 9; transition paradigm 8; variations in mobilization across cases 6–8; videos of beatings and shootings 8

consociational democracy, attempt to build 125;

Contentious Politics (CP) 115

"crescent of state weakness" 26

cross-ideological coalitions *see* social movements, protest movements and cross-ideological coalitions

crowd-control policing 60

INDEX

"culture wars" 75, 84
"cycles of violence" 60

Dawa Party 119, 121
"De-Baathification" programme 120
democracy: bourgeois 96, 105; compromised 58; consociational 125; low intensity 159; movements 154–5; -spotting 16, 18; Western 92, 139–40
"democratic Godot" 19
democratization theory (DT) 1
diffusionist model 131
dynasticism 9

economic dependency 94
economic globalization 132
Egypt: anti-regime protest movements in 45; burgeoning cooperation among regime opponents in 40; Cairo's Maspero television building, protesters killed at 63; class forces 99–102; greatest expansion of state violence in 63; history of revolution 100; insider-outsider coalitions in 8; "liberalized autocracies" of 36–7; onset of neoliberalism in 7; reversed transition 165–7; statist Islamism in 82
Egyptian Independent Trade Union Federation (EITUF) 101
Eita, Kamal abu 101
Ennahda party 47
"era of postdemocratization" 17
Essebsi, Beji Caid 48

'Facebook' youth 42
Fatteh, Esraa Abdel 42
food riots 5
"foreign fighters" 85
Forum for Democracy and Labour 42
"fourth wave of democratization" 18, 58
fragmenting states, new regimes *see* militarized state violence (in regime re-making)
"free-form collective action" 41
Free Syrian Army (FSA) 123
Freedom and Justice Party (FJP) 82
Front of Coptic Youth 43
"fundamentalism" 77

Gaza, Israeli-Palestinian war in 25
geopolitical dependency 94
geopolitical rivalries 125
Ghannouchi, Rached 48, 77

Ghazzali, Muhammad al- 77
Ghonim, Wael 42
government-organized non-governmental organizations (GONGOs) 21
grassroots Islamism 73, 78, 79
Gulf Cooperation Council (GCC) 62, 143

Hashemi, Tarek 121
"hijackers" of the revolutions 81
Hizbollah, 121, 145; alliance 123; Assad regime and 144; strategic loss 124
Houthi movement 44
"humanitarian" interventionism 148
Hussein, Saddam 111, 118
hybrid governance 163–4

infitah 99
information technology (IT) penetration 7
insider-outsider coalitions 8, 10, 164
international financial institutions (IFIs) 137, 158
International Monetary Fund-driven "structural adjustment" 5
Iranian revolution, 74
Iraq, colonial domination in 117; Kurds enjoying de facto autonomy 119; Supreme Islamic Council 120; US invasion of 76, 140
Islamic State of Iraq and Syria (ISIS) 84, 111, 145
Islamism 72–89; "anachronistic" regimes 74; "buying off" tribal authorities 85; centrist trend 78; "culture wars" 75, 84; evolving models of governance and development 74–6; "foreign fighters" 85; "fundamentalism" 77; grassroots movements 73, 78, 79; "hijackers" of the revolutions 81; Islamic Salvation Front 78; jihadi movements 73, 79, 80, 84; models of state governance 73; neoliberalism, post-populist turn towards 75; non-statist Islamism 78–80, 84–8; political Islam 73; political liberalization 78; pseudo-democratic politics 75; regime change, Islamism following 80–6; regional "state weakening" 76; religious solidarity, model of 74; Saudi model, growing influence of 74; socio-historical changes 72–4; statist Islamism 77–8, 80–4; US invasion of Iraq 76; variations 76–80; violence 76; "war on terror" 75, 76
Israel 6, 124, 142

INDEX

Israeli-Palestinian war 25
Issawi, Rafi al- 121

Jadid, Salah 118
jihadi movements 73, 79, 80, 84
Joint Meetings Party (JMP) 44

Khaldun, Ibn 2
"kingdom of tear gas" 62
Kurds, de facto autonomy of 119

Lebanon 120, 142
less developed countries (LDCs) 133
"liberal imperialism" 134
Libya 163; protest movement in 44–5; Qadhafi regime in 56
"low intensity democracy" 131, 134, 159

Maghreb, authoritarianism in 23
Maliki, Nuri al- 121, 125
Marxist theory 5
MENA (Middle East North Africa) failed democratization, international factor in 131–53; Adalet ve Kalkınma Partisi government 143; Cold War, second wave of globalization following, 147; competitive interference amidst the regional struggle for power 142–6; democratization within the frame of globalization 132–5; diffusionist model 131; economic globalization 132; global level precipitants 140–1; globalization, 137; "humanitarian" interventionism 148; imperialism, expansion of European international society through 132; international financial institutions 137; less developed countries 133; "liberal imperialism" 134; linkage 135; "lopsided political liberalization" 138; "low intensity democracy" 131, 134; neo-liberal globalization, MENA under 136–40; "New Arab Cold War" 141; new struggle for Syria 144–5; non-governmental organization networks 133; "offshore balancing" (US) 134; outcome hybridity 135; paradox 134; political economy of MENA 136–8; populist authoritarian regimes 136; "post-populist authoritarianism" 138; regional trans-state level 141–2; Saudi Arabia and the Gulf Cooperation Council 143; "sovereignty of God" 135; Sunni-Shia conflict 141; Turkey (failed liberal hegemon) 143–4; uprising (democratization between structure and agency) 140–6; Western democracy promotion in MENA 139–40; Western imperialism 136; Western intervention 143

Middle East North Africa (MENA) 1, 37; see also MENA failed democratization, international factor in
militarized state violence (in regime re-making) 55–71; anti-coup coalition 64; cases from the Arab uprisings 61–5; coalition 57; "compromised democracy" 58; crowd-control policing 60; "cycles of violence" 60; "Fourth Wave of democracy and dictatorship" 58; fragmenting state 56; "kingdom of tear gas" 62; "More Murder in the Middle" theory 58; opposition radicals, empowerment of 60; role of state violence in Arab uprisings 59–61; "slow violence" 58; "sultanistic" starting point 57; theoretical approaches 56–9; "Third Wave of Democratization" 55; transitology 65; "violence specialists" 61
"military/industrial complex" 26
modernization theory (MT) 4
modest harvest" 1
Mohsen, Ali 44
"More Murder in the Middle" (MMM) theory 58
Morsi 47, 64, 82, 142
"movements of movements" 37, 49
Mubarak, Hosni 18, 42, 63, 76, 99
multi-dimensional re-politicization of Arab politics 25
Muslim Brotherhood: brand 85; elections 78, 113; empowerment of 156; and fall of Mubarak 46; hardliner coalition excluding 11; as insider-outsider coalitions 8; and Islamic identity 141; media campaign against 160; Obama administration interest in 100; orientations 73; political offshoot 82; repression of 27, 74; split between allies and 47, 50; strategy 124; variant of Islamism exemplified by 77; Youth of 43
Mutlak, Saleh al- 121
"myth of authoritarian stability" 113

National Constituent Assembly (NCA) 47
National Democratic Party (NDP) 98

INDEX

nationalist corporatism 101
neoliberalism, post-populist turn towards 75
neopatrimonialism 9
"New Arab Cold War" 141
new social movements (NSMs) 35, 39
non-governmental organizations (NGOs) 40, 133
non-statist Islamism 78–80, 84–8

"offshore balancing" (US) 134
opportunity structure 7
outcome hybridity 135

paradogma 17, 24–7
patrimonialism 10, 97
Pearl Roundabout 62
Poland, Solidarity movement in 41
political cultural variable 159–61
political Islam 73
politics *see* self-reflections
polyarchic governance 164–5
populist authoritarian (PA) regimes 136
post-democratization approaches (PDT) 1
post-uprising regimes (emerging) *see* agency, context and emergent post-uprising regimes
"praetorianism" 162
privatization 97
protest movements *see* social movements, protest movements and cross-ideological coalitions
proto-democratic experiment 120
pseudo-democratic politics 75
pseudo-liberalizations 19

Qadhafi, Muammer 56, 62
Qaradawi, Yusuf al- 77
Qatar 100, 124, 141
Qutb, Sayyid 77

Rassemblement Constitutionnel Démocratique (RCD) 98
regime erosion 111, 117
regime re-making *see* militarized state violence (in regime re-making)
religious solidarity, model of 74
rival powers, competitive interference of 161
Russia, regional influence of 141

Sadat assassination 74
Sa'id, Khalid 59

satellite TV 7
Saudi Arabia, Wahhabi interpretation of Islam in 114
Saudi model, growing influence of 74
Saudi "Sahwa" movement 77
self-reflections 14–34; analytical implications of Arab uprisings 15; "authoritarian-democratic hybrid" 22; civil-military relations 26; classic debates and old toolboxes 25–27; combining traditions and integrating insights 22–3; "crescent of state weakness" 26; democracy-spotting 16, 18; "democratic Godot" 19; "era of postdemocratization" 17; "fourth wave of democratization" 18; framing types 14, 15; "genuine science of politics" 15; government-organized non-governmental organizations 21; how-do-we-synthesize-and-upgrade framing 20–4; likelihood of democratic transitions 22; multi-dimensional re-politicization of Arab politics 25; paradogma 17, 24–7; political order in changing societies 26; post-democratization 16–17; problematique, framing of 28; pseudo-liberalizations 19; reflecting on our self-reflections 27–8; region of surprises (Arab uprisings, 2011) 18; re-politicized Arab world 24–5; revisiting and revising existing approaches 21–2; specifying when and where what works 23; "transition to nowhere" 19, 20; upgrades and revisions within existing debate 23–4; "vast sound chamber", Arab world as 27; who-has-been-vindicated-and-made-obsolete framing 18–20
Sisi, Abd al-Fattah al- 63, 82
social movement organizations (SMO) 38
social movement theory (SMT) 6, 35
social movements, protest movements and cross-ideological coalitions 35–54; anti-regime coalitions in the aftermath of regime change 45–49; cultural sub-systems 41; "Day of Rage" 43; definitional approaches 38; insurrectionary movements 40; labour mobilization 43; mobilization types 40; "movements of movements" 37, 49; new social movements 35, 39; political opportunity theory 36; political vacuum 46; politics of "the informal people" 39;

INDEX

social movement theory and the Middle East and North Africa 37–41; social movements, coalitions, and the Arab uprisings 41–5; "symbolic direct actions" 39; "technocrats" 48; "whole-society" opposition 46
Solidarity movement (Poland) 41
"sovereignty of God" 135
Soviet "totalitarianism", imitations of 4
state violence *see* militarized state violence (in regime re-making)
statist Islamism 77–8, 80–4
"Sultanism" 9, 22, 97
Sunni Islamist militants 121
Sunni-Shia conflict 141
Supreme Council of the Armed Forces (SCAF) 47, 57, 63, 92, 100
"symbolic direct actions" 39
Syria, class forces 102–5; colonial domination in 117; corporatist state unions 104; failed transition, failed state 165; French-occupied 59; geopolitical rivalries over 125; Local Coordination Committees 104; new struggle for 144–5; record of labour organization 96
Syrian National Council (SNC) 123

Tahrir Square 47, 57
Tamarod 64
Tantawi, Hussein al- 63
"technocrats" 48
"third wave" democratizations 55, 112
"Tikitization" of the Baath 118
Tilly, Charles 38
Trabelsi, Leila 97
transition paradigm 8, 16
"transnational power relations" 94
Tunisia, anti-regime protest movements in 45; class forces 96–9; Constituent Assembly 96; insider-outsider coalitions in 8; key protagonists in uprisings in 42; "liberalized autocracies" of 36–7; onset of neoliberalism in 7; role of political parties in 42; social mobilization 4; statist Islamism in 83; transition and institutionalization 167–9; UGTT 98
Turkey 124, 143–4

"unblockage" of investment propensities 159
Union Générale Tunisienne du Travail (UGTT) 37, 42, 93
United States, alignment with 6; funded military 157; hegemon 147; imports from 62; invasion of Iraq 76, 140
urban working class 94, 95

"vast sound chamber", Arab world as 27
videos of beatings and shootings 8
"violence specialists" 61

Wahhabi interpretation of Islam 114
"war on terror" 75, 76
"We are all Khalid Sa'id" Facebook page 42, 59
Weber, Max 2, 115
Western democracy 92
Western imperialism 136
Western influence 98
"whole-society" opposition 46
working class, empowerment of 95; urban 94, 95
World Trade Organization 132

Yemen 142, 163; anti-regime protest movements in 45; migration of AQAP to 80; social mobilization 4; Socialist Party 44
Youth of the Muslim Brotherhood 43

Zaydi revivalist movement 44